S N C C

SNCC

THE NEW ABOLITIONISTS

by Howard Zinn

BEACON PRESS BOSTON

Library of Congress catalog card number: 64-20493

Published simultaneously in Canada by
S. J. Reginald Saunders and Co., Ltd., Toronto

Beacon Press books are published under the auspices
of the Unitarian Universalist Association

Second edition, August 1965

Printed in the United States of America

To Ella Baker

A Note, and Some Acknowledgments

This book is not a "history" of the Student Nonviolent Coordinating Committee in any formal sense. It leaves out too much for that. I have not attempted to deal with the Cambridge, Maryland, movement, for instance, and the remarkable Gloria Richardson. That deserves a book in itself. So does the story of Danville, Virginia, and, in fact, that extraordinary attorney Len Holt is writing it. I omit, with regrets, the work of Bill Hansen and others in Pine Bluff, and too many more places and people whose heroism goes unnoticed. What I *am* attempting to do here is to catch a glimpse of SNCC people in action, and to suggest the quality of their contribution to American civilization.

I am very much aware of the magnificent work done by people in the other civil rights organizations: one thinks of Dave Dennis and Tom Gaither in CORE, of Annell Ponder and James Bevel in SCLC, of Amzie Moore and Aaron Henry in the NAACP, and so many others, black and white, who belong to no organizations, who are asked for no interviews, but whose sacrifice is tossed, anonymously, into the common pool.

Perhaps I pay special attention to SNCC because these are the people I know best; some of them are former students of mine; many of them are my friends. Perhaps I write about SNCC also because I believe that its young people are the nation's most vivid reminder that there is an unquenchable spirit alive in the world today, beyond race, beyond nationality, beyond class. It is a spirit which seeks to embrace all people everywhere.

Much of my information is gained first-hand, from being where SNCC people work, watching them in action, talking to them. A good deal of the documentation comes from SNCC's extensive files in the Atlanta office. I owe a great debt to Julian Bond and Dorothy Zellner, two talented young writers, who generously turned over material they were going to use (and one day perhaps will) in a great history of SNCC, which they have served so devotedly.

Many other people have helped: Guy and Candie Carawan have let me use material from their moving collection of freedom songs, *We Shall Overcome,* as well as from Candie's reminiscences of sit-in days in Nashville. Marilyn Young interviewed Bob Zellner with the perspicacity of a first-rate historian, which she is. Tom Hayden's excellent pamphlet, *Revolution in Mississippi,* was very helpful. Sheila Kessler's research on Leflore County was valuable, as was Ronnie Dugger's research on Selma. Tom Rose, who has done his own fine study of the Negro student in the United States, offered his tapes and other materials. Staige Blackford and Leslie Dunbar of the Southern Regional Council were, as usual, warmly cooperative in giving me access to their incomparable files. Alan Ribback was kind enough to let me have some of the tapes he made at trouble spots in the Deep South; I only regret that my readers can't hear the singing of the Freedom Choruses on these tapes.

Everyone in the Atlanta SNCC office was helpful in countless ways: Jim Forman and Ruby Doris Smith and Mary King and Worth Long, and others. I could not begin to mention all the SNCC people in the field who helped me in one way or another: in Greenwood, in Greenville, in Selma, in Hattiesburg, in Albany.

In this book, as in everything I have written, my most

judicious and perceptive editorial advisor has been my wife, Roslyn.

And finally, there is the lady to whom this book is dedicated, who is more responsible than any other single individual for the birth of the new abolitionists as an organized group, and who remains the most tireless, the most modest, and the wisest activist I know in the struggle for human rights today.

Contents

1. The New Abolitionists 1
2. Out of the Sit-ins 16
3. The Freedom Rides 40
4. Mississippi I: McComb 62
5. Mississippi II: Greenwood 79
6. Mississippi III: Hattiesburg 102
7. Southwest Georgia: The Outsider as Insider 123
8. Alabama: Freedom Day in Selma 147
9. The White Man in the Movement 167
10. "I Want To Know: Which Side Is the Federal Government On?" 190
11. The Revolution Beyond Race 216
12. An Independent Radicalism 242

Index 276

Preface to the Second Edition

One year is a long time to the young, especially when they are in battle, and it has been a year since I turned in my manuscript on the young people in SNCC for the hardcover edition of this book. I have therefore added a chapter for this edition, at the end of the book, to discuss the "Mississippi Summer" of 1964, with its tragedy and its triumph, the sensational entrance into national politics of the Freedom Democratic Party, and the explosion of Selma, Alabama, seventeen months after the Selma story I narrated in the body of the book. In the midst of all this, the place of SNCC in the civil rights movement, and in the nation, has become a matter of sharp controversy, and I dwell, in the final chapter, on that, in order to try to understand (for myself, as much as for my readers) why SNCC appears to be on a collision course with the traditional values of American society.

May, 1965

1. The New Abolitionists

For the first time in our history a major social movement, shaking the nation to its bones, is being led by youngsters. This is not to deny the inspirational leadership of a handful of adults (Martin Luther King and James Farmer), the organizational direction by veterans in the struggle (Roy Wilkins and A. Philip Randolph), or the participation of hundreds of thousands of older people in the current Negro revolt. But that revolt, a long time marching out of the American past, its way suddenly lit up by the Supreme Court decision, and beginning to rumble in earnest when thousands of people took to the streets of Montgomery in the bus boycott, first flared into a national excitement with the sit-ins by college students that started the decade of the 1960's.

And since then, those same youngsters, hardened by countless jailings and beatings, now out of school and living in ramshackle headquarters all over the Deep South, have been striking the sparks, again and again, for that fire of change spreading through the South and searing the whole country.

These young rebels call themselves the Student Nonviolent Coordinating Committee, but they are more a movement than an organization, for no bureaucratized structure can contain their spirit, no printed program capture the fierce and elusive quality of their thinking. And while they have no famous leaders, very little money, no inner access to the seats of national authority, they are clearly the front line of the Negro assault on the moral comfort of white America.

To be with them, walking a picket line in the rain in Hattiesburg, Mississippi or sleeping on a cot in a cramped "office" in Greenville, Mississippi; to watch them walk out of the stone jailhouse in Albany, Georgia; to see them jabbed by electric prod poles and flung into paddy wagons in Selma, Alabama, or link arms and sing at the close of a church meeting in the Delta—is to feel the presence of greatness. It is a greatness that comes from their relationship to history, and it does not diminish when they are discovered to be human: to make mistakes or feel fear, to act with envy, or hostility or even violence.

All Americans owe them a debt for—if nothing else—releasing the idealism locked so long inside a nation that has not recently tasted the drama of a social upheaval. And for making us look on the young people of the country with a new respect. Theirs was the silent generation until they spoke, the complacent generation until they marched and sang, the money-seeking generation until they renounced comfort and security to fight for justice in the dank and dangerous hamlets of the Black Belt.

Princeton philosopher Walter Kaufmann, writing in *The Faith of a Heretic,* called the young people born during World War II the "uncommitted generation." He said: "What distinguishes them is that they are not committed to any cause." But this was written in 1960. And in that year, out of that same generation which Kaufmann described, there emerged the first rebels of the decade. They came out of unexpected places: they were mostly black and therefore unseen until they suddenly became the most visible people in America; they came out of Greensboro, North Carolina and Nashville, Tennessee and Rock Hill, South Carolina and Atlanta, Georgia. And they were committed. To the point of jail, which is a large commitment. And to the point of death, which hovers always near a heretic in a police state and which turns to stare a Deep South Negro directly in the face at that moment when he utters that word so long taboo for Negroes in America, "*No.*"

How do you measure commitment? Is it the willingness to take a day out of life and sacrifice it to history, to plunge for one morning or one afternoon into the unknown, to engage in one solitary act of defiance against all the arrayed power of established society? Then tens of thousands of young people, mostly black, some white, have committed themselves these past four years, by the simple act of joining a demonstration. Is commitment more than that—the willingness to wrench yourself out of your environment and begin anew, almost alone, in a social jungle which the most powerful forces in the nation have not dared to penetrate? Then the number is reduced to sixteen: those sixteen college youngsters who, in the fall of 1961, decided to drop everything—school and family and approved ambition—and move into the Deep South to become the first guerrilla fighters of the Student Nonviolent Coordinating Committee.

By early 1964, the number was up to 150. In the most heated days of abolitionism before the Civil War, there were never that many dedicated people who turned their backs on ordinary pursuits and gave their lives wholly to the movement. There were William Lloyd Garrison and Wendell Phillips and Theodore Weld and Frederick Douglass and Sojourner Truth and a handful of others, and there were hundreds of part-time abolitionists and thousands of followers. But for 150 youngsters today to turn on their pasts, to decide to live and work twenty-four hours a day in the most dangerous region of the United States, is cause for wonder. And wherever they have come from—the Negro colleges of the South, the Ivy League universities of the North, the small and medium colleges all over the country—they have left ripples of astonishment behind. This college generation as a whole is not committed, by any means. But it has been shaken.

These 150—who next year will be 250 or more, because the excitement grows daily on the college campuses—are the new abolitionists. It is not fanciful to invest them with a name that has the ring of history; we are always shy about recognizing the historic worth of events when they take place before our eyes, about recognizing heroes when they are still flesh and blood and not yet transfixed in marble. But there is no doubt about it: we have in this country today a movement which will take its place alongside that of the abolitionists, the Populists, the Progressives—and may outdo them all.

Their youth makes us hesitant to recognize their depth. But the great social upsurge of post-war America is the Negro revolt, and this revolt has gotten its most powerful impetus from young people, who gave it a new turn in 1960 and today, as anonymous as infantrymen everywhere, form the first rank in a nonviolent but ferocious war against the old order.

It would be easy to romanticize them, but they are too young, too vulnerable, too humanly frail to fit the stereotype of heroes. They don't match the storybook martyrs who face death with silent stoicism; the young fellows sometimes cry out when they are beaten; the girls may weep when abused in prison. Most often, however, they sing. This was true of the farmer and labor movements in this country, and of all the wars; but there has never been a singing movement like this one. Perhaps it is because most of them were brought up on the gospel songs and hymns of the Negro church in the South, perhaps also because they are young, probably most of all because what they are doing inspires song. They have created a new gospel music out of the old, made up of songs adapted or written in jail or on the picket line. Every battle station in the Deep South now has its Freedom Chorus, and the mass meetings there end with everyone standing, led by the youngsters of SNCC, linking arms, and singing "We Shall Overcome."

The mood of these young people, which they convey to

everyone around them in the midst of poverty, violence, terror, and centuries of bitter memories, is joy, confidence, the vision of victory: "We'll walk hand in hand . . . we are not afraid. . . ." Occasionally there is sadness, as in "I Been 'Buked and I Been Scorned." But most often there is an exuberant defiance: "Ain't Gonna Let Chief Pritchett Turn Me Round. . . ." They are happy warriors, a refreshing contrast to the revolutionaries of old. They smile and wave while being taken off in paddy wagons; they laugh and sing behind bars.

Yet they are the most serious social force in the nation today. They are not playing; it is no casual act of defiance, no irresponsible whim of adolescence, when young people of sixteen or twenty or twenty-five turn away from school, job, family, all the tokens of success in modern America, to take up new lives, hungry and hunted, in the hinterland of the Deep South. Jim Forman was a teacher in Chicago before he joined the SNCC, and an aspiring novelist; Bob Moses was a graduate of Harvard, teaching in New York; Charles Sherrod was a divinity school graduate in Virginia; Mendy Samstein, a graduate of Brandeis University, was on the faculty of a Negro college, working for his Ph.D. in history at the University of Chicago. Others found it easier—and harder—for they came right out of the Black Belt and, even though they tasted college, they had nowhere then to go but back towards danger and freedom: John Lewis, Sam Block, Willie Peacock, Lafayette Surney, MacArthur Cotton, Lawrence Guyot and too many more to name.

In his study *Young Man Luther*, the psychologist Erik Erikson ponders the "identity crisis" which young people face. "It occurs in that period of the life cycle when each youth must forge for himself some central perspective and direction, some working unity, out of the effective remnants of his childhood and the hopes of his anticipated adulthood; he must detect some meaningful resemblance between what he has come to see in himself and what his sharpened awareness tells him others judge and expect him to be." It would be hard to imagine a more startling contrast than that between the young Negro as the old South saw him (or rather half-saw him, blurred and not quite human) and the vision of himself he suddenly perceived in the glare of the 1960's.

The entire nation, caught suddenly in the intersection of two images where it always thought there was only one, has begun slowly to refocus its own vision. So that what started as an identity crisis for Negroes turned out to be an identity crisis for the nation. And we are still resolving it. It is one of the conditions of effective psychotherapy that the patient must begin to see himself as he really is, and the United States, now forced by the young Negro to see itself through *his* eyes (an ironic reversal, for the Negro was always compelled to see himself through the eyes of the white man), is coming closer to a realistic appraisal of its national personality.

All young people, in their late teens or early twenties, face this "identity crisis" which Erik Erikson describes. As Erikson points out: "Some young individuals will succumb to this crisis in all manner of neurotic, psychotic, or delinquent behavior; others will resolve it through participation in ideological movements passionately concerned with religion or politics, nature or art." We have seen the delinquent responses, or simply the responses of non-commitment, on the part of millions of young people of this generation who have not been able to find their way. Young Negroes were among these, were perhaps even the most delinquent, the most crisis-ridden of all. But today, by the handful, or the hundreds, or perhaps the thousands, they are making their way through this crisis with a firm grip on themselves, aided immeasurably by the fact that they are anchored to a great social movement.

We ought to note, however, that this "participation in ideological movements" today has a different quality than that of earlier American student movements—the radical movements of the thirties, for instance. The young people in the

Student Nonviolent Coordinating Committee have not become followers of any dogma, have not pledged themselves to any rigid ideological system. Unswerving as they are in moving towards certain basic goals, they wheel freely in their thinking about society and how it needs to be changed. Erikson writes of a very few young people who, making their way through their identity crisis, "eventually come to contribute an original bit to an emerging style of life; the very danger which they have sensed has forced them to mobilize capacities to see and say, to dream and plan, to design and construct, in new ways." And this is true of those in the SNCC. They are radical, but not dogmatic; thoughtful, but not ideological. Their thinking is undisciplined; it is fresh, and it is new.

One must listen to Jane Stembridge speaking, a white girl from Virginia, part of that little band of black and white students who organized SNCC out of the turmoil of the 1960 sit-ins:

> . . . finally it all boils down to human relationships. It has nothing to do finally with governments. It is the question of whether we . . . whether *I* shall go on living in isolation or whether there shall be a we. The student movement is not a cause . . . it is a collision between this one person and that one person. It is a *I am going to sit beside you* . . . Love alone is radical. Political statements are not; programs are not; even going to jail is not. . . .

These new abolitionists are different from the earlier ones. The movement of the 1830's and 1840's was led by white New Englanders, bombarding the South and the nation with words. The present movement is planted firmly in the deepest furrows of the Deep South, and it consists mostly of Negroes who make their pleas to the nation more by physical acts of sacrifice than by verbal declamation. Their task is made easier by modern mass communication, for the nation, indeed the whole world, can *see* them, on the television screen or in newspaper photos—marching, praying, singing, *demonstrating* their message. The white people of America, to whom Negroes were always a dark, amorphous mass, are forced to see them for the first time sharply etched as individuals, their features —both physical and moral—stark, clear, and troubling.

But in one important way these young people are very much like the abolitionists of old: they have a healthy disrespect for respectability; they are not ashamed of being agitators and trouble-makers; they see it as the essence of democracy. In defense of William Lloyd Garrison, against the accusation that he was too harsh, a friend replied that the nation was in a sleep so deep "nothing but a rude and almost ruffian-like shake could rouse her." The same deliberate harshness lies behind the activities of James Forman, John Lewis, Bob Moses, and other leaders of SNCC. What Samuel May once said of Garrison and slavery might be said today of each of these people and segregation: "He will shake our nation to its center, but he will shake slavery out of it."

When SNCC leader Gloria Richardson in Cambridge, Maryland, refused, under a rain of criticism, to subject the issue of segregation to popular vote, one was reminded of the words of Wendell Phillips, explaining the apparent strange behavior of the abolitionists: "The reformer is careless of numbers, disregards popularity, and deals only with ideas, conscience, and common sense. . . . He neither expects, nor is overanxious for immediate success." Phillips contrasted the reformer with the politician, who "dwells in an everlasting now. . . ." In a similar mood, poet James Russell Lowell wrote: "The Reformer must expect comparative isolation, and he must be strong enough to bear it."

Yet the staff member of the Student Nonviolent Coordinating Committee can never be isolated as was the New England abolitionist of the 1830's, who was far from slave territory, and surrounded by whites unconcerned for the slave. The SNCC youngster is in the midst of his people, surrounded by them, protected by them. To be cut off, by harsh criticism of his "extremism," from Northern white intellectuals or from those in national political power is a minor blow, cushioned by a popularity based on the poor and the powerless, but perhaps even more comforting because of that.

Oddly enough—or perhaps naturally enough—the student movement has left the campuses where it began in those sit-ins of early 1960. The sit-in leaders have either graduated from or left college, and the fact that they call themselves the *Student* Nonviolent Coordinating Committee is primarily a reflection of their backgrounds, their youth, and perhaps their hope to return one day and bring a new dynamism to college education. Some go back to college after a year or two with the movement; others find a less formal but more genuine intellectual satisfaction in the movement. All live in a state of tension: there is the recognition that academic life is too far removed from the social struggle, alongside the frustration that exists for any intellectually aroused youngster separated from books and concentrated learning. At the same time, having exchanged college attire and the tree-lined campus for overalls and the dusty back roads of the rural South, they are getting the kind of education that no one else in the nation is getting.

There is another striking contrast to Garrison and Phillips, Lewis Tappan and Theodore Weld: these young people are not middle-class reformers who became somehow concerned about others. They come themselves from the ranks of the victims, not just because they are mostly Negroes, but because for the most part their fathers are janitors and laborers, their mothers maids and factory workers.

In late 1963 I checked the backgrounds of forty-one field workers for SNCC in Mississippi (roughly one-third of the total SNCC force in the Deep South). Thirty-five of them were Negro, and twenty-five of them came from the Deep South. Of the six white staff members two were from the Deep South.

The white youngsters and most of the Northern Negroes came from middle-class homes; their fathers were ministers or teachers or civil service workers. All of the Southern Negroes, and some of the Northern Negroes (twenty-one out of thirty-five) came from homes where the mothers were maids or domestics, the fathers factory workers, truck drivers, farmers, bricklayers, carpenters. Twenty-nine (about three-fourths) of the total SNCC Mississippi staff were between fifteen and twenty-two years old. There were twelve between twenty-two and twenty-nine, and one person each in his thirties, forties, and fifties. Twenty-six, or about two-thirds, of the Mississippi SNCC staff were either college graduates or had some college education. Ten had finished high school or had some high school education and two had no more than part of an elementary school education. If one were to generalize roughly about the SNCC staff in the Deep South, one would say they are young, they are Negro, they come from the South, their families are poor and of the working class, but they have been to college. Northern middle-class whites and Negroes are a minority.

As of mid-1964, about 150 people worked full-time for SNCC, roughly 80 percent of them Negro. Of the whites, most were Northerners, but the few white Southerners played important roles (Jane Stembridge, the first office secretary in Atlanta; Bob Zellner and Sam Shirah, assigned to white college campuses; Sandra Hayden, in the Jackson, Mississippi office). Of the Negro staff people, most were Southern born; more and more, young Negroes were being recruited out of Deep South towns to become SNCC field secretaries right there at home.

By 1963, the annual budget of SNCC was about $250,000, almost all of this coming from the contributions of individuals and organizations (churches, colleges, foundations). About one-fourth of this income was being used to pay the salaries of field secretaries, $10 a week for most of them, with a few married people in the Atlanta office receiving $50 or $60 a week. Most of the remaining income went to pay for field operations in Mississippi, southwest Georgia, and the other areas of concentration.

The two chief officers of SNCC are the Chairman (John Lewis) and the Executive Secretary (James Forman). One of the field secretaries in each major geographical area is known as a Project Director. An Executive Committee of twenty-one members, including two older "advisors," is the top policy-making body, and is elected at an annual conference in the spring.

Where do the 150 or so SNCC workers operate? Perhaps a dozen man the central office in Atlanta, a buzzing jumble of rooms above a tailor shop in the Negro section of Atlanta, not far from the Negro college campuses. Long-distance phone connections keep Jim Forman and John Lewis, the two top officers of SNCC, in day-to-day, sometimes hour-to-hour touch with crisis situations in those parts of the Deep South where SNCC maintains headquarters and "field secretaries" (as its staff members are called).

One of the two main areas of concentration is Mississippi, where SNCC's first penetration of the Deep South was made by Bob Moses and a few Negro youngsters from the Delta. A half-dozen spots in Mississippi have had varying degrees of attention: Greenwood, Hattiesburg, Jackson, Liberty, Greenville, Clarksdale. The other major focus of activity is southwest Georgia, where Charles Sherrod, a divinity school student from Virginia, came in the fall of 1961 and stayed to become a legend. Albany has been the center there, and, radiating from it, SNCC workers have moved into the terror-ridden towns of the old Cotton Kingdom: Americus, Dawson, Camilla, Sasser. Outside of Mississippi and Southwest Georgia, SNCC groups function in Selma, Alabama; Danville, Virginia; Cambridge, Maryland; Pine Bluff, Arkansas; and other places; they register voters, distribute food and clothing, lead demonstrations, conduct classes, vitalize long-dormant communities.

To visit SNCC field headquarters in these rural outposts of the Deep South is like visiting a combat station in wartime. Living conditions are crude. Sometimes there is a "Freedom House," an old frame dwelling with cots and blankets for the field secretaries and whoever else is staying over for the night. At other times, field people stay in homes in the Negro community. It may take weeks or months to dispel the initial fear on the part of local Negroes now aware of impending change and trouble. Negro women in town often become mothers to the SNCC youngsters far from home and family; they put them up, make meals for them, tend them when they are sick, go out on the line with them in demonstrations. One thinks of Mrs. Boynton in Selma, Mrs. Woods in Hattiesburg, and Mrs. Daniels in Dawson. (Sheriff Jim Clark in Selma, hoping to arrest SNCC leader Prathia Hall, went straight to the home of Mrs. Boynton to find her.)

Over every one of these headquarters in the field, whether a "Freedom House" rented by SNCC, or a home or office donated by a local supporter, there hangs the constant threat of violence. The first SNCC headquarters in Selma was burned down; in Greenwood, two SNCC workers found themselves under siege by a mob of armed men and had to make their way over rooftops to safety; in Danville, police simply marched into the SNCC office and arrested everyone in sight.

"These are beautiful people down here," Sandra Hayden wrote to me from Mississippi shortly after she arrived there to work for SNCC. She was speaking about the Negroes of the Delta, aroused to take their first steps out of the past—but she was not speaking of color or of that ordered set of physical characteristics which American society has characterized as "beauty." She was speaking of the souls of black folk—and of white folk too. She was speaking of a beauty of spirit, of a courage beyond comprehension, which pervades the ranks of the new abolitionists in the Deep South. It is expressed in Sandra Hayden herself, tall, blonde, slender, a Texas girl who moved from the University of Texas into the student movement; it is expressed in the rugged, black, smiling face of Chuck McDew, peering through the bars of Baton Rouge jail; or the tawny, delicate features of Peggy Day in Terrell County; or the agonized, shining eyes of Mrs. Fannie Hamer, a middle-aged woman thrown off her land in Ruleville, Mississippi, who has gone to work for SNCC.

Those who join the SNCC staff agree to work for subsistence wages; this usually means $10.00 a week ($9.64 after deductions), and often weeks going by with no checks coming from Atlanta. It may mean knocking on doors for food, scrounging around for a pair of shoes, riding a mule along a country road because the car donated by some sympathizer has broken down. A typical SNCC automobile has always just run out of gas, and the driver has no money left to buy more. "You know it's like they're in another world," a college girl said after visiting SNCC headquarters in Greenwood, Mississippi.

These are young radicals; the word "revolution" occurs again and again in their speech. Yet they have no party, no ideology, no creed. They have no clear idea of a blueprint for a future society. But they do know clearly that the values of present American society—and this goes beyond racism to class distinction, to commercialism, to profit-seeking, to the setting of religious or national barriers against human contact—are not for them.

They are prepared to use revolutionary means against the old order. They believe in civil disobedience. They are reluctant to rely completely on the niceties of negotiation and conciliation, distrustful of those who hold political and economic power. They have a tremendous respect for the potency of the demonstration, an eagerness to move out of the political maze of normal parliamentary procedure and to confront policy-makers directly with a power beyond orthodox politics—the power of people in the streets and on the picket line.

They are nonviolent in that they suffer beatings with folded arms and will not strike back. There have been one or two rare exceptions of discipline being broken, yet this must be laid against hundreds of instances of astounding self-control in the face of unspeakable brutality.

Next to the phrase "nonviolence," however, what you hear most often among SNCC workers is "direct action." They believe, without inflicting violence, and while opening themselves to attack, in confronting a community boldly with the sounds and sights of protest. When it is argued that this will inevitably bring trouble, even violence, the answer is likely to be that given by James Bevel, who in his activity with the Southern Christian Leadership Conference works closely with SNCC in Alabama and Mississippi: "Maybe the Devil has got to come out of these people before we will have peace. . . ."

They have no closed vision of the ideal community. They are fed up with what has been; they are open to anything new and are willing to start from scratch. Erik Erikson talks about young rebels with a "rock-bottom" attitude, who "want to be reborn in identity and to have another chance at becoming once-born, but this time on their own terms." Nineteen-year-old SNCC veteran Cordell Reagan, brown-skinned, slender, explains himself this way:

> It's not hard to interpret what our parents mean by a better world. You know, go to school, son, and get a good education. And what do you do with this? You get a degree, you move out into some little community housing project, you get married, five kids and two cars, and you don't care what's happening. . . . So I think when we talk about growing up in a better world, a new world, we mean changing the world to a different place.

Is it any wonder that Cordell Reagan and so many other SNCC workers have been put in jail again and again by Deep-South sheriffs for "contributing to the delinquency of minors"?

A young white student, explaining why he wanted to join SNCC, wrote about his new-found view of life:

> I have never felt so intense, alive, such a sense of well-being, which is not to be confused with the illusion of "happiness" equated to "having fun." I have chosen to be outside of society after having been very much inside. I intend to fight that society which lied to and smothered me for so long, and continues to do so to vast numbers of people. . . . My plans are unstructured in regards to anything but the immediate future. I believe in freedom, and must take the jump; I must take the chance of action.

The nation has suddenly become aware that the initiative today is in the hands of these 150 young people who have moved into the Deep South to transform it. Everyone waits on their next action: the local police, the state officials, the national government, the mass media of the country, Negroes and whites sitting at their radios and television sets across the land. Meanwhile, these people are living, hour by hour, the very ideals which this country has often thought about, but not yet managed to practice: they are courageous, though afraid; they live and work together in a brotherhood of black and white. Southerner and Northerner, Jew and Christian and agnostic, the likes of which this country has not yet seen. They are creating new definitions of success, of happiness, of democracy.

It is just possible that the momentum created by their enormous energy—now directed against racial separation—may surge, before it can be contained, against other barriers which keep people apart in the world: poverty, and nationalism, and all tyranny over the minds and bodies of men. If so, the United States may truly be on the verge of a revolution—nonviolent, but sweeping in its consequences—and led by those who, perhaps, are most dependable in a revolution: the young.

2. Out of the Sit-ins

"My stomach always hurt a little on the way to a sit-in. . . . I guess it's the unexpected." Candie Anderson, a white girl attending Fisk University as an exchange student from Pomona College in California, had joined her Negro classmates to demonstrate against segregation in Nashville, Tennessee. It was the explosion of sit-ins throughout the South in early 1960 that led to the formation of the Student Nonviolent Coordinating Committee.

On February 1, 1960, four freshmen at A & T College in Greensboro, North Carolina, took seats at a lunch counter downtown, not knowing they were starting a movement that would soon take on the proportions of a revolution. "For about a week," David Richmond recalled later, "we four fellows sat around the A & T campus, talking about the integration movement. And we decided we ought to go down to Woolworth's and see what would happen." They spent an hour sitting at the Woolworth's counter, with no service. Then the counter was closed for the day, and they went home.

In a matter of days, the idea leaped to other cities in North Carolina. During the next two weeks, sit-ins spread to fifteen cities in five Southern states. Within the following year, over 50,000 people—most were Negroes, some were white—had participated in one kind of demonstration or another in a hundred cities, and over 3600 demonstrators spent time in jail. But there were results to show: by the end of 1961, several hundred lunch counters had been desegregated in scores of cities—in Texas, Oklahoma, the border states of the South, and even as far as Atlanta, Georgia. A wall of resistance, however, apparently impenetrable, faced the student in the rest of Georgia, South Carolina, Alabama, Mississippi, Louisiana—the hard-core Deep South.

It is hard to overestimate the electrical effect of that first sit-in in Greensboro, as the news reached the nation on television screens, over radios, in newspapers. In his Harlem apartment in New York City, Bob Moses, a former Harvard graduate student and mathematics teacher, saw a picture of the Greensboro sit-inners. "The students in that picture had a certain look on their faces," he later told writer Ben Bagdikian, "sort of sullen, angry, determined. Before, the Negro in the South had always looked on the defensive, cringing. This time they were taking the initiative. They were kids my age, and I knew this had something to do with my own life. . . ."

In Atlanta, Morehouse College student Julian Bond, who wrote poetry and thought about being a journalist, reacted quickly to the Greensboro sit-in. He and another student, discussing it in the Yates & Milton drug store across the street from the campus, decided to summon Morehouse men to a meeting. Out of that grew the Atlanta student movement, which six weeks later erupted in one of the largest and best organized sit-in demonstrations of all.

Also in Atlanta, seventeen-year-old Ruby Doris Smith, a sophomore at Spelman College, heard about the Greensboro sit-in and ran home that evening to see it on television:

> I began to think right away about it happening in Atlanta, but I wasn't ready to act on my own. When the student committee was formed in the Atlanta University Center, I told my older sister, who was on the Student Council at Morris Brown College, to put me on the list. And when two hundred students were selected for the first demonstration, I was among them. I went through the food line in the restaurant at the State Capitol with six other students, but when we got to the cashier, she wouldn't take our money. She ran upstairs

to get the Governor. The Lieutenant-Governor came down and told us to leave. We didn't, and went to the county jail.

Charles ("Chuck") McDew, a husky former athlete from Massilon, Ohio, was studying at South Carolina State College in Orangeburg. McDew had never adjusted to South Carolina; he had been arrested three times in his first three months there, and was struck by a policeman for trying to enter the main YMCA. When, during Religious Emphasis Week at the College, some visiting white Protestant ministers had responded negatively to his question about attending their churches, and a rabbi invited him to the temple, he converted to Judaism. With the news of Greensboro being discussed all around him, McDew read in the Talmud: "If I am not for myself, then who is for me? If I am for myself alone, then what am I? If not now, when?" He became a leader of the local sit-in movement.

To these young people, the Supreme Court decision of 1954 was a childhood memory. The Montgomery bus boycott of 1955, the first mass action by Southern Negroes, though also dimly remembered, was an inspiration. The trouble at Little Rock in 1957 was more vivid, with the unforgettable photos of the young Negro girl walking past screaming crowds towards Central High School. The Greensboro sit-ins struck a special chord of repressed emotion, and excitement raced across the Negro college campuses of the South.

Bob Moses, Julian Bond, Ruby Doris Smith, Chuck McDew: all were to become stalwarts in the Student Nonviolent Coordinating Committee. And for so many others in SNCC, the Greensboro sit-in—more than the Supreme Court decision, more than the Little Rock crisis, more than the Montgomery bus boycott, more than the recent declarations of independence by a host of African nations, and yet, perhaps, owing its galvanic force to the accumulation of all these events—was a turning point in their lives. James Forman, studying French in graduate school in the North, began turning his thoughts southward. Exactly what was going on in the minds of so many other students, soon to leave school for "The Movement," remains unknown.

Out of the Nashville, Tennessee, sit-ins, a battalion of future SNCC people took shape. Tall, quiet, Marion Barry, a graduate student in chemistry at Fisk University, who would later become the first chairman of SNCC, took a leading part in the Nashville sit-ins from the beginning. His father, a Mississippi farmer, migrated to Memphis, Tennessee, and Barry went to school there. As an undergraduate at LeMoyne College in Memphis, he publicly protested an anti-Negro remark made by a prominent white trustee of the college, created an uproar in the city, and barely avoided being expelled.

> I came to Fisk . . . inquired about forming a college chapter of the NAACP. . . . But we didn't do much. . . . We had not at any time thought of direct action. . . . In the meantime in Greensboro, N.C., the student movement began February 1, 1960. So we in Nashville decided we wanted to do something about it. . . . I remember the first time I was arrested, about February 27. . . . I took a chance on losing a scholarship or not receiving my Master's degree. But to me, if I had received my scholarship and Master's degree, and still was not a free man, I was not a man at all.

John Lewis, short, fiery, from a small town in Alabama, was also in Nashville as a seminary student when the sit-ins began. He immediately became involved and went to jail four times. "My mother wrote me a letter and said 'Get out of the movement,' but I couldn't. . . . I wrote her and said, 'I have acted according to my convictions and according to my Christian conscience. . . . My soul will not be satisfied until freedom, justice, and fair play become a reality for all people.' " Lewis later followed Marion Barry and Chuck McDew to become Chairman of SNCC.

"Do show yourself friendly on the counter at all times.

Do sit straight and always face the counter. Don't strike back, or curse back if attacked. Don't laugh out. Don't hold conversations. Don't block entrances." These were the instructions to sit-in demonstrators in Nashville. They demanded a careful balance of quiet non-resistance and a determined militancy, and perhaps no one better expressed this than Diane Nash, a tiny, slender, campus beauty queen at Fisk, one of the pillars of the Nashville student movement and later a founder of SNCC. When students were being cross-examined at the trials that followed the Nashville demonstrations, one of the standard questions was: "Do you know Diane Nash?" Friendship with her was apparently full of perils.

Twelve days after the Greensboro incident, forty students sat in at Woolworth's in Nashville. There was at first some discussion about whether the white exchange students should go along, but finally the prevailing opinion was in favor. Candie Anderson recalls:

> That first sit-in was easy. . . . It was a Thursday afternoon and it was snowing. There were not many people downtown. Store personnel ran around nervously. . . . My friends were determined to be courteous and well-behaved. . . . Most of them read or studied while they sat at the counters, for three or four hours. I heard them remind each other not to leave cigarette ashes on the counter, to take off their hats, etc. . . . When the sit-in was over we all met in church. There must have been five hundred kids there, and we all sang together. . . .

By the fourth sit-in, tension was mounting rapidly. There was violence that day. Lighted cigarettes were pushed against the backs of girls sitting at the counter. A white sit-inner, on a stool beside a Negro girl, became a special object of attention by the crowd nearby. Someone kept calling him a "nigger-lover." When he didn't respond he was pulled off the stool, thrown to the floor, and kicked. At McClellan's variety store, a white man kept blowing cigar smoke into the face of a Negro sitting at the counter, a Fisk University student named Paul LePrad, who made no move. This infuriated the man. He pulled the student from his stool and hit him. LePrad got back on the stool. He was pulled off again and hit. The police came and arrested LePrad and the seventeen students sitting in with him.

The group at Woolworth's, where Candie Anderson was, heard about this incident. They decided to go to McClellan's to protest.

> There was a rope around the stools, showing that the counter was closed. We climbed over the rope. A policeman stood there and said quite clearly, "Do not sit down," and we sat down. . . . I became suddenly aware of the crowd of people standing behind us. . . . Young kids threw french fried potatoes at us, and gum, and cigarette butts. I looked down the counter at Barbara Crosby in a straight pink skirt and nice white blouse, and at Stephen in a dark suit, with a calculus book. . . . The policemen simply lined up behind us and peeled us two by two off the stools. . . . The crowd in the store . . . shouted out approval. They said about Barbara and me. . . . Oh, white . . . WHITE, WHITE, WHITE! Three paddy wagons were blinking at us from the street. Once more we had to walk through those crowds. Someone spit right in front of me. . . . The TV cameras took lots of pictures and we drove off to the Nashville city jail.

With seventy-six students in jail, a group of NAACP people in Nashville met the next day and pledged support. Fisk University President Stephen Wright said: "Students have been exposed all their lives to the teachings of the great American scriptures of democracy, freedom, and equality, and no literate person should be surprised that they reflect these teachings in their conduct."

But at white Vanderbilt University in Nashville, where a thirty-one-year-old Negro named James Lawson was enrolled in the Divinity School, it was different. Lawson, a conscientious objector and a pacifist, believed in nonviolent resistance. When the first mass arrests took place, newspapermen quoted him as saying he would advise students to violate the law. The *Nashville Banner* immediately called this "incitation to anarchy" and added: "There is no place in Nashville for flannel-mouthed agitators, white or colored—under whatever sponsorship, imported for preachment of mass disorder; self-supported vagrants, or paid agents of strife-breeding organizations." The Vanderbilt trustees, one of whom was the publisher of the *Nashville Banner*, another of whom was president of one of the large department stores where sit-ins had taken place, voted the next day to give Lawson the choice of withdrawing from the movement or dismissal from the University.

Charging the press with distorting his statements, Lawson refused to leave the movement, and in early March he was expelled, three months before his scheduled graduation. Most of the sixteen faculty members of the divinity school, all white, protested. By May, eleven of them, as well as Dean J. Robert Nelson, had resigned over the refusal of the school to re-admit Lawson, leaving four persons on the divinity school faculty. The *Richmond News Leader* commented: "Good riddance . . . Vanderbilt University will be better off. . . ."

The Nashville sit-ins continued, with arrests, trials, and students deciding to stay in jail in protest rather than pay fines or put up bond. Chief defense lawyer for the students was sixty-two-year-old Z. Alexander Looby, a distinguished Negro attorney, born in Trinidad, and a member of the Nashville City Council.

On April 19, at five o'clock in the morning, while Looby and his wife were asleep in the backroom of their home, one block away from Fisk University's campus, a bomb exploded on his porch. In her dormitory room, Candie Anderson was awakened by the noise. "Only one time in my life have I heard a sound worse than the one when Mr. Looby's house was bombed," she wrote later. "That was when a girl fainted and I heard her head hit the floor. That's the kind of feeling it left when we heard the explosion. . . . It would have seemed unreal, I think, if the sirens had not kept insistently coming. . . ."

One hundred and forty-seven windows were blown out in Meharry Medical School across the street, and the front part of the Looby's house was demolished, but the attorney and his wife were not hurt. Perhaps, as James Bevel (who married Diane Nash) said, "The Devil has got to come out of these people." For after the bombing, and after a protest march of 2000 Negroes on City Hall, negotiations for desegregation got under way in earnest. In early May, four theaters and six lunch counters downtown declared an end to the color line. In the meantime, the sit-ins had spread to Chattanooga, Knoxville, Memphis, and Oak Ridge. By late spring, seven Tennessee cities had desegregated some of their lunch counters.

CORE, with its long emphasis on nonviolent direct action, played an important part, once the sit-ins began, as an educational and organizing agent. Tom Gaither, of Claflin College in Orangeburg, South Carolina, tells of CORE classes which started there, inspired by the Rock Hill sit-ins. (Those, the first in South Carolina, took place even before the first Nashville sit-ins, with one hundred students from two Negro junior colleges sitting in.)

The Orangeburg students held classes in nonviolence over a period of three or four days for students from Claflin College and South Carolina State, both Negro colleges, and then picked forty students who felt confident in the use of nonviolent techniques. Here is a sample of the instructions to people being schooled in nonviolence:

> You may choose to face physical assault without protecting yourself, hands at the sides, unclenched; or you may choose to protect yourself, making plain you do not intend to hit back. If you choose to protect yourself, you practice positions such as these:

> To protect the skull, fold the hands over the head.
>
> To prevent disfigurement of the face, bring the elbows together in front of the eyes.
>
> For girls, to prevent internal injury from kicks, lie on the side and bring the knees upward to the chin; for boys, kneel down and arch over, with skull and face protected.

The Kress five and dime store in Orangeburg became the object of careful plans. Students checked the store entrances, counted the number of stools at the lunch counter, calculated exactly the number of minutes it took to walk from a central point on campus to the Kress store. On February 25, the sit-ins began, and lunch counters closed in downtown Orangeburg. A thousand students were being trained meanwhile, and a mass march through the streets of the city took place, with no violence, no arrests.

When lunch counters reopened on March 14, followed by another great march designed to support a new wave of sit-ins, the police moved in with tear gas bombs and water hoses. The weather was sub-freezing. Students were drenched and knocked off their feet by the water pressure. One of these was a blind girl. Over five hundred were arrested and, with the jails full, three hundred and fifty were jammed into a chicken coop and enclosed by a seven-foot wire fence. There was no shelter against the bitter cold.

Meanwhile, students jammed into the basement of the city jail were sweating in 90-degree temperatures from the nearby boiler room. One student, drenched from head to toe, was locked in solitary confinement with water three inches deep covering the cell floor. Requests for dry clothing were denied. A Claflin College nurse came to give first aid, and had to force her way inside. Two hundred students marched around the courthouse in protest. Tom Gaither, the movement's leader (and today a professional civil rights worker with CORE), was marching with them when he was seized and put into jail.

The sit-ins were spreading southward now. They were also becoming larger and better organized. In Atlanta, where they were preceded by many meetings and by a sensational full-page ad of eloquent protest in the *Atlanta Constitution* addressed to a startled white community, the sit-ins were planned like a military operation. On March 15, at exactly 11:00 A.M., two hundred students moved into ten downtown restaurants which had been carefully selected because they were connected with city or county or federal government, and were therefore subject to the Fourteenth Amendment's requirement that *public* places may not discriminate. Seventy-six students were arrested, and the city of Atlanta was never the same again.

There was some violence in those first months of the sit-ins. In Jacksonville, Florida, the city was in turmoil for three days: a white sit-in student was attacked in jail and his jaw was broken; a sixteen-year-old Negro boy was pistol-whipped by the Ku Klux Klan; a Negro man unconnected with the demonstrations who went through a police roadblock was shot to death by a white service station attendant. In Atlanta, acid was thrown at sit-in leader Lonnie King. In Frankfort, Kentucky, the gymnasium of a Negro college was set afire. In Columbia, South Carolina, a Negro sit-in student was stabbed. In Houston, Texas, a twenty-seven-year-old Negro was kidnaped and flogged with a chain, and the symbol KKK was carved on his chest.

Mississippi responded with a special savagery. When students marched down the street in Jackson, police used clubs, tear gas, and police dogs. Women, children, and a photographer were beaten by police and bystanders, and some demonstrators were bitten by dogs. In Biloxi, Mississippi, Negroes trying to use a public beach were attacked with clubs and chains by crowds of whites, and ten were wounded by gunfire.

Yet, considering the number of people involved in demonstrations and the intense psychological tremors accompanying this sudden attack by long-quiescent Negroes on the old way of life, violence was minimal. The restraint of the demonstrators themselves was one factor; they gave the least possible excuse for club-happy and trigger-happy policemen, and the most the police could justify, in most cases, was carting them off to jail. The ratio of social change, both immediate and long-term, to the resulting violence, was extremely high.

The sit-ins marked a turning point for the Negro American, subordinate for three hundred years. He was rebelling now, not with the blind, terrible, understandable hatred of the slave revolts, but with skill in organization, sophistication in tactics, and an unassailable moral position. With these went a ferocious refusal to retreat. What had been an orderly, inch-by-inch advance via legal processes now became a revolution in which unarmed regiments marched from one objective to another with bewildering speed.

The idea so long cherished by Southern whites—and by many Northerners too—that the Southern Negro (whether through ignorance or intimidation or a shrewd recognition of reality) was content with the way things were, that only a handful of agitators opposed the system of segregation, was swept aside by the mass marches, demonstrations, meetings. Montgomery had been the first sign of this, and now it was made clear beyond argument that Negroes all across the South had only been waiting for an opportunity to end their long silence.

Impatience was the mood of the young sit-in demonstrators: impatience with the courts, with national and local governments, with negotiation and conciliation, with the traditional Negro organizations and the old Negro leadership, with the unbearably slow pace of desegregation in a century of accelerated social change.

A Negro never before seen by white Americans was brought into the national view. The young educated Negro was raised inside a ghetto, then went off to a Negro college, where he or she was kept behind the ivy-colored walls by conservative Negro college administrators. Ostensibly this was to protect the sensitive Negro student, but, as a by-product, it protected white society from the possibility of rebellion. And in addition, the separation left unmarred the images in white American minds of the faithful, hard-working Negro maid or handyman or the lazy drunk. In early 1960, the Negro student climbed over the wall and into view on millions of television screens all over the country. The picture was impressive, even to those not really convinced these youngsters were doing the right thing. The *Richmond News Leader* (the same paper which had declared "Good riddance" to Lawson, *et al.*) said in an editorial on February 22, 1960:

> Many a Virginian must have felt a tinge of wry regret at the state of things as they are, in reading of Saturday's "sit-downs" by Negro students in Richmond stores. Here were the colored students, in coats, white shirts, ties, and one of them was reading Goethe and one was taking notes from a biology text. And here, on the sidewalk outside, was a gang of white boys come to heckle, a ragtail rabble, slack-jawed, black-jacketed, grinning fit to kill, and some of them, God save the mark, were waving the proud and honored flag of the Southern States in the last war fought by gentlemen. Eheu! It gives one pause.

Ralph McGill, long a believer—in the face of bitter attack by segregationists—in the deliberate processes of law to effect an equalitarian society, did not immediately endorse the sit-ins. But by the time he wrote his book, *The South and the Southerner*, he had come to a blunt conclusion:

> The sit-ins were, without question, productive of the most change. . . . No argument in a court of law could have dramatized the immorality and irrationality of such a custom

> as did the sit-ins. . . . The sit-ins reached far out into the back country. They inspired adult men and women, fathers, mothers, grandmothers, aunts and uncles, to support the young students in the cities. Not even the Supreme Court decision on the schools in 1954 had done this. . . . The central moral problem was enlarged.

Actually, the sit-ins represented an intricate union of economic and moral power. To the store owner, they meant a disruption of normal business; liberal and moderate people in the city and in the nation now, perhaps for the first time, faced their own status as a privileged group in American society.

The sit-ins were an important learning experience for white Southerners, and also for those Northerners who were convinced of some mystical, irremovable germ of prejudice in the Southern mind: when the first lunch-counters were desegregated, the world did not come to an end. Whites and Negroes could use public facilities together, it was shown, without violent repercussions, without white withdrawal. Southern whites, once a new pattern became accepted and established in the community, would conform to it as they conformed to the old. Men and women seeking a sandwich at a lunch counter, as young Negroes could see readily in many of the sit-ins, were more interested in satisfying their hunger or their thirst than in who sat next to them. After two months of desegregation in Winston Salem, North Carolina, the manager of a large store said: "You would think it had been going on for fifty years. I am tickled to death over the situation."

There were potential repercussions on the American social structure of enormous scope, far beyond the problem of race. For what happened in the sit-ins is that Americans were resorting to civil disobedience on a national scale, ignoring local statutes, applying the direct pressure of masses of aggrieved people to the nerve centers of the opposition, without using the intermediary of normal political channels. To move outside the American governmental structure in order to effectuate social change, to assert the power of the popular demonstration as superior to that of the parliamentary process, was dangerously suggestive. And, in fact, civil disobedience as a technique spread in a matter of weeks from sit-ins in restaurants to stand-ins at movies, kneel-ins at churches, wade-ins at beaches, and a dozen different kinds of extra-legal demonstrations against segregation.

The sit-ins took the established Negro organizations by surprise. The NAACP had a large membership in the Southern states, had handled thousands of legal cases there, and was a long-established center for Negroes wanting to share their dissatisfactions. But it had not carried on any widespread campaigns of direct protest in the South. The Congress of Racial Equality, or CORE, was a Northern-based organization, with just a few staff members below the Mason-Dixon line. The Southern Christian Leadership Conference, which grew out of the Montgomery boycott and was led by Martin Luther King, Jr., had an office in Atlanta, and was planning various actions in the South, but had engaged in no large-scale movement since Montgomery. Spontaneity and self-sufficiency were the hallmarks of the sit-ins; without adult advice or consent, the students planned and carried them through.

What happened then was that the student movement galvanized the older organizations into a new dynamism, won the support of some of the established Negro leaders who quickly sensed that a new wind was blowing, and left far behind those leaders who could not break either old habits of thinking, or old ties with the white elite.

From the beginning, the students found strong backing in the generation just ahead of them—young Negro professionals in their thirties or early forties, who helped mobilize community support behind the young people. One thinks of Carl Holman, Dr. Clinton Warner, and Whitney Young in Atlanta; also of Dr. Anderson, Slater King and C. B. King in Albany; and of Martin Luther King himself.

On the other hand, the self-interest of some elements in the Negro community had long become enmeshed with that of the whites who held political and economic power, and even the explosive force of the sit-ins could not break that tie. Presidents of state-supported Negro colleges, with an eye on trustees, regents, and state legislatures, lashed out at their student rebels. Faculty members, fearful for their jobs, remained silent. At Southern University in Baton Rouge, whose 5000 students made it the largest Negro institution in the nation, eighteen sit-in leaders were suspended. At Albany State College in Albany, Georgia, the president eventually got rid of forty student demonstrators. At Alabama State and Florida A & M, punishment was swift. Even at some private, church-supported institutions, like Benedict and Allen Colleges in South Carolina, college administrators threatened expulsion for students who joined the sit-in movement and fired the few faculty members who spoke their minds.

Between the unequivocal supporters and the conservative die-hards in the adult Negro community was a third group, whose response to the new militancy of the college generation was complex and curious. These were Negroes ranking high in the social structure of the community, who were beset by a number of conflicting pressures: that of the white side of town, where they had some useful relationships; that of the Negro community at large, which embraced the sit-ins, and on which they were dependent socially and politically; that of their own long resentment against segregation; of a conservatism fundamental to their lofty position; of an uncomfortable feeling of being left in the shadows by the immature upstarts of the student movement. In this confusion of interests, the reaction of such people was often to support the movement publicly, and try privately to keep it within respectable limits.

Atlanta is a case in point. Here, a number of the college presidents in the Atlanta University Center, while publicly expressing their support, tried to discourage their students from direct action activities. Some ministers and businessmen reacted similarly. Jeremy Larner, writing in the *New Leader* at the time of the sit-ins, reports a meeting that spring of five student leaders summoned to a conference with the Negro old guard of Atlanta.

> While the students wore slacks and sport shirts, their elders were dressed like New York bankers. Their faces were somber and the atmosphere was somewhat like that of an emergency meeting of the General Motors board of directors. From a high table in front, the meeting was presided over by a man with a pleasant face and remarkably light skin who spoke and looked like President Eisenhower. He was flanked by an Episcopalian minister, a banker, a realtor, and a lawyer. One by one they rose and delivered sober, articulate speeches. I was impressed by the absence of Southern accents, and later discovered that they sent their own children to Northern universities.

Whether Larner's report of what these "elders" said to the sit-in leaders is an exact quote, or a paraphrase, it catches the spirit of what so many of the students heard from well-placed adults in those hectic days:

> So you see, kids, we've been in this a long time. We want the same things you do, but we know by now they can't be gotten overnight. It's our experience that you have to work slowly to get lasting results. We'd hate to see your movement backfire and spoil the things we've worked so hard for. You need guidance, and we hope you'll have the vision to accept it.

The response of the students was brief, unpolished, to the point. "We are continuing the movement as best we know how. We hope you will join us."

They did continue the movement, and the important men

of the Negro community, whatever qualms they had, let it be known to the public that they had joined.

As pointed out earlier, there was no central direction to the sit-ins. The sparks from that first almost-innocent sit-in of four college freshmen in Greensboro showered the South and caught fire in a hundred localities. But hardly a month had passed before Ella Baker, in charge of the Southern Christian Leadership Conference office in Atlanta and observing the wild spread of the sit-ins, decided that something should be done to coordinate them.

Ella Baker, middle-aged, dark-skinned, beautiful, with a deep-throated voice that seemed suited for the stage, had grown up in a little town in North Carolina. As a girl, she had listened to stories of slave revolts told by her ninety-year-old grandmother, who as a slave had been whipped for refusing to marry the man picked out for her by her master. Miss Baker was a champion debater in high school, and valedictorian of her graduating class at Shaw University in Raleigh. She wanted to go to medical school and become a medical missionary, then dreamed of teaching sociology at the University of Chicago. But family difficulties intervened. Instead, she went to New York.

There, she found that despite her college education, jobs were closed to her because of her color; she worked as a waitress, or found a job in a factory. She lived in Harlem in the 1930's, worked for the WPA on consumer education, started consumers' cooperatives in Philadelphia and Chicago, and then in 1940 turned to the NAACP, spending six years with them as a field secretary. Then she worked for the Urban League and other groups.

When the Southern Christian Leadership Conference was organized by Martin Luther King, Bayard Rustin, and Stanley Levinson in 1957, Ella Baker came South to organize a series of mass meetings for them. In early 1958 she set up the SCLC office in Atlanta and was its first full-time executive-secretary. Deciding, in late February of 1960, that the sit-in leaders should be brought together, she asked the SCLC to underwrite it financially. With $800 of SCLC money, the prestige of Martin Luther King, the organizing wisdom of Ella Baker, and the enthusiasm of the rare young people who were leading the new student movement, the Student Nonviolent Coordinating Committee was born.

Ella Baker went to Raleigh and got her Alma Mater, Shaw University, to provide facilities for a meeting of about a hundred students. But by the time of the conference on Easter weekend, April 15–17, 1960, demonstrations had spread so fast that there were sixty centers of sit-in activity. Also, nineteen northern colleges were interested enough to send delegates. The result was that over two hundred people came to the conference, one hundred twenty-six of them student delegates from fifty-eight different Southern communities in twelve states.

Jane Stembridge, from Virginia, later described her feelings that first night in Raleigh:

> The most inspiring moment for me was the first time I heard the students sing "We Shall Overcome" . . . It was hot that night upstairs in the auditorium. Students had just come in from all over the South, meeting for the first time. February 1 was not long past. There was no SNCC, no *ad hoc* committees, no funds, just people who did not know what to expect but who came and released the common vision in that song. I had just driven down from Union Seminary in New York—out of it, except that I cared, and that I was a Southerner. . . . It was inspiring because it was the beginning, and because, in a sense, it was the purest moment. I am a romantic. But I call this moment the one. . . .

James Lawson, the divinity school student just expelled from Vanderbilt University, gave the keynote address. At the organizing sessions, there was some tension over whether to have an official connection with SCLC. It was finally decided to maintain a friendly relationship with SCLC and other organizations but to remain independent. This urge for freedom from adult fetters and formal ties had marked the student movement from the beginning, so the decision was important, reflecting a mood which has continued in SNCC to this day. The conference set up a temporary committee, which would meet monthly through the spring and summer, and would coordinate the various student movements around the South. Ed King, who had been a leader in the Frankfort, Kentucky sit-ins, was asked to serve, at least temporarily, as administrative secretary.

The first meeting after the Raleigh Conference was held in May, 1960, on the campus of Atlanta University. About fifteen of the student leaders were there, as were Martin Luther King, Jr., James Lawson, Ella Baker, Len Holt (a CORE lawyer from Norfolk, Virginia), and observers from the National Student Association, the YWCA, the American Friends Service Committee, and other groups. They now called themselves the Temporary Student Nonviolent Coordinating Committee, and elected Marion Barry, at this time doing graduate work at Fisk, as chairman. A statement of purpose was adopted, of which the first paragraph states the theme:

> We affirm the philosophical or religious ideal of nonviolence as the foundation of our purpose, the pre-supposition of our faith, and the manner of our action. Nonviolence as it grows from Judaic-Christian traditions seeks a social order of justice permeated by love. Integration of human endeavor represents the first step towards such a society. . . .

It was decided to set up an office, hire a secretary to man it over the summer months, begin to raise money, plan nonviolent institutes for the summer, print a newsletter, and try to coordinate the various student activities throughout the South. Marion Barry told reporters that the sit-in movement "demonstrates the rapidity with which mass action can bring about social change. This is only the beginning."

They called Jane Stembridge at Union Theological Seminary in New York and asked her if she would serve as SNCC's first office secretary. In early June, 1960, she arrived in Atlanta. Bob Moses, recalling his first trip South that summer of 1960, described later how "SNCC and Jane Stembridge were squeezed in one corner of the SCLC office. . . . I was licking envelopes, one at a time, and talking—Niebuhr, Tillich and Theos—with Jane, who was fresh from a year at Union. . . . Miss Ella Baker was in another corner of the office."

In June, the first issue of *The Student Voice* appeared. Three years later it would be beautifully printed and designed (though still small, direct, terse) and illustrated by remarkable photos of SNCC in action. At this time it was crudely mimeographed, carrying news of the Raleigh Conference and the May meeting. It was not so intensely organizational that it could not find room for a poem, written by one of the founders of SNCC, later to be its chief writer of press releases and editor of *The Student Voice*, Julian Bond:

> I too, hear America singing
> But from where I stand
> I can only hear Little Richard
> And Fats Domino.
> But sometimes,
> I hear Ray Charles
> Drowning in his own tears
> or Bird
> Relaxing at Camarillo
> or Horace Silver doodling,
> Then I don't mind standing
> a little longer.

The new SNCC organization, that summer and early fall of 1960, found that "coordinating" was not easy. Jane Stembridge later recalled:

> A great deal of time was spent trying to find out exactly what was going on in the protest centers. . . . Response was next to nil. . . . This was because the students were too busy protesting and because they did not understand the weight of the press release (thank God some still don't). . . . No one really needed "organization" because we then had a movement. . . . Members of the first SNCC were vague simply because they were right damn in the middle of directing sit-ins, being in jail, etc., and they did not know what was going on anywhere outside of their immediate downtown. . . . We had no one "in the field" either. SNCC called for demonstrations once or twice. The response was extremely spotty and then the news was not sent in. We could not afford phone calls and so it went. SNCC was not coordinating the movement. . . . I would say the main thing done then was to let people know we existed. . . . We were not sure, and still aren't, "what SNCC is" . . .

In July, in Los Angeles, where the National Democratic Convention was about to nominate John F. Kennedy and Lyndon Johnson, Marion Barry appeared for SNCC before the Platform Committee of the Convention, recommending strong federal action: to speed school desegregation, to enact a fair employment law, to assure the right to vote against Southern economic reprisal and violence, to protect demonstrators against false arrest and police repression by invoking that clause of the Fourteenth Amendment which says: "No state shall make or enforce any law which shall abridge the privileges and immunities of citizens of the United States."

The sit-ins, Barry told the Platform Committee, "in truth were peaceful petitions to the conscience of our fellow citizens for redress of the old grievances that stem from racial segregation and discrimination." Characteristically, the statement was not coldly organizational, but carried some of the poetic freshness of the new student movement:

> . . . The ache of every man to touch his potential is the throb that beats out the truth of the American Declaration of Independence and the Constitution. America was founded because men were seeking room to become. . . . We are again seeking that room. . . . We want to walk into the sun and through the front door. For three hundred and fifty years, the American Negro has been sent to the back door. . . . We grew weary. . . .

Barry spoke directly to the charge made by ex-President Harry Truman during the sit-ins, that the student movement was somehow connected with communism. He said:

> To label our goals, methods, and presuppositions "communistic" is to credit Communism with an attempt to remove tyranny and to create an atmosphere where genuine communication can occur. Communism seeks power, ignores people, and thrives on social conflict. We seek a community in which man can realize the full meaning of the self which demands open relationship with others.

In October of 1960, at a conference of several hundred delegates in Atlanta, SNCC was put on a permanent basis. It was not (and never has become) a membership organization. This left the adhesion of individuals to the group fluid and functional, based simply on who was carrying on activity. The Student Nonviolent Coordinating Committee consisted of a delegate from each of sixteen Southern states and the District of Columbia, plus a few voting members and many observers from various national student and race relations organizations, such as CORE, SCLC, the YWCA, the National Student Association, the NAACP, and the Southern Conference Educational Fund.

Again, the purpose was to coordinate the student movement. But the movement, still with a quality of abandon, still spontaneous and unstructured, refused to be put into a bureaucratic box. The twig was bent, and the tree grew that way. For SNCC, even after it had a large staff, its own office, and money for long-distance phone calls, managed to maintain an autonomy in the field, an unpredictability of action, a lack of overall planning which brought exasperation to some of its most ardent supporters, bewilderment to outside observers, and bemusement to the students themselves.

Throughout the winter of 1960–1961, sit-ins continued, linked only vaguely by SNCC, but creating a warmth of commitment, a solidarity of purpose which spurred awareness of SNCC by students all over the South. They also sustained a vision—or perhaps, knowing SNCC, a set of various visions, which kept Marion Barry, Jane Stembridge, Julian Bond, Diane Nash, Charles Sherrod, Charles Jones, and others, going.

When ten students were arrested in Rock Hill, South Carolina, in February, 1961, the SNCC steering committee, meeting in Atlanta, made its boldest organizational decision up to that date. Four people, it was agreed, would go to Rock Hill to sit in, would be arrested, and would refuse bail, as the first ten students had done, in order to dramatize the injustice to the nation. The Rock Hill action was the start of the jail-no bail policy.

Sit-in veterans Charles Sherrod (Petersburg, Virginia), Charles Jones (Charlotte, North Carolina) and Diane Nash were to go. The fourth person was a relative novice in the movement, Spelman College student Ruby Doris Smith, who talked her older sister out of the trip so she could go instead. "I went home that night to explain to my mother. She couldn't understand why I had to go away—why I had to go to Rock Hill."

Ruby Doris and the others spent thirty days in prison, the first time anyone had served full sentences in the sit-in movement. "I read a lot there: *The Ugly American, The Life of*

Mahatma Gandhi, Exodus, The Wall Between. . . . Every day at noon we sang 'We Shall Overcome'. . . ." The fellows had been put on a road gang: Tom Gaither of CORE, Charles Sherrod and Charles Jones of SNCC, and nine others. The captain of the guards took their textbooks away, saying: "This is a prison—not a damned school." He turned out to be wrong.

"Jail-no bail" spread. In Atlanta, in February, 1961, eighty students from the Negro colleges went to jail and refused to come out. I knew some, but not all, of the participants from Spelman, where I taught history and political science. That fall, when a very bright student named Lana Taylor, fair-skinned, rather delicate looking, joined my course on Chinese Civilization, I learned she had been in jail. In early 1964 I came across a reminiscence of Jane Stembridge:

> . . . the most honest moment—the one in which I saw the guts-type truth—stripped of anything but total fear and total courage . . . was one day during 1961 in Atlanta. . . . Hundreds went out that day and filled every lunch counter. . . . There was much humor—like A. D. King coordinating the whole damn thing with a walkie-talkie. . . The moment: Lana Taylor from Spelman was sitting next to me. The manager walked up behind her, said something obscene, and grabbed her by the shoulders. "Get the hell out of here, nigger." Lana was not going. I do not know whether she should have collapsed in nonviolent manner. She probably did not know. She put her hands under the counter and held. He was rough and strong. She just held and I looked down at that moment at her hands . . . brown, strained . . . every muscle holding. . . . All of a sudden he let go and left. I thought he knew he could not move that girl—ever. . . ."

The sit-ins of 1960 were the beginning. They left not only excitement, but a taste of victory. The spring and summer of 1961 brought, for the youngsters in SNCC and for many others, an experience of a different kind: an ordeal by fire and club. These were the Freedom Rides.

3. The Freedom Rides

Stokely Carmichael, tall, slim, brown-skinned, gives the impression he would stride cool and smiling through Hell, philosophizing all the way. Arriving in the Jackson, Mississippi, train terminal as a Freedom Rider in the spring of 1961 (he was twenty, and a student at Howard University) Stokely and a young woman Rider made their way past what seemed an endless mob of howling, cursing people who screamed and threw lighted cigarettes; then they went into the white waiting room, where they were arrested. They were part of that extraordinary group of Americans who, in the Freedom Rides of 1961, embarked on a dramatic attempt to expose and challenge segregation in interstate travel in the Deep South.

In Parchman jail, the state penitentiary, Stokely almost drove his captors crazy: when they decided to take away his mattress because he had been singing, he held tightly to it while they dragged it—and him—out of the cell, and they had to put wristbreakers on him to try to make him relinquish his grip; after six fellow Riders had been put in solitary confinement, he demanded the same treatment, and kept banging loudly on his cell door until his wish was granted. When, after 49 days, Stokely and the others left Parchman, the sheriff and his guards were somewhat relieved.

At the time of the Freedom Rides in the spring and summer of 1961, SNCC was one year old and still loosely put together; it had an office in Atlanta with two full-time workers who maintained sporadic communication with affiliated student movements all over the South. But the students who went on the Rides—most of them veterans of the sit-ins—came out of jail to become central figures in a stronger SNCC organization that would now take up forward positions in a no-man's-land untouched since Reconstruction.

The sit-ins had begun a new phase of the Negro upsurge, in which students—matured overnight into social revolutionaries—started to play the leading role. These same students, in the brutal training ground of the Freedom Rides, became toughened, experienced. And in the course of it all, they somehow decided that the Deep, Deep South, out of which they had just barely escaped alive, was the place where they must go back to do their work.

To CORE should go most of the credit for the Freedom Rides. Formed in Chicago in 1942 to conduct nonviolent direct action against racial discrimination, CORE worked successfully in Chicago, in St. Louis, in New Jersey, to end segregation in restaurants and other public places. In 1947, CORE and the Fellowship of Reconciliation, in order to follow up a Supreme Court decision outlawing discrimination in interstate travel, sponsored a Freedom Ride which they called a "Journey of Reconciliation." Bayard Rustin, a Negro and a fiercely eloquent pacifist, and James Peck, white (he had startled his Harvard classmates years back by bringing a Negro date to the freshman dance), also a pacifist, were among sixteen Negro and white riders. They rode two buses through the upper South, with very little violence and only a few arrests, and established that most passengers and drivers would not go out of their way to make trouble for people who chose to sit where they pleased.

Again, in 1961, fourteen years later, a Supreme Court decision—this time in the Boynton Case, extending desegregation from carriers themselves to terminal facilities—stimulated action. Early that year, Tom Gaither (mentioned previously as the CORE man in the Rock Hill sit-in) spoke to Gordon Carey, also of CORE, about a "Freedom Ride," after which a national council meeting of CORE agreed to undertake it, and CORE's new national director, James Farmer, issued a call on March 13. Farmer himself and James Peck were the first two volunteers, and on May 1, 1961, a group of thirteen, seven Negroes and six whites, assembled in Washington, D.C. for a briefing session on nonviolence. Part of the group riding a Greyhound bus and the others a Trailways bus, they started the long trip from Washington to New Orleans on May 4.

On the Greyhound bus was John Lewis of SNCC, who had participated in the Nashville sit-ins. They made it through Virginia and North Carolina with little trouble, but at the Greyhound bus station in Rock Hill, South Carolina (as James Peck relates the story in his gripping book, *Freedom Ride*) twenty toughs were waiting. John Lewis was the first to be slugged as he approached the white waiting room. Behind him was Albert Bigelow (famous as the pacifist skipper of the *Golden Rule,* which sailed into an atomic testing area in the Pacific to protest nuclear warfare), who was attacked by three men. Police first watched, then stopped the beatings, and the group entered the white waiting room. The two buses went on, through Augusta and Athens, Georgia, with long lay-overs en route, and on May 13 arrived in Atlanta, where they stopped for the night before heading into Alabama and Mississippi.

Sunday, May 14, when the buses left Atlanta and crossed into Alabama, was Mother's Day. That day the Greyhound bus was stopped, its tires slashed, outside of Anniston, Alabama, and surrounded by a mob. An incendiary device hurled through a window set the bus on fire, and those on board had to make their way out, choking, through the dense smoke, while the bus burned to a charred iron skeleton. Twelve of the passengers were hospitalized briefly for smoke inhalation, but the riders assembled again and took another bus into Birmingham.

In the meantime, the Trailways bus, an hour behind the

other, was arriving in Anniston, the driver insisting he would not go on unless the group sat segregated. Eight hoodlums climbed aboard the bus and began beating the Negroes in the front seats. When James Peck and retired professor Walter Bergman moved forward to try to dissuade them, Peck was knocked to the ground, bleeding, and Bergman received a crushing blow on the head. The whole group was forced to the back of the bus, which went on to Birmingham.

Peck tells of his group's arrival in Birmingham, of the mob lined up on the sidewalk near the loading platform as they got off, with young men carrying iron bars following them as they went into the white waiting room and towards the lunch counter. Then the attack came. Peck and Charles Person, an Atlanta Negro student who had been in the sit-ins there, were dragged into an alleyway, six men working on Peck, five men on Person, with fists and pipes. Peck, battered into unconsciousness, awoke to find the alleyway empty, blood flowing down his face. His friend Bergman came along and they managed to get a cab to Rev. Fred L. Shuttleworth's house, where they saw Person, a gash in the back of his head, his face swollen.

Peck was taken to the hospital and lay on an operating table for several hours while reporters plied him with questions and doctors sewed fifty-three stitches in his head. At 2:00 A.M. Peck was discharged from the hospital, and then a brief nightmarish episode followed. Waiting outside the hospital for Rev. Shuttlesworth to arrive in a car, he was told by police to get off the street or be arrested for vagrancy. Returning to the hospital, he was told by a guard that discharged patients were not permitted in the hospital. He went back into the street, and, fortunately, the car arrived to pick him up.

A Southern Regional Council report on the Freedom Rides, discussing the bus-burning and beatings in Anniston and Birmingham, commented that all this took place "while police were either inactive, not present, or strangely late in arrival." Police knew in advance of the arrival of the buses in these cities, but they simply were not on hand as the violence unfolded. When Birmingham police chief Bull Connor was questioned on this, he replied that protection was not available because so many of his men were off for Mother's Day.

The entire Freedom Ride group assembled in Birmingham the next afternoon, ready to go on to Montgomery. No bus driver would take them. They waited for an hour on the loading platform while a mob gathered, then sat down in the white waiting room. It became clear that they would not get out of Birmingham, so they decided to fly on to New Orleans to participate in a mass rally there marking the May 17, 1954, Supreme Court decision. A bomb threat cancelled their first plane, and another mob gathered at the airport. After six difficult hours, they finally left Birmingham at 11:00 P.M. and arrived in New Orleans at midnight.

That was the end of the first Freedom Ride. It was at this point that SNCC and the Nashville student movement entered the picture. A new phase of the Freedom Rides began.

Ruby Doris Smith, spending more of her sophomore year at Spelman in the SNCC office than with her books, recalls clearly the tension in Atlanta when news came of the Mother's Day violence in Anniston and Birmingham.

> I remember Diane Nash called the Department of Justice from Nashville, and Lonnie King—you know he was head of the Atlanta student movement—also called the Department. Both of them asked the federal government to give protection to the Freedom Riders on the rest of their journey. And in both cases the Justice Department said no, they couldn't protect anyone, but if something happened, they would investigate. You know how they do. . . .

When the news came that the Riders could not go on by bus, that they were flying to New Orleans, an excited discussion went on over long distance between Nashville and

Atlanta, the two centers where SNCC had its strongest contingents. The Ride, they decided, should continue. If it didn't, it would prove that violence could overcome nonviolence.

The indomitable Diane Nash was quickly assembling a group of students in Nashville, determined to go to Birmingham and continue the Freedom Ride from there to Montgomery, then into Mississippi, then into New Orleans. They were joined by some members of the first Ride, including John Lewis and Henry Thomas. Ruby Doris Smith raced around Atlanta trying to raise money so that she could go along, but many Atlanta Negroes thought it was too dangerous, and tried to dissuade her from going.

Meanwhile the Nashville group had left, early in the morning of May 17, 1961. Eight Negroes and two whites were aboard a bus headed for Birmingham. Police got on the bus on the outskirts of Birmingham, ordered two students to change their seats, and arrested them when they refused. The rest of the group was arrested (the reason given was "protective custody") in the Birmingham terminal, after making their way through a crowd and trying in vain to get a bus driver to agree to take them on to Montgomery.

The Riders spent a night in jail. Then, early the next morning they were driven 120 miles to the Tennessee border by Birmingham police chief "Bull" Connor, and let out in the middle of nowhere. Diane and the others made their way back to Nashville and started all over, joined by more students, including three whites, so that there were now seventeen in the group. That same afternoon they were back, by bus, in the Birmingham terminal. It was May 19. Five days had passed since Mother's Day.

Ruby Doris Smith, her money finally in hand, flew from Atlanta to Birmingham to join the Nashville group:

> I was alone. . . . When I got to Birmingham I went to the bus terminal and joined the seventeen from Nashville. We

> waited all night trying to get a bus to Montgomery. Every time we got on a bus the driver said no, he wouldn't risk his life. The terminal kept crowding up with passengers who were stranded because the buses wouldn't go on. The Justice Department then promised Diane that the driver of the 4:00 A.M. bus would go on to Montgomery. But when he arrived he came off the bus and said to us: "I have only one life to give, and I'm not going to give it to NAACP or CORE!"

The students sat outside on the ramp for three hours, and sang Freedom Songs as dawn broke over Birmingham. Then they were startled to see the same bus driver return and, still grumbling, begin to collect tickets for the trip to Montgomery. Joined by two Birmingham Negroes and some newspapermen, but with no other white passengers aboard, the bus headed for Montgomery.

That trip to Montgomery took place on Saturday, May 20. The day before, a political drama was enacted on the long-distance wires between Washington, D.C. and Montgomery, Alabama. On Friday, President John Kennedy, concerned ever since the bus-burning and beatings of Mother's Day, telephoned the Capitol Building at Montgomery to talk to Governor John Patterson. Patterson had said, just before the Anniston-Birmingham violence: "The people of Alabama are so enraged that I cannot guarantee protection for this bunch of rabble-rousers." Patterson was not available to answer the phone and President Kennedy spoke to the Lieutenant-Governor.

The President said, in this conversation, that it was the federal government's responsibility to guarantee safe passage of people in interstate travel, and that he hoped Alabama could restore this right without the need for federal action. That same evening, a representative of the President, Justice Departmentman John Siegenthaler, flew to Montgomery to confer with Governor Patterson. Then he telephoned Attorney General Robert Kennedy in Washington, relaying Patterson's assurance that he had "the will, the force, the men, and the equipment to fully protect everyone in Alabama." Apparently, this promise of safe conduct led the Justice Department to arrange for a bus driver to leave the Birmingham terminal with the Freedom Riders. The F.B.I. notified the Montgomery police that the students were coming, was promised that precautionary steps would be taken, and told Washington that therefore no federal action was needed.

Ruby Doris Smith tells of the students' arrival in Montgomery:

> There were police cars all around the bus, and helicopters flying overhead. But when we got inside the Montgomery city limits, it all disappeared. It was around noon when we got to the terminal and got off the bus. Paul Brooks went to call cabs for us. People were meantime gathering nearby, and a CBS cameraman was taking pictures. Suddenly a large man with a cigar hit the cameraman. He kept dragging him all over the street, beating him. The cameraman was small. There was not one policeman around.

About three hundred persons had gathered at the terminal, but apparently only about twenty-five or thirty participated in the actual violence that followed. These had clubs and sticks. Fifteen of them clubbed one newspaperman, Norman Ritter, head of the Time-Life News Bureau, when he tried to come to the help of another newsman.

One of the first of the Riders to get off the bus was James Zwerg, a young white man from Appleton, Wisconsin, tall, slender, dressed neatly in an olive-green business suit. Several women screamed, "Kill the nigger-loving son of a bitch," and a group of white youngsters moved in, pounded at Zwerg with fists and sticks, and sent him bleeding to the pavement. Then others stomped his face into the hot tar of the roadway, while women shouted encouragement.

"Zwerg never attempted to defend himself in any way,"

Ruby Doris Smith recalls. "He never put his hands up or anything. Every time they knocked him down, he got back up." At just about that time, the cabs arrived for them.

> The mob turned from Zwerg to us. Someone yelled: "They're about to get away!" Then they started beating everyone. I saw John Lewis beaten, blood coming out of his mouth. People were running from all over. Every one of the fellows was hit. Some of them tried to take refuge in the post office, but they were turned out. . . . We saw some of the fellows on the ground, John Lewis lying there, blood streaming from his head. . . .

A few of the Riders escaped in the crowd. Others, trying to get through, were caught. Suitcases were torn from the students' hands; clothing and mail were scattered over the street. (Later, onlookers gathered the clothing together, along with an English composition book that belonged to one of the students, and set the pile on fire.)

One of the white girls was chased by the mob. John Siegenthaler, the President's emissary to Montgomery, was on the scene, and as he tried to get the girl into his car, someone struck him from behind and knocked him unconscious. He lay on the street while people milled around. In the meantime the police had arrived. Siegenthaler still lay unconscious on the pavement. A newspaperman asked Police Commissioner L. B. Sullivan why an ambulance wasn't called for Zwerg and for Siegenthaler. Sullivan replied: "Every white ambulance in town reports their vehicles have broken down." After Siegenthaler lay there twenty-five minutes, police put him in a car and took him to a downtown hospital.

Jim Zwerg got no medical attention for more than two hours. A Negro woman who saw him lying on the street called an ambulance, but none would come. For a long time he sat in a parked car in a state of semi-shock, the blood streaming from his mouth and nose. A reporter again suggested to Police

Commissioner Sullivan that Zwerg get medical attention. Sullivan retorted: "He hasn't requested it."

One Negro student, William Barbee, from the American Baptist Theological Seminary in Nashville, was knocked unconscious by a group using baseball bats. He lay on the loading platform of the bus terminal for twenty minutes before a Negro ambulance came. He would spend several weeks in the hospital.

Accounts vary about how long it took the police to arrive after the violence began. The Associated Press reported that it took them twenty minutes. Even after their arrival the violence continued; the police then used three or four tear gas bombs to disperse the mob, which had grown to over a thousand. Governor Patterson issued a statement in which he said that "state highway patrolmen responded in force seconds after they were called. Within five minutes, we had sixty-five state patrolmen on the scene. Officers restored order quickly. . . ."

As the news came to Washington, Robert Kennedy telephoned Governor Patterson, but was told by a secretary that the governor was out of town, that no one knew where he was or when he would return. The Attorney General now took several moves: he had Justice Department attorneys go into federal district court in Montgomery to enjoin the KKK, the National States Rights Party, and anyone supporting them from interfering with peaceful interstate travel; he had the F.B.I. send in an extra team to intensify its investigation of the violence connected with the Freedom Ride; he sent a contingent of U.S. marshals to Montgomery under Deputy Attorney General Byron White.

President John F. Kennedy issued a statement in which he called the situation "a source of the deepest concern," asked Alabama to prevent further violence, expressed the wish that citizens would refrain "from any action which would in any way tend to provoke further outbreaks," and said that he hoped local officials would meet their responsibilities, that the United States "intends to meet its."

Their heads bandaged, their wounds treated, the Freedom Riders stayed overnight in Montgomery, in the homes of local Negroes. The next day was Sunday, May 21, and they all appeared at Ralph Abernathy's First Baptist Church in Montgomery for a mass meeting to be held that evening. Martin Luther King, Jr., flew in from Chicago to speak at the meeting. Over 1200 Negroes and a few whites were there. In the church basement, the Freedom Riders gathered and clasped hands. Someone called out: "Everybody say Freedom!" The group responded. "Say it again!" someone shouted, and the cry "Freedom!" went up once more in the church basement. Then they all went upstairs and sat on the platform as the meeting began.

A crowd of whites, gathering outside the church, began throwing bottles and rocks at the church door. National Guardsmen stood by, for the Governor had that day declared martial law, and some local police were on duty. A group of U.S. marshals faced the crowd. After a while the marshals lobbed a few tear gas bombs into the crowd and it thinned out. But it was still too dangerous to let people come out of the church.

While all this was going on, two Atlanta students, who had heard about the violence that noon and had immediately taken a Greyhound bus for Montgomery, made their way through the National Guardsmen into the church. One of them was Frank Holloway, a SNCC worker, who later described that night in Abernathy's First Baptist Church:

> Inside were three or four times as many people as the church was supposed to hold, and it was very hot and uncomfortable. Some people were trying to sleep, but there was hardly room for anybody to turn around. Dr. King, other leaders, and the Freedom Riders were circulating through the church talking to people and trying to keep their spirits up. But it was a relief and like a haven to be among friends. . . .

Everyone stayed in the church until six the next morning and then left.

The students planned now to continue the Ride into Mississippi and then on to New Orleans. While they waited in Montgomery for several days, staying at the homes of Negro families there, more students arrived to join them—from Nashville, Atlanta, Washington. Five CORE people came into Montgomery from New Orleans. Twenty-seven Riders were now ready to go on to Jackson, Mississippi, where Governor Ross Barnett had said: "The Negro is different because God made him different to punish him."

At seven-thirty in the morning on Wednesday, May 24, with National Guardsmen lining both sides of the street near the bus terminal, twelve Freedom Riders (eleven Negro, one white), accompanied by six Guardsmen and sixteen newspapermen, left Montgomery for Jackson. Before leaving, they tasted victory by eating in the "white" cafeteria at the Trailways terminal. On the road, a convoy of three airplanes, two helicopters, and seven patrol cars accompanied the bus while, inside, James Lawson held a workshop on nonviolence. On arrival in Jackson, escorted into the city by National Guardsmen, the group was arrested trying to use white rest rooms and waiting rooms. The charges were the customary ones for civil rights demonstrators: breach of peace, refusal to obey an officer.

Several hours after the arrest of the first contingent of Riders in the Jackson terminal, the rest of the group, including James Farmer, arrived from Montgomery, also with National Guard escort, and entered the Jackson bus terminal. Frank Holloway wrote later in *New South* about this experience:

> Behind all these escorts, I felt like the President of the United States touring Russia or something. . . . At the door of the waiting room a policeman stood there like the doorman of the Waldorf Astoria and opened the door for us. . . . I guess the

> crooks in the city had a field day because all the Jackson police were at the bus station . . . opening doors for us. . . .

Standing in line at the terminal cafeteria, the Riders in this second group were arrested too, and joined their friends in the city jail. All twenty-seven were found guilty, given two-month suspended sentences, and fined $200. They decided to go to prison rather than pay, and were taken to the Hinds County jail across the street. "When we went in," Holloway recalls, we were met by some of the meanest looking, tobacco-chewing lawmen I have ever seen. They ordered us around like a bunch of dogs and I really began to feel like I was in a Mississippi jail." Then they were transferred to the penal farm out in the country:

> When we got there we met several men in ten-gallon hats, looking like something out of an old Western, with rifles in their hands, staring at us. . . . Soon they took us out to a room, boys on one side and girls on the other. One by one they took us into another room for questioning. . . . There were about eight guards with sticks in their hands in the second room, and the Freedom Rider being questioned was surrounded by these men. Outside we could hear the questions, and the thumps and whacks, and sometimes a quick groan or a cry. . . . They beat several Riders who didn't say "Yes, sir. . . ." Rev. C. T. Vivian of Chattanooga was beaten pretty bad. When he came out he had blood streaming from his head. . . . We could hear somebody slap a girl Freedom Rider, and her quick little scream. . . . She was about five feet tall and wore glasses. . . .

In the meantime, the newspapers were full of excited talk about the Freedom Rides. Attorney General Robert Kennedy, while seeking an injunction in federal court to prohibit Bull Connor and other policemen from interfering with interstate travel, issued a call for a "cooling-off period." The reaction of moderate opinion in the country (for instance, the *New York Times* and the *Charlotte Observer*) was to support this. On the other hand, the very next day saw the arrival in Montgomery of Negro and white ministers headed by William Coffin, Yale University chaplain, all of whom were arrested trying to use the facilities of the bus terminal. Wyatt Walker of SCLC, the Rev. Ralph Abernathy from Montgomery, and the Rev. Fred L. Shuttlesworth from Birmingham—were all arrested that day in Montgomery.

Charges flew back and forth. Governor Patterson of Alabama denounced the Riders and the Federal Government. Twenty-six white students from Auburn University, a state-supported college in Alabama, wrote in a letter to the *Montgomery Advertiser*: "Governor Patterson referred to the freedom riders as 'rabble rousers.' He is entitled to his opinion, but is Alabama to glory in the fact that it furnishes sufficient rabble to be roused?"

In the Atlanta *Constitution*, editor Eugene Patterson, although criticizing the "theatrical approach" of the Freedom Riders, said:

> But that is not the point of what happened in Alabama. Any man in this free country has the right to demonstrate and assemble and make a fool of himself if he pleases without getting hurt. If the police, representing the people, refuse to intervene when a man—any man—is being beaten to the pavement of an American city, then this is not a noble land at all. It is a jungle. But this is a noble land. And it is time for the decent people in it to muzzle the jackals.

Meeting in Atlanta, the executive committee of Martin Luther King, Jr.'s Southern Christian Leadership Conference turned down the Attorney General's plea for a "cooling-off period," but said there would be a "temporary lull" in the Freedom Rides. It was very temporary, because students kept arriving in Jackson, by train and by bus. Through June, July, and August, the pilgrimage continued, with students, ministers, and many others, white and Negro, coming into Jackson, where police, with monotonous regularity, arrested all comers as they tried to desegregate the terminal facilities. Forty-one Negroes from Jackson joined the Riders. By the end of the summer, the number of arrested persons reached over three hundred.

In early June, Ruby Doris Smith started her two-month sentence in Hinds County jail, sharing a four-bunk cell first with thirteen others, then with seventeen others, then with twenty-three others. She told me later, smiling, speaking softly as she always does:

> It was a nice set-up. When the windows were open we could talk to the fellows. We sang. We wrote Freedom Songs. A Negro minister from Chicago sang: "Woke Up In The Mornin' With My Mind Set On Freedom" so everyone began singing it. It started there. . . . Other songs were composed—"I Know We'll Meet Again" was written by a fellow I knew from Nashville and Rock Hill. We would do ballet lessons in the morning to keep ourselves fit. There were different people from different areas. Somebody was giving Spanish lessons. But then, after about two weeks, we were awakened at 4:00 A.M. to find out that we were all going to Parchman State Penitentiary. . . . It was a long ride in the night. We sang Freedom Songs. . . .

Parchman was tougher. The prisoners had all their belongings taken from them; they were stripped down and searched, not left with a comb or cigarettes. Even their shoes were taken from them. The women were issued skirts with stripes, then put in the maximum security unit of the penitentiary, reserved for the most dangerous criminals, with whites and Negroes in alternate cells. Each was given a towel, a bar of soap, a toothbrush, sheets, and pillow cases. The cells, Ruby Doris says, were filthy, full of bugs.

The prisoners were only allowed to speak softly, and when they began to sing the guards threatened to take their mattresses away. Elizabeth Wyckoff, a white woman from the North, was quietly telling some of the Greek myths, and a guard said she was disturbing people and began to take their mattresses away. They started to sing *The Star-Spangled Banner,* and then their sheets were taken away. They kept singing, and their towels and toothbrushes were confiscated. The singing kept getting louder all the time. They slept on steel for three nights, without coverings, with cold air deliberately blown into their cells all night long.

One time, Ruby Doris recalls, she and nine other Negro girls were taken to live in the prison infirmary, where conditions were better. Through their windows they could see the men prisoners going out to work in the fields every morning. "There were fifty, sixty Negro men in striped uniforms, guarded by a white man on a white horse. It reminded you of slavery."

In jail with Ruby Doris, on the men's side, were Stokely Carmichael and Bill Mahoney of Howard University. Bill Mahoney had been one of the driving forces behind the decision of students at Howard to continue the Freedom Ride after the CORE group flew to New Orleans. "By that time," Stokely recalls, "Bill Mahoney decided we should all go South. Bevel said, 'What do you think?' and I said, 'Let's go on through.' Here we were, discussing what we were going through and then the call came in that they had sent the first bus off. . . ."

Stokely Carmichael was brought up in New York, where his parents had moved from the West Indies.

> My father really worked hard, day and night. There were times when I didn't see him for a week. He'd get up in the morning and leave for his regular job—he was a carpenter—then he'd have an odd job on the side, so he'd probably eat at my aunt's house downtown and go to his odd job, and after that he'd drive a taxi, and then he'd come back and go to sleep. By that time, I'd be in bed. . . . He died in early 1962.

He was a man in his late forties. It was a heart attack. We think he died of hard work. . . .

A very bright student, Stokely was admitted to the Bronx High School of Science, which was reserved for the top students in New York. "I was an avid reader, but had no discipline. All the other kids I went to school with, their fathers were professors, doctors, they were the smartest kids in the world. Their fathers had libraries. . . . We had *Huckleberry Finn*. That was our highest book." In his later high school years, Stokely read Marx; pondered and debated radical ideas.

He was a senior in high school when the Greensboro sit-ins occurred. Soon after, he joined some of his classmates who went to Washington, D.C., to picket the House Un-American Activities Committee. "I was shocked to see Negroes at a H.U.A.C. demonstration. It turned out they had been involved in the sit-in demonstrations I was reading about in Virginia. I was very happy and decided, well, I can try it."

At Howard University in Washington, Stokely joined an affiliate of the newly-formed SNCC. It was called NAG, the Nonviolent Action Group, and in it were Bill Mahoney (to whom the others looked for leadership), Courtland Cox (tall, handsome, bearded, dark), Joan Trumpauer (tiny, blonde, and soon a Freedom Rider), and Dion Diamond (who later, as a SNCC field secretary, would be locked up for a long time in a Baton Rouge jail). The NAG conducted sit-ins and demonstrations to desegregate public places all around the Washington area. Then came the Freedom Rides.

Bill Mahoney, writing later in *Liberation*, described their arrival at Parchman penitentiary in mid-June, shortly after Ruby Doris had gotten there. As they got off the trucks, they were surrounded by men who brandished guns and spat at them and cursed. Two white men, Terry Sullivan and Felix Singer, refusing to cooperate, kept going limp as guards tried to move them along. They were thrown from the truck onto the wet sand-and-gravel drive, dragged through wet grass and mud puddles across a rough cement walk, into a building. Then a guard in a Stetson hat approached them carrying a long black rubber-handled tube. It was a cow-prodder, battery operated, which sears the flesh with an electric charge. When the two men refused to undress, the prodder was applied to their bodies. They squirmed in pain but would not give in. Their clothes were ripped from them and they were thrown into a cell.

Stokely talks of their time in Parchman:

> I'll never forget this Sheriff Tyson—he used to wear those big boots. He'd say, "You goddam smart nigger, why you always trying to be so uppity for? I'm going to see to it that you don't ever get out of this place." They decided to take our mattresses because we were singing. . . . So they dragged Hank Thomas out and he hung on to his mattress and they took him and it and dropped him with a loud klunk on his back. . . . And then they put the wristbreakers on Freddy Leonard, which makes you twist around and around in a snake-like motion, and Tyson said, "Oh you want to hit me, don't you," and Freddy just looked up at him meekly and said, "No, I just want you to break my arm." And Sheriff Tyson was shaken visibly, and he told the trusty, "Put him back." I hung on to the mattress and said, "I think we have a right to them and I think you're unjust," and he said, "I don't want to hear all that shit nigger," and started to put on the wristbreakers. I wouldn't move and I started to sing "I'm Gonna Tell God How You Treat Me," and everybody started to sing it and by this time Tyson was really to pieces. He called to the trusties, "Get him in there!" and he went out the door and slammed it, and left everybody else with their mattresses. . . .

James Farmer said later: "Jails are not a new experience for the Riders, but the Freedom Riders were definitely a new experience for Mississippi jails."

The students from Nashville, Atlanta, Washington, and

other places who came out of jail as Freedom Riders in July and August of 1961 sought one another out, wondering what they would do next. There was the SNCC office in Atlanta which had linked them all loosely, uncertainly. A volunteer SNCC worker named Bob Moses, just down from the North, was setting up voter registration schools around McComb, Mississippi. Two other SNCC people, Reggie Robinson from Baltimore and John Hardy from Nashville, had joined him.

Through the summer of 1961, fifteen or twenty people on the Coordinating Committee were meeting every month: at Louisville in June, at Baltimore in July, at the Highlander Folk School, Tennessee, in August. Tim Jenkins, a slim, energetic, bright young Negro who was vice-president of the National Student Association, came to the June meeting with a proposal that SNCC make the registration of Negro voters in the South its main activity. That started a controversy which simmered, unsettled, throughout the summer. It came to a boil at the Highlander meeting in August, where the issue was posed sharply: would SNCC concentrate on a methodical, grinding campaign to register Negro voters in the Black Belt? Or would it conduct more sensational direct-action campaigns—sit-ins, kneel-ins, wade-ins, picket lines, boycotts, etc.—to desegregate public facilities?

Even before the Freedom Rides began, Jenkins had been attending a series of meetings in which representatives of several foundations, including the Taconic and the Field Foundations, discussed the raising of substantial funds to support a large-scale voter registration effort in the South. Present at these meetings were Burke Marshall, Assistant Attorney General in charge of the Civil Rights Division, and Harris Wofford, special assistant to President Kennedy on civil rights. Jenkins was asked by the Foundation people to broach the idea to his friends in SNCC.

The Negro students who had gone through the sit-ins and Freedom Rides were somewhat distrustful of white liberals with money and of the national government. The fact that both these elements were behind the idea of concentrating on voter registration, on top of Robert Kennedy's call for a "cooling-off" period during the Freedom Rides, reinforced the suspicion that an attempt was being made to cool the militancy of the student movement and divert the youngsters to slower, safer activity. Led by Diane Nash and Marion Barry, many of the SNCC people at the Highlander meeting held to the idea that "direct action" should continue to be the primary policy.

Tim Jenkins was also aware of the interest of the Justice Department in moderating the temper of the student movement. He knew that the Department's conservative interpretation of civil rights law led it to argue that only in connection with voter registration activities could it go into federal court for injunctive relief against local and state governments in the South which tried to suppress the civil rights movement. But he felt that voter registration *was* the crucial lever which could set progress in motion in the South, and if white liberals and the government were willing to help, why not take advantage of this? Over the summer, he convinced a number of people in SNCC that he was right.

At the Highlander meeting, it seemed for a while that an impasse had been reached between the "direct action" people and the "voter registration" people, and that SNCC might even split into two groups. Ella Baker, advisor to SNCC since it was founded at Raleigh in 1960, helped reconcile the opposing viewpoints. The result was a compromise. Two arms of SNCC were created: Diane Nash was put in charge of direct action projects. Charles Jones (from Charlotte, North Carolina, and the Rock Hill jail-in), fair-skinned, blue-eyed, and self-assured, was put in charge of voter registration work.

In McComb, Mississippi, Bob Moses was already beginning voter registration schools when this decision was made, and about the middle of August, 1961, SNCC people began to converge on McComb. Moses recalls: "I became a member of the staff during a hectic hiring session in McComb in August, when staff hired staff or some such nonsense."

Money raised by Harry Belafonte began to come through now, and a number of people decided not to return to school in the fall but to go to work full-time for SNCC: Diane Nash, Charles Jones, James Bevel, Charles Sherrod, and others. With Ed King leaving the Atlanta office to go to law school (Jane Stembridge had returned to school earlier), the organization desperately needed an Executive Secretary. Diane Nash telephoned James Forman in Chicago and asked him to come to work for SNCC.

Forman, a thirty-three-year-old teacher, was born in Chicago but spent part of his childhood in Mississippi. He served four years in the Air Force, received a degree from Roosevelt College in Chicago, did graduate work on Africa at Boston University, studied French at Middlebury College, and somewhere inbetween wrote a novel (unpublished). Forman also spent a year working with sharecroppers in Fayette County, and made occasional trips to Nashville, where he met Diane Nash and talked with her about the future of SNCC. She had been impressed by him, and so called on him now.

Forman was just back from Monroe, North Carolina, where he had participated in demonstrations and been badly beaten. In Chicago, he was teaching school and thinking of doing some more writing; Diane Nash, James Bevel and Paul Brooks asked him to come to direct the SNCC office in Atlanta for sixty dollars a week. Forman (strongly built, handsome, with a big shock of curly hair, brown skin, an easy smile, and the features of an Indian) agreed to start working for SNCC in October.

Thus, in August of 1961, SNCC was ready to move. The sit-ins and Freedom Rides had been successful in the Upper South. They had ground to a bloody halt in the Deep South, leaving the participants wounded but determined, the opposition unsettled, the nation expectant. The excitement of the

Rides was still in the atmosphere. The students and ex-students in SNCC had a staff, a new Executive Secretary, and a vague idea of general strategy. Now, with their characteristic instinct for both challenge and danger, they turned towards the state of Mississippi.

4. Mississippi I: McComb

> The hundred and fifteen students stopped in front of the city hall to begin praying one by one, Brenda first, and then Curtis, and then Hollis, and then Bobby Talbert and then finally all of us herded up the steps and into the city courthouse, and Bob Zellner, who was the only white participant, attacked on the steps as he went up, and then a mob outside, waiting, milling around, threatening. And inside, they brought the people down, the white people, the so-called good citizens of the town, one by one, to take a look at this Moses guy. And they would come down and stand in front of the jail and say, "Where's Moses? Where's Moses?"

That scene is recalled by Robert Parris Moses, twenty-nine years old, of medium height and sturdy build, with light brown skin and a few freckles near his nose, who looks at you directly out of large tranquil eyes, who talks slowly, quietly, whose calm as he stands looking down a street in Mississippi is that of a mountain studying the sea. It took place in the fall of 1961, shortly after he arrived in Mississippi and threw state officials into great nervousness with the fantastic suggestion that Negroes should register to vote.

Bob Moses was raised in Harlem, one of three boys in the family. He went to Hamilton College in upstate New York, majoring in philosophy, and then went to Harvard where he did graduate work in philosophy and received a Master's Degree in 1957. He began teaching mathematics at Horace Mann High School in New York. Two years later there occurred the most cataclysmic event of his life, the kind against which perhaps all of the painful scenes he would watch later in the

Delta of Mississippi might measure small: his mother, aged forty-three, died of cancer. It was a steep and sudden fall, for she and Bob's father had just had their first real vacation, which he described:

"Did I say vacation, no, our honeymoon. A beautiful bubble that the two of us floated in . . . the world locked outside that thin filament. . . . I would close my eyes and it would seem to me that we two would be singing. . . . But bubbles burst."

Gregory Moses wrote down for his sons what life had been like with their mother. He is a working man, and has been all his life, a remarkable man, grey-haired, handsome, soft of voice, with a keen intelligence and a gift for language which another world, another time, would have put to splendid use. But it was no waste to pour all of himself into the lives of his three sons.

Gregory Moses recalls that Bob, as a baby, took all sorts of incredible risks cavorting on his high chair, "but somehow knew the laws of balance and never fell." Today, after three years on the Mississippi high wire, with all the officialdom of the state tugging at it, Bob Moses still keeps his balance.

It was only a few months after his mother's death that the first sit-ins took place, and Bob Moses read about them in the newspapers. "I knew for sure I would have to come South to take a first-hand look." During the spring break from his teaching job he went to visit his uncle in Hampton, Virginia. "I slipped into the crowd of students picketing and sitting-in at Newport News . . . my first introduction to the movement." Back in New York, talking to Bayard Rustin about the Southern Christian Leadership Conference, Moses prepared to go South that summer.

After arriving in Atlanta, Moses stuffed envelopes until he and Jane Stembridge decided that, on his own money (for SNCC had none), he would make a field trip to Mississippi, gathering people to go to the October conference which SNCC was going to hold in Atlanta. In Cleveland, Mississippi, he met a wise and rock-like Negro man named Amzie Moore, and that started a train of events that would leave Mississippi not quite the same. Moore was head of the NAACP in his town, and he and Moses sat down that summer of 1960 and planned a campaign to begin registering Negroes to vote.

Anywhere else, such a campaign might mean a certain amount of leg-work, persuasion, and organization; in Mississippi it would require a revolution. While 50 percent of the voting-age whites in Mississippi were registered to vote, only 5 percent of the Negroes were registered. Negroes were 43 percent of the population of the state—but held zero percent of the political offices, zero percent of the political power of the state. The median income of Negro families in Mississippi (U.S. Census figures for 1960) was $1100. White family income was three times as high. Negroes were laborers, sharecroppers, farm laborers, maids, servants of various kinds. More than half of them lived in houses with no running water; for two-thirds of them there was no flush toilet, no bathtub or shower. They lived in tarpaper shacks and rickety wooden boxes sometimes resembling chicken coops. Most whites were also poor, though not so poor; Mississippi was a feudal land barony, in which a small number of whites controlled the political power and the wealth of the state, using a tiny part of this wealth to pay the salaries of thousands of petty local officials who kept the system as it was by force.

Negroes had been sheriffs and judges and state legislators and even lieutenant-governors in those few years of Radical Reconstruction after the Civil War when Negroes, supported by federal troops, voted in Mississippi. They never dominated Mississippi politics, but in those years, linked to the economic power of Republican white Southerners like Governor James L. Alcorn, they had a voice, and their record as public servants was a good one, as historian Vernon Wharton has pointed out in his study, *Reconstruction in Mississippi*. But the reform spirit that accompanied the Civil War vanished; the political leaders of the nation began to see greater advantage in an alliance with powerful Southern white Democrats than with poor Southern Negroes, and in 1877 the great Compromise was reached between Northern white politicians and Southern white politicians, at the expense of the Negro. It was agreed, among other things, that the Fourteenth Amendment, which wrote into supreme law that no state could discriminate among its citizens, would be considered dead in the Deep South. The national government would leave the Negro helpless in his semi-slavery now, as it had left him in slavery before the Civil War; it would not interfere with the desires of Southern politicians no matter what the Constitution said.*

By 1890, Mississippi was to take the leadership of the Southern states in enacting a whole series of laws which legalized the system of segregation from the cradle to the grave. Negro voting was squeezed down to nothing. To any who violated the code, the punishment was swift (between 1890 and 1920, about four thousand Negroes were put to death in the South, without benefit of trial, and Mississippi accounted for a good part of these). With the threat of death, mutilation, or imprisonment at worst, economic destitution at best, the Negro was held down. Segregated Mississippi became as closed a society as slave Mississippi had been.

And now, in the summer of 1960, two Negroes, one a Mississippi farmer, the other a New York school teacher, sat in a farmhouse in the Delta and planned a campaign to dismantle, stone by stone, the prison that was Mississippi.

* The Compromise arose partly out of the disputed presidential election of 1876, and arranged for the Republican candidate, Rutherford Hayes, to become President in return for certain concessions to the South. But, more fundamentally, it came out of the general conditions of the post-Civil War era, in which Northern politicians and businessmen needed Southern white support for peaceful national development along the lines they desired. The Compromise of 1877 gave an affirmative answer to the question, as C. Vann Woodward puts it in *Reunion and Reaction*: "... could the South be induced to combine with the Northern conservatives and become a prop instead of a menace to the new capitalist order?"

After his talks with Amzie Moore, Bob Moses returned to Mississippi the following July, 1961, now as a SNCC staff member. An NAACP leader named C. C. Bryant in the city of McComb, in Pike County, read in *Jet* Magazine about Moses' voter registration plans, and wrote to him suggesting McComb as a place to work. Pike County was in Southern Mississippi, just north of the Louisiana border. Moses came to live in McComb, went around town getting Negro ministers and storekeepers to agree to supply room, board, and transportation expenses for ten students to come to McComb to work on voter registration.

In the meantime SNCC was meeting at Highlander Folk School, and deciding to work on voter registration in the Deep South, along with "direct action" projects. Through Harry Belafonte and others, money was being raised to hire SNCC's first field secretaries. And students who had been in the Freedom Rides were coming out of jail. Somehow, they began, little by little, to drift into McComb. Two of SNCC's first field secretaries now came in to help Moses: Reggie Robinson from Baltimore, slim, dark, animatedly cheerful; and John Hardy, of the Nashville student movement. On August 7, 1961, the first voter registration school was opened in Pike County and Negroes, in a slow release of resolve bottled up for a hundred years, began to study the complexities of registering to vote in Mississippi.

Mississippi law requires that a person wanting to vote must fill out a twenty-one–question form. He must interpret any section of the Constitution of Mississippi chosen by the registrar, who has complete authority to decide if the interpretation is correct—there are 285 sections in the Mississippi Constitution. But in the schools people patiently went over the questionnaire and the Constitution, and the first Negroes made the trek to the county courthouse.

Sixteen Negroes went down to the county seat of Magnolia to register, and six passed the test. Word got out to two neighboring counties, Amite and Walthall Counties, and people began to ask for schools in their areas. Three Negroes from Amite County—an old farmer and two middle-aged ladies—decided to go to Liberty, the county seat, to register. Bob Moses went with them.

> We left early morning August 15. It was a Tuesday. We arrived at the courthouse about 10 o'clock. The registrar came out. I waited by the side, waiting for either the farmer or one of the two ladies to say something to the registrar. He asked them: What did they want? What were they here for? In a very rough tone of voice. They didn't say anything. They were literally paralyzed with fear. So after a while I spoke up and said they would like to come to try to register to vote. So he asked: Who are you? What do you have to do with them? Do you want to register? I told him who I was and that we were conducting a school in McComb, and these people had attended the school, and they wanted an opportunity to register. Well, he said, they'll have to wait. . . . Our people started to register, one at a time. In the meantime a procession of people began moving in and out of the registration office: the sheriff, a couple of his deputies, people from the far office, the people who do the drivers' licenses—looking in, staring, moving back out, muttering. Finally finished the whole process about 4:30; all three of the people had had a chance to register—at least to fill out the form. This was a victory.

As the four drove back on the road to McComb, a highway patrolman whom they had seen in the registration office flagged them down. Moses got out of the car to find out what was wrong and was told by the policeman to get back in. He wrote down the name of the patrolman, who then pushed him back, saying, "Get in the car, nigger," and ordered all of them to follow him to McComb. There Moses was placed under arrest on a charge of interfering with an officer, but was given a quick trial and a suspended sentence with a five-dollar fine after they heard him complaining on the telephone to the

Justice Department in Washington. He described the incident later: "Well, I refused to pay . . . since I was obviously not guilty. I was taken to jail then—this was my first introduction to Mississippi jails."

On the farm of an Amite County NAACP leader, Mr. E. W. Steptoe, a school was set up, and on August 29, Bob Moses again accompanied two persons to Liberty. There he was attacked on the street by Billy Jack Caston (cousin of the sheriff and son-in-law of a state representative named E. H. Hurst) who proceeded to hit Moses again and again with the butt end of a knife. "I remember very sharply that I didn't want to go immediately back into McComb because my shirt was very bloody and I figured that if we went back in we would probably frighten everybody." So Moses and the two men with him went back to Mr. Steptoe's farm, before going anywhere else. He washed up, and they made their way to McComb. Later, Moses had his head wound sewn up with eight stitches.

McComb was at this time in a state of excitement. The two arms of SNCC (voter registration and direct action) had begun to move, hardly days after the decision at Highlander. Marion Barry, one of the "direct action" advocates, arrived in McComb on August 18 and began to hold workshops on nonviolent action. Three days before the beating of Moses, two eighteen-year-olds, Curtis Hayes and Hollis Watkins, sat-in at the Woolworth lunch counter in McComb—the first such act of defiance in the area's history. They were arrested on a charge of breaching the peace and sentenced to thirty days in jail. The evening that Moses returned to McComb two hundred Negroes attended a mass meeting, where they heard James Bevel speak, and made plans for further sit-ins and registration attempts. "We felt that it was extremely important that we go back to Liberty immediately so the people wouldn't think we'd been frightened off by the beating."

Now McComb, Mississippi saw another "first": a Negro

—Robert Moses—filed charges of assault and battery against a white—Billy Jack Caston.

> Well, it turned out that . . . we did have his trial, that they had a six-man Justice of the Peace jury, that the courthouse in a twinkling was packed. That is, the trial was scheduled that day and within two hours farmers, all white, came in from all parts of the county, bearing their guns, sitting in the courthouse. We were advised not to sit in the courthouse except while we testified—otherwise we were in a back room. After the testimony was over the sheriff came back and told us that he didn't think it was safe for us to remain there while the jury gave its decision. Accordingly he escorted us to the county line. We read in the papers the next day that Billy Jack Caston had been acquitted.

Meanwhile, there were more sit-ins in McComb. A fifteen-year-old Negro girl named Brenda Travis had walked the streets from noon to five every afternoon with the SNCC people, under the hot sun, had become exasperated with the apathy or the fear shown by Negroes in McComb, and decided they needed to be awakened. She and five other high school students sat-in and were arrested. Her companions were sentenced to eight months in jail for "breach of peace." Brenda Travis was turned over to juvenile authorities and sentenced to a year in a state school for delinquents. Her high school principal immediately expelled her from school.

More SNCC workers were arriving in McComb. One of them was Travis Britt, a student from New York City. Not long after his beating, Bob Moses went with Britt and four Negroes eager to register to the county courthouse in Liberty. "It was around the fifth of September," Moses recalls,

> and I stood around and watched Travis get pummeled by an old man, tall, reedy, and thin, very very mean with a lot of hatred in him. . . . Travis and I had been sitting out front of

> the courthouse and then decided to move around back because people had started to gather around front. Finally about fifteen people gathered around back and began questioning Travis and myself. My own reaction in all those instances is simply to shut up, to be silent. I get very, very depressed. The people were talking to Travis . . . asking him where was he from and how come a nigger from New York City could think that he could come down here and teach people how to register to vote. . . .

Travis Britt reported the incident as follows:

> I reached into my pocket and took out a cigarette. A tall white man . . . wearing a khaki shirt and pants stepped up to me and asked: "Boy, what's your business?"—at which point I knew I was in trouble. The clerk from the hallway came to the back door . . . with a smile on his face and called to the white man. . . . At this point, the white man whom they called Bryant hit me in my right eye. Then I saw this clerk motion his head as if to call the rest of the whites. They came and all circled round me and this fellow Bryant hit me on my jaw, then my chin. Then he slammed me down . . . I stumbled on to the courthouse lawn. The crowd followed, making comments. Bryant . . . just kept hitting and shouting, "Why don't you hit me, nigger?" I was beaten into a semi-conscious state. My vision was blurred. . . . I heard Bob tell me to cover my head. . . . Bryant released me. Moses then took me by the arm and took me out to the street. . . .

Two days later, John Hardy, twenty-one, from Nashville, where his father worked as a porter and his mother as a maid, was beaten with a pistol by the registrar of Walthall County and then arrested for disturbing the peace. With the aid of SNCC worker MacArthur Cotton (tall, husky, born in Kosciusko, Miss., a student at Tougaloo Southern Christian College) and others, Hardy had been running a voter registration school in Walthall County. Two people who attended the school said they wanted to go down to Tylertown to register, and Hardy said he would go with them.

> The next morning they stopped by for me between 8:30 and 9:00 A.M. Mr. Wilson, Mrs. Peters, MacArthur Cotton and I drove into town together in a pick-up truck . . . parked in the street down by the fish market, and I went in with Mrs. Peters and Mr. Wilson to the Courthouse. . . . I stood just outside the door to the inner office, about four or five feet away from the registrar's desk. The registrar asked what they wanted. Mrs. Peters stated they had come to register to vote. Mr. Wood said he wasn't registering anyone. . . . I stepped into the doorway to the inner office and looked at Mrs. Peters and asked her what the trouble was. . . . Mr. Woods said, "What right do you have coming down here messing in these people's business, and why don't you go back where you came from? . . ." He reached behind a desk . . . and pulled a gun from the drawer . . . and said, "I want you to get the hell out of this office and never come back. . . . I was frightened and turned and started to walk out of the office. . . . I felt a blow on my head. I can only remember being very dazed, and the next thing I knew Mr. Wilson and Mrs. Peters were helping me across the street and up an alleyway. I felt something running down my head and saw blood dripping on the ground. . . ."

Out on the street, Hardy was taken into custody by the sheriff and charged with inciting to riot and resisting arrest. The rest of the day, Hardy was in a prison cell, or being interviewed by the District Attorney and others. It wasn't until 4:30 that afternoon that he was finally taken to a doctor at the Walthall County Hospital who pronounced it a superficial wound, said it required no stitches, and charged Hardy $3.00. He was held overnight in jail, then released on bond. Later, the Justice Department brought a successful suit to block Hardy's prosecution, on the grounds that it constituted intimidation of voters under the 1957 Civil Rights Act.

"Well, the Travis Britt incident, followed by the John Hardy incident . . . just about cleaned us out," says Bob Moses.

"The farmers in both those counties were no longer willing to go down. The people down in McComb were in an uproar over the sit-in demonstrations and the fact that Brenda Travis, a fifteen-year-old girl, was in jail. And for the rest of the month of September, we just had a tough time. There wasn't much we could do." The youngsters in jail on sit-in charges had $5000 bail hanging over them, and the chief problem now was to raise that money and get them out of jail, and then somehow figure out what the next set of steps would be. In the midst of this, a man was murdered. As Moses tells it:

> The boom lowered on September 25; Herbert Lee, a Negro farmer, was killed in Amite County. I was down at Steptoe's with John Doar from the Justice Department and we asked Steptoe—was there any danger in that area—who was causing the trouble, and who were the people in danger? Steptoe told us that E. H. Hurst, who lived across from him, had been threatening people and that specifically people said that he, Steptoe, Herbert Lee, and George Reese were in danger of losing their lives. We went out, but didn't see Lee that afternoon. That night, John Doar and the other lawyers from the Justice Department left. The following morning about twelve o'clock, Dr. Anderson came by the voter registration office and said a man had been shot in Amite County. They had brought him over to McComb and he was lying on a table in a funeral home in McComb and he asked me if I might have known him. I went down to take a look at the body, and it was Herbert Lee. There was a bullet hole in the left side of his head, just above the ear. He had on his farm clothes.

Moses waited until it was dark, then went out with a few others into Amite County, riding past night-shrouded cotton fields from one Negro home to another until three or four in the morning, trying to find witnesses to the killing of Herbert Lee. They continued this four or five nights, driving through the darkness, fighting off sleep, waking up Negro families in the hours before dawn to try to piece together what happened.

They found three Negro farmers who had seen the shooting and who told essentially the same story. They had been standing at the cotton gin early in the morning when Herbert Lee drove up in a truck with a load of cotton. E. H. Hurst was following directly behind in an empty truck. (This truck, incidentally, was owned by Billy Jack Caston.) Hurst got out of the truck and came up to Lee, who was sitting in the cab of his truck, and began arguing with him. Hurst gesticulated, pulled a gun from under his shirt. Lee said he wouldn't talk to Hurst unless he put the gun away, and Hurst put the gun under his coat. Then Lee slid out of the cab on the side away from Hurst. Hurst ran around in front of the cab, took his gun out, pointed it at Lee and fired.

"This was the story that three Negro witnesses told us on three separate nights as we went out, in Amite County, tracking them down, knocking on doors, waking them up in the middle of the night." These witnesses also told another story: that the sheriff, the deputy sheriff, and some white people in town had put pressure on them to say that Lee, who was about five feet four, had tried to hit Hurst, who was about six feet two, with a tire tool.

Only at one point in Bob Moses' detailed, quiet recounting of the killing of Herbert Lee did his voice show emotion:

> Lee's body lay on the ground that morning for two hours, uncovered, until they finally got a funeral home in McComb to take it in. No one in Liberty would touch it. They had a coroner's jury that very same afternoon. Hurst was acquitted. He never spent a moment in jail. . . . I remember reading very bitterly in the papers the next morning, a little item on the front page of the McComb *Enterprise Journal* said that a Negro had been shot as he was trying to attack E. H. Hurst. And that was it. Might have thought he'd been a bum. There was no mention that Lee was a farmer, that he had a family, nine kids, beautiful kids, and that he had farmed all his life in Amite County.

One of the three Negro witnesses to the murder of Herbert Lee was Louis Allen, who shortly after the murder was whisked from the scene by a white man, driven to the coroner's jury hearing, and told what to say to the jury: that Hurst was right in claiming he had killed Lee in self-defense. The coroner's jury accepted Hurst's story. A month after the killing of Lee, a federal grand jury met to consider indicting Hurst. Louis Allen drove to McComb to tell Bob Moses that he had lied at the coroner's jury hearing, that he wanted to tell the truth at the grand jury hearing, but wanted protection.

Moses says: "We called the Justice Department in Washington. We talked to responsible officials in that department. They told us that there was no way possible to provide protection for a witness at such a hearing and that probably in any case it didn't matter what he testified—that Hurst would be found innocent." Allen gave the grand jury the same story he had told the coroner's jury, and Hurst was exonerated, the grand jury deciding there was insufficient evidence to indict. About six months later a deputy sheriff told Allen he knew he had told the F.B.I. that his story about the killing was a lie. The deputy hit Allen with a flashlight and broke his jaw. Moses says: "It's for reasons like these that we believe the local F.B.I. are sometimes in collusion with the local sheriffs and chiefs of police, and that Negro witnesses aren't safe in telling inside information to local agents of the F.B.I."

That was not the end of the affair. On a Friday night, January 31, 1964, Louis Allen was found dead in his front yard. Three shotgun blasts had killed him.

The force of SNCC revolutionaries in McComb grew. Chuck McDew, with his powerful frame and ever-present look of deep thoughtfulness, came into town. So did Bob Zellner, a college student from Alabama, SNCC's first white field man, whose job was to work among white college students in the South, but who couldn't stay away from the Negro community. About ten days after the slaying of Herbert Lee, 115 high school students in McComb marched through town to express their feelings about the expulsion of their classmate Brenda Travis and the killing of Herbert Lee.

Bob Moses and the other SNCC people went with them, through the Negro neighborhoods, into downtown McComb, where they stopped and began to pray on the steps of City Hall. White men in shirt sleeves stood by and watched. The street was thick with cars circling the block continuously. The police asked them to leave, but they refused, and were arrested one by one. Marching up the steps to be booked, Bob Zellner was attacked by a white man. Moses and McDew were hit also, then dragged into the station by police. Moses, McDew, Zellner, and six other SNCC people, charged with "contributing to the delinquency of minors," Moses recalls, were brought downstairs into a large room to be questioned.

> I was again very quiet all the way down. . . . I remember when I went in, the room was very tense; all of the people were sort of sitting around on the edges, on benches, in the dark, and the sheriff was standing, and at one point threatened me about saying "Yassuh" and "Nossir," and I remember that I finally just answered the questions without saying "yes" or "no."

The prisoners slept on a concrete bunker and on the floor before being assigned to cells. In jail, their spirit was high. They sang. McDew and Moses made a chessboard on the floor, shaping chess pieces out of cigarette butts. They swapped stories and told jokes until they were let out on bond a few days later.

Over a hundred high school students in McComb, in response to their principal's demand that they pledge not to participate in demonstrations, stayed out of school. The principal gave them an ultimatum: return to school by 3:00 P.M. on October 16 or be expelled. At a quarter of three on that day, 103 students returned to school, turned in their books, and walked out. "Nonviolent High" opened up in Pike County to take care of their education, with Moses teaching algebra and geometry, Dion Diamond teaching physics and chemistry, and McDew teaching history, until several weeks later Campbell Junior College in Jackson agreed to take the students. It was just in time, for in late October the SNCC staff in Pike County was found guilty of the charges connected with the march in McComb, and spent the next few months in jail, unable to raise the $14,000 required to keep them free pending appeal. In November, Bob Moses managed to slip a message from his jail to a local Negro who got it to SNCC headquarters in Atlanta:

> We are smuggling this note from the drunk tank of the county jail in Magnolia, Mississippi. Twelve of us are here, sprawled out along the concrete bunker; Curtis Hayes, Hollis Watkins, Ike Lewis and Robert Talbert, four veterans of the bunker, are sitting up talking—mostly about girls; Charles McDew ("Tell the story") is curled into the concrete and the wall; Harold Robinson, Stephen Ashley, James Wells, Lee Chester Vick, Leotus Eubanks, and Ivory Diggs lay cramped on the cold bunker; I'm sitting with smuggled pen and paper, thinking a little, writing a little; Myrtis Bennett and Janie Campbell are across the way wedded to a different icy cubicle.
>
> Later on, Hollis will lead out with a clear tenor into a freedom song, Talbert and Lewis will supply jokes, and McDew will discourse on the history of the black man and the Jew. McDew—a black by birth, a Jew by choice, and a revolutionary by necessity—has taken on the deep hates and deep loves which America and the world reserve for those who dare to stand in a strong sun and cast a sharp shadow. . . .
>
> This is Mississippi, the middle of the iceberg. Hollis is leading off with his tenor, "Michael row the boat ashore, Alleluia; Christian brothers don't be slow, Alleluia; Mississippi's next to go, Alleluia." This is a tremor in the middle of the iceberg —from a stone that the builders rejected.

Out of jail finally in December, Moses and the others pondered their next moves. They had learned something in the flurry of events centered in McComb that summer and fall of 1961. Direct action ran head-on into the stone wall of absolute police power in Mississippi. After the beatings of Moses and Britt and Hardy, and the killing of Herbert Lee, there had been continuing violence in the city of McComb: in October, two young white men, Paul Potter of the National Student Association and Tom Hayden of Students for a Democratic Society, were dragged from their car and beaten in the street; in November, four CORE people were brutally beaten by a mob of whites when they tried to eat at the lunch counter of the Greyhound bus terminal (this was a week after the Interstate Commerce Commission ruling went into effect, but FBI men merely stood by taking notes as the beating took place); also that month, someone fired a shotgun into the bedroom of Dion Diamond and John Hardy; in December, four white men attacked three newspapermen in the street, and three more CORE people were attacked at the Greyhound bus terminal.

Voter registration was presumably a milder form of activity than a sit-in or a march downtown or a Freedom Ride, but here the SNCC people found more frustration. In all of Amite County, there was one Negro officially registered. But, as McDew said wryly: "We haven't been able to find him." Negro ministers, Negro businessmen, those people in the black community who had the most resources, were also most vulnerable to economic pressure from the white community, and they could not be counted on to give anything but undercover help. It became clear that the only way to carry on voter registration campaigns was, as Moses put it, "to build a group of young people who would not be responsible economically to any sector of the white community and who would be able to act as free agents."

With youngsters from the towns and countryside of Mississippi clustering now in growing numbers around the handful of SNCC staff people, and with perhaps one courageous businessman, one minister or farmer in the Negro community willing to take risks, they might move. McComb, with all its bitter legacy, was a beginning for SNCC in Mississippi. "We had, to put it mildly, got our feet wet," Moses said. They now moved north, deeper into the Delta.

5. Mississippi II: Greenwood

Leaving McComb in early 1962, the winter in Mississippi not yet over, Bob Moses wrote to the Atlanta office:

> The movement from the rural to the urban is irresistible and the line from Amite to McComb to Jackson straight as the worm furrows. Accordingly, I have left the dusty roads to run the dusty streets. In short, I'm now installed in Jackson—subject to reproval or removal—and am duly reporting. Jackson is to be the center for a new newspaper, the *Mississippi Free Press.* . . . A group of Jackson businessmen are backing it. . . . The third and fourth congressional districts are to see Negro candidates for Congress, and I'm up to be the submerged campaign director for the Rev. R. L. Smith, who is running for the fourth district . . . we will scuffle like hell to get as many poll taxes paid as possible in the next six weeks, while the hunting season lasts. After the hunting comes the killing and if we're all dead, I want to be cremated and snuck into the next sun-circling satellite for my last rites. . . .

A group of SNCC staff people had rented a house in Jackson, and Moses stayed there, with Paul Brooks and his wife, James and Diane Nash Bevel (newly wed), Lester McKinnie and Bernard Lafayette. With his old friend Amzie Moore, Moses went on a field trip through the state. With Reverend Smith, the candidate for Congress, he visited a session of the Mississippi state legislature and tried to sit in the white section of the gallery, but was turned away. With Tom Gaither of CORE, a plan was drafted for CORE, SNCC, SCLC, and NAACP to carry on a unified voter registration program in Mississippi, joined together in a Council of Federated Organizations (COFO). Moses wrote,

"Most of the winter was lean. We were just hanging on in Jackson . . . laying foundations, getting ready for the next drives in the summer." Meanwhile, Mississippi continued in its ways. To Jackson in February came the story told to SNCC people by a young Negro woman, Bessie Turner, aged nineteen, who lived in Clarksdale:

> About four o'clock Sunday afternoon, January 21, two policemen came to my house, one short and stocky with silver teeth at the bottom, and a tall slender policeman. They told me to get in their car and they carried me to the City Hall into a small room and began questioning me about some money they said I had taken. . . . The short policeman told me to lay down on the concrete floor in the jail and pull up my dress and pull down my panties. He then began to whip me. . . . He then told me to turn over. . . . He hit me between my legs with the same leather strap. . . . He told me then to get up and fix my clothes and wipe my face, as I had been crying. . . .

In May, Diane Nash Bevel was tried in Jackson for teaching the techniques of nonviolence to Negro youngsters; the charge was "contributing to the delinquency of minors" and she was sentenced to two years in jail. Four months pregnant, she insisted on going to jail rather than putting up bond, saying: "I can no longer cooperate with the evil and corrupt court system of this state. Since my child will be a black child, born in Mississippi, whether I am in jail or not he will be born in prison." After a short stay in prison, she was released.

Two Negro students from Jackson were in the courtroom during the trial of Mrs. Bevel. One was Jesse Harris, tall and serious, who had attached himself to SNCC ever since James Bevel came to Jackson in the Freedom Rides. The other was seventeen-year-old Luvaghn Brown. They refused to move to the "colored" side of the courtroom and were arrested. En route to jail, Harris was beaten by a deputy. Out on the prison farm, both were singled out for special attention. A guard ordered other prisoners to hold Jesse Harris while he whipped him with a length of hose. At another time, he was beaten with a stick, handcuffed and removed to the county jail where he was put in the "sweatbox" on a bread and water diet. Brown was also beaten. After forty days of such treatment, they were released.

In Jackson that spring, Moses, with an enlarged SNCC staff, began to plan voter registration operations for the summer. The money that Tim Jenkins had spoken about was on its way, contributed by the Taconic and Field Foundations, administered by the Southern Regional Council in Atlanta, through a new Voter Education Project. Money was going to SNCC, CORE, NAACP, SCLC and the Urban League. Moses planned to set up voter registration projects in seven different Mississippi towns in a "crash program" for the summer months.

Lester McKinnie was already working in Laurel, from where he wrote to James Forman in Atlanta: "Jim, the Negroes in Laurel are like many other cities, waiting until someone else starts something, and then if it is effective they will get on the band wagon. Every minister seems to be uncle Tomish; it's absurd really. So I am working mostly with the common layman. . . ." And in June, Frank Smith, a wiry, agile Morehouse College student from Atlanta, set up shop in Holly Springs, where tiny Rust College, a Negro school, was a kind of haven. His first report back to Atlanta gives an idea of how a SNCC worker goes about his business when he arrives in a Deep South town:

> Two days were spent just loafing around in all sections of the County in an effort to find out just who the most trusted and respected leaders were. . . . On June 27, a letter was sent to seventeen people in Marshall County announcing a meeting. It was very vague and mentioned only slightly voter registration. Sixteen people came out and among them was Father

> Monley, who let us have the meeting at the Catholic School. It was quite a success and everyone was very enthusiastic. Mr. O. C. Pegues is a middle-aged man of about forty. He has seven kids and is renting a 200-acre farm. . . . He has a high school diploma and served three years during World War II. He has a very prosperous farm and a wonderful family. He is one of the few that is known by the white community as a "crazy nigger." He doesn't stand any pushing around. . . . The door-to-door committee was set into motion on July 8. . . . Transportation was provided for all persons and we contacted about 1000 people and got about 150 of them to take the voter registration test. . . . It did not take the sheriff and the police force long to discover that Smith was in town. . . . We are dealing with very subtle problems here, not one of shootings and hangings, but of lowering of cotton acreage allotments and the raising of taxes. The Chancery Court sells the land for taxes and the farmer is forced to move. In the meantime the banks refuse to give him a loan. . . . Here we have the problem of the sheriff riding by a place where meetings are being held and writing down the tag numbers. The next week, any person at the meeting who does public work is fired. . . . Perhaps something should be said about handicaps at this point. Perhaps the greatest one could be spelled out in one word, MONEY. . . . There were times when my buddy and I walked as many as fifteen miles per day, and we rode a mule for almost a week. These things were good psychologically for the community, but I don't think they did the asses and the feet of two of us any good. . . .

Thus, the original nucleus that had gathered in McComb after the Freedom Rides had spread out in the summer of 1962 to Holly Springs, Laurel, and other places. Curtis Hayes and Hollis Watkins were in Hattiesburg; other staff members were in Greenville, Cleveland, Vicksburg, and Ruleville.

But it was the city of Greenwood, seat of Leflore County, that was to become the focus of attention in Mississippi for the next year. To Greenwood came, in June, 1962, a twenty-three-year-old native of Cleveland, Mississippi, named Sam Block, the son of a construction worker, tall, black, gaunt, silent, who sings in a deep voice and looks at you with eyes large and sad.

As Sam Block walked through the Negro section of Greenwood, knocking on doors, a police car followed him around and people were afraid to talk to him. The Elks Club gave him a meeting place, and people began to gather there around Sam. But he wrote to Jim Forman in mid-July: "We lost our meeting place at the Elks Club. The members did not approve of our meeting there and singing Freedom songs." One day three white men beat Sam; another day he had to jump behind a telephone pole to escape a speeding truck.

Willie Peacock, also from Mississippi, dark, muscular, handsome, who joined Block in Greenwood, spoke of their hard times together:

> We were hungry one day and didn't have anything to eat and didn't even have a pair of shoes hardly, and we went down and started hustling and a fellow gave me a pair of shoes. Then we had to ride a mule. . . . Didn't even have transportation. But we kept begging for transportation. Came up to Memphis and had to stay five days and still didn't get a car. But we're not worryin'. We ain't complaining. We just go on and raise hell all the time. We don't have to ride, we can walk, we don't care.

A profile of Leflore County is very much a profile of the rural Deep South. The county in 1960 had about 50,000 people, of whom approximately two-thirds were Negro. Whites owned 90 percent of the land and held 100 percent of the political offices; their median income was three times that of Negroes. (But most whites were poor; thirty-six white families made over $25,000 a year, earning a total amount of money greater than the 3600 poorest families.) Of 168 hospital beds in the county, 131 were reserved for whites. Ninety-five percent of the whites of voting age were registered to vote; 2 percent of the Negroes of voting age were registered.

Soon after his arrival in Greenwood, Sam Block became interested in a police brutality case. Late in July, the police picked up a fourteen-year-old Negro boy and accused him of breaking into a white woman's house. The boy told them: "I go to the cotton field all the time and back home," but they took him to the police station, where they forced him to strip and beat him with a bull whip as he lay naked on the concrete floor. They kicked him, beat him with fists, a billy club, and a blackjack until knots and welts were raised all over his body. When someone came near, a buzzer was sounded, and a television set was turned on to drown out the boy's screams. Finally, his father came for him. Police told him to stop crying, wash his face, dress, and go to the courtroom. He entered the wrong room, and a policeman struck him on the head, pushed him into the courtroom, saying: "That room, nigger."

Sam Block took affidavits from the boy, took photos of his wounds, and dropped them into the bottomless, bucketless well of the Justice Department. "From then on," says Bob Moses, "it was Sam versus the police." Sam's courage began to be contagious; more people began to show up at the SNCC office at 616 Avenue I in Greenwood, and to go down to the county courthouse to register. The newspapers now reported that a voter registration drive was being organized among Negroes in town, and gave the address of the office.

On August 17, 1962, Bob Moses was in Cleveland, Mississippi, when a collect telephone call came at midnight from Greenwood. Sam Block, Luvaghn Brown and Lawrence Guyot were working late in the second story SNCC office there. It was Sam Block on the line:

> Sam said there were some people outside, police cars, about twelve o'clock at night . . . white people riding up and down the street, and they felt something was going to happen. I

told him to keep in touch with us, hung up, called a member of the Justice Department. We gave him Sam's number and he had some instructions about calling the local FBI. And Sam called back again. The police had gone, and white people had come in their cars, were standing outside the office. He was crouched in the office, looking out the window, talking on the phone in a very hushed voice, describing people downstairs with guns and chains, milling around down there, outside his office. He had to hang up. . . . We didn't know what to do. . . . Willie Peacock and I decided then to drive over to Greenwood. We got there about three-thirty or four. The office was empty, the door was knocked down, the window was up, Sam was gone, so was Guyot and Luvaghn. Well, the next morning when they came in they told us what had happened. People had charged up the back stairs, had come into the office and they had escaped out the window, across the roof to an adjoining building, and down a TV antenna into somebody else's home.

Sam Block went to Hattiesburg the day after that incident, and returned to Greenwood to find the SNCC office a shambles. The owner told him he couldn't stay there any longer. For the next two nights he slept in a junkyard on the seat of a wrecked auto. Then he found a room to sleep in. It would be five months before they could find another office, but he and Willie Peacock stayed in town, visiting people every day. They were, as Moses put it, "breaking down the psychological feeling on the part of the Negroes that these boys are just coming in here, they're going to be in here for a short time, and then they're going to leave, and we're going to be left holding the bag."

One day, while taking Negroes down to register in Greenwood, Block was stopped by the sheriff, and the following conversation took place:

SHERIFF: Nigger, where you from?
BLOCK: I'm a native of Mississippi.

SHERIFF: I know all the niggers here.
BLOCK: Do you know any colored people?
(The sheriff spat at him.)
SHERIFF: I"ll give you till tomorrow to get out of here.
BLOCK: If you don't want to see me here, you better pack up and leave, because I'll be here.

That he wasn't murdered on the spot is something of a miracle. The next day, Sam Block took some more Negro men and women down to the county courthouse to try to register.

As the stream of voting applicants in Greenwood increased (though in Block's first six months there, only five Negroes were actually declared by the registrar to have passed the test), the economic screws tightened on the Negro community. Winters were always lean in the farming towns of Mississippi, and people depended on surplus food supplied by the Government to keep them going. In October, 1962, the Board of Supervisors of Leflore County stopped distributing surplus food, cutting off 22,000 people—mostly Negro—who depended on it. By mid-winter, conditions were desperate. Willie Peacock and Sam Block wrote to Jim Forman in Atlanta:

> Saturday, January 19, 1963 . . . these people here are in a very, very bad need for food and clothes. Look at a case like this man, named Mr. Meeks, who is thirty-seven years old. His wife is thirty-three years old, and they have eleven children, ages ranging from seventeen down to eight months. Seven of the children are school age and not a one is attending school because they have no money, no food, no clothes, and no wood to keep warm by, and they now want to go register. The house they are living in has no paper or nothing on the walls and you can look at the ground through the floor and if you are not careful you will step in one of those holes and break your leg.

From Atlanta, the word went out to the cities of the North, to college campuses, wherever SNCC had friends, that food and other supplies were needed in Mississippi. People began to respond. Two Negro students at Michigan State University, Ivanhoe Donaldson and Ben Taylor, drove a truckload of food, clothing and medicine a thousand miles to the Mississippi Delta during Christmas week. They were stopped in Clarksdale, arrested, charged with the possession of narcotics, and held in jail under $15,000 bond. The bond was reduced after nationwide protests, and after they had spent eleven days in jail they were released. Their cargo was confiscated. The "narcotics" in the shipment consisted of aspirin and vitamins. After that Ivanhoe Donaldson became a one-man transport operation; twelve times he drove truckloads of supplies the thousand miles from Michigan to Mississippi.

Bob Moses had written from the Delta to Martha Prescod, a pretty Negro coed at Ann Arbor:

> We *do* need the actual food. . . . Just this afternoon, I was sitting reading, having finished a bowl of stew, and a silent hand reached over from behind, its owner mumbling some words of apology and stumbling up with a neckbone from the plate under the bowl, one which I had discarded, which had some meat on it. The hand was back again, five seconds later, groping for the potato I had left in the bowl. I never saw the face. I didn't look. The hand was dark, dry, and wind-cracked, a man's hand, from the cotton chopping and cotton picking. Lafayette and I got up and walked out. What the hell are you going to do when a man has to pick up a left-over potato from a bowl of stew?

In January, Sam Block reported to the Atlanta office:

> *Dear Jim,*
>
> Man, I am so glad we now have transportation here in Greenwood. . . . We carried five people down to register. In addition to that we are now able to get around to these people who have been cut off from the surplus food deal, and some of them will make you cry to see the way they have been trying

> to live. We went to about ten people's houses who lived up in little nasty alleys, it was cold, cold outside, and some of them were sitting beside of the fireplace with a small amount of wood burning trying to keep warm. They had little babies that had no shoes to put on their feet in that cold, cold house. . . . We found out that the people . . . had to tell their kids that Santa Claus was sick and that he would be able to see them when he gets well.

The food drive turned out to be a catalyst for the voter registration campaign in Mississippi. It brought the SNCC workers into direct contact with thousands of Negroes, many of whom came forward to help with the distribution of food, and stayed on to work on voter registration. Thus SNCC became identified in the minds of Negroes in Mississippi not simply with agitation, but with direct aid. The more food was distributed, the more people began to go down to the courthouse to register. Eventually, federal pressure led Leflore County to resume the distribution of surplus food.

Bob Moses wrote, on February 24, to thank the Chicago Friends of SNCC, who, with the aid of Dick Gregory, had sent food and clothing and medicine to Mississippi:

> . . . we have been on a deep plateau all winter, shaking off the effects of the violence of August and September and the eruption that was Meredith at Old Miss. . . . You combat your own fears about beatings, shootings and possible mob violence; you stymie by your mere physical presence the anxious fear of the Negro community, seeded across town and blown from paneled pine and white sunken sink to windy kitchen floors and rusty old stoves, that maybe you *did* come only to boil and bubble and then burst out of sight . . . you create a small striking force capable of moving out when the time comes. . . . After more than six hundred lined up to receive food in Greenwood on Wednesday, 20 February, and Sam's subsequent arrest and weekend in prison on Thursday, 21 February, over one hundred people overflowed city hall to

> protest at his trial, over two hundred and fifty gathered at a mass meeting that same night, and on Tuesday by 10:30 A.M. I had counted over fifty people standing in silent line in the county courthouse; they say over two hundred stood in line that day. This is a new dimension. . . . Negroes have never stood en masse in protest at the seat of power in the iceberg of Mississippi politics. . . . We don't know this plateau at all. We were relieved at the absence of immediate violence at the courthouse, but who knows what's to come next?

The evening after he wrote that letter, about 10:00 P.M., Bob Moses left the SNCC office in Greenwood and got into an automobile with two other men, heading for Greenville. One was Randolph Blackwell, of the Voter Education Project in Atlanta, tall, of powerful build and voice, who was doing a tour of the voter registration areas. The other was Jimmy Travis, twenty years old, a native Mississippian and a former Freedom Rider, who had come out of the Rides to join the SNCC staff.

A 1962 Buick with no license tags had been sitting outside the SNCC office all day, with three white men in it—nothing unusual for SNCC. As they pulled away, the Buick followed. They stopped at a filling station for gasoline, and the Buick followed and circled the block. Then they headed out on the main highway toward Greenville, all three sitting in front: Jimmy Travis at the wheel, Bob Moses next to him, Blackwell on the outside. It was about 10:30 P.M., and there was a good deal of traffic on the road. As the traffic began to thin, the Buick pulled up alongside and then came the deafening sound of gunfire. Thirteen 45-calibre bullets ripped through the car shattering the front left window, missing Bob Moses and Randolph Blackwell by inches, smashing through the window on the other side. Two bullets hit Jimmy Travis. The Buick sped off, and Moses grabbed the controls to pull the car to a stop as Travis crouched in his seat, bleeding.

They drove to a hospital, and phoned the news to Atlanta.

Ruby Doris Smith sent wires the next morning to SNCC workers in the field: "Jimmy Travis was shot in the Delta last night. Twice in shoulder and neck. Will be operated on today to remove bullet which is lodged behind spinal cord." Travis lived, but the doctor said that if the bullet had penetrated with just slightly more force, he would have died instantly.

From Jackson, David Dennis, who came out of the Freedom Rides to be CORE's representative in Mississippi, wired Attorney General Kennedy asking for "immediate action by the federal government" to protect voter registrants and civil rights workers. The head of the NAACP in Mississippi, Aaron Henry, also issued a statement of protest. Jim Forman wrote to President Kennedy from Atlanta, requesting protection. But, as in all other acts of violence in Mississippi, the national government carefully confined its work to the filing of occasional lawsuits, and left the police power of the state of Mississippi to its own devices.

One immediate consequence of the shooting was that Wiley Branton, the civil rights lawyer in charge of the Voters Education Project in Atlanta, asked registration workers all over Mississippi, from all civil rights groups, to move into Greenwood immediately. (Branton, a very fair-skinned Negro, was, coincidentally, a descendant of the remarkable white millionaire slave-owner Greenwood LeFlore, after whom both the city and the county were named, who built a mansion styled after the palace of Empress Josephine, and who supported the Union from his plantation in the Delta all through the Civil War, dying on his front porch with four grandchildren holding Union flags above him.) For the next year, Leflore County was to be the point of concentration for all civil rights work in Mississippi. Said Branton: "The State of Mississippi has repeatedly thrown down a gauntlet at the feet of would-be Negro voters. . . . The time has come for us to pick up the gauntlet. Leflore County has elected itself as the testing ground for democracy."

With the whole Mississippi Voter Education Project staff clustered in Greenwood now—dozens of SNCC people, a few from CORE and SCLC—violence continued. A week after the shooting of Travis, a station-wagon pulled up near SNCC headquarters and someone blasted away with a shotgun into a parked car where Sam Block and three other young people were sitting. The car windows were smashed, but no one was injured. And on March 24, 1963, the voter registration office used by SNCC and the other civil rights organizations was destroyed by fire. All of the office equipment was ruined, records were burned, a phone was ripped from the wall—Greenwood police said there was no evidence of arson. With the owner urging them to leave, SNCC had to look again for another office. Two nights later, someone fired a shotgun into the home of George Greene, a SNCC worker whose family lived in Greenwood. Three children slept as the shots tore into the wall of their bedroom.

Meanwhile, in other parts of Mississippi, there was more trouble. The windows in Aaron Henry's drug store in Clarksdale were broken, as they had been many times before. Dave Dennis' car was fired into in Jackson, three bullets boring through the windshield, but fortunately no one was in the car.

The day after the shooting up of the Greene home, Wednesday, March 27, 1963, Bob Moses, Jim Forman, Willie Peacock, Frank Smith and six others were arrested leading a march to the county courthouse.

Moses recalls:

> The march that took place in Greenwood was not planned. . . . Now the morning of the march we were at the church there and began singing. Forman came by; he was actually on his way out of town, he was driving. So he suggested that maybe we ought to go down to city hall and protest the shooting. We did not anticipate that the police would react as they did. We were simply going to the police station and request a conference with the police chief asking for police protection

> in light of the shooting. And they met us there with the dogs and with guns and so forth and I guess, as Jim says, they simply went berserk for a little while. . . .

As about a hundred Negro men, women, and youngsters, singing and praying, approached the Leflore County Courthouse, the police appeared, wearing yellow helmets, carrying riot sticks, leading police dogs. One of the dogs bit twenty-year-old Matthew Hugh, a demonstrator. Another, snarling and grunting, attacked Bob Moses, tearing a long gash in his trousers. Marian Wright, a young Negro woman studying law at Yale, was on the scene that day:

> I had been with Bob Moses one evening and dogs kept following us down the street. Bob was saying how he wasn't used to dogs, that he wasn't brought up around dogs, and he was really afraid of them. Then came the march, and the dogs growling and the police pushing us back. And there was Bob, refusing to move back, walking, walking towards the dogs.

Demonstrations continued around the county courthouse for the next few days, with more arrests. Comedian Dick Gregory joined the demonstrators. Moses, Forman, and the others were found guilty of disorderly conduct and given the maximum sentence, four months in prison and a $200 fine. They were released in return for a Justice Department agreement to postpone its suit against local officials.

To the SNCC headquarters in Greenwood, through the spring and early summer of 1963, came a stream of reports of events happening all over the state: an explosive tossed into the window of NAACP leader Aaron Henry's home in Clarksdale, then an explosion ripping into the roof of his drugstore, then bullets fired from a passing car into his home; firebombs thrown into the home of Hartman Turnbow, first Negro voter applicant in Holmes County, after which Bob Moses and three others were arrested on "suspicion of arson"; SNCC worker Milton Hancock clubbed by a Greenwood policeman; a sit-in student beaten and kicked at a Jackson lunch counter; an NAACP official clubbed to the ground at a demonstration in Jackson; and, on June 12, Medgar Evers murdered in the driveway of his home in Jackson.

But the evidence began to appear, here and there throughout the state of Mississippi, that what Bob Moses had called the "Mississippi iceberg" was beginning to crack. The evidence was not yet in changes in the social structure of the state, but in the people who emerged slowly, as rocks appear one by one out of a receding sea.

Mrs. Fannie Lou Hamer, forty-seven, married, the mother of two children, has been all her life a sharecropper in Ruleville, Mississippi (Sunflower County, where James Eastland has his plantation). I spoke to her at a SNCC staff meeting in Greenville, Mississippi, in late 1963, on a sunny Sunday afternoon, over the noise of Negro boys practicing in a brass band, blowing trumpets and pounding on drums just outside the door. She told how she got into the movement:

> I went to a meeting at this church, and they announced about this important mass meeting, something we wasn't used to, and they said James Bevel would be speaking that night. So I went to church that Monday night in Ruleville. . . . James Bevel did talk that night and everything he said, you know, made sense. And also, Jim Forman was there. So when they stopped talking, well, they wanted to know, who would go down to register you see, on this particular Friday, and I held up my hand.

Mrs. Hamer is short and stocky, her skin like weather-beaten copper, her eyes soft and large; she walks with a limp because she had polio as a child, and when she sings she is crying out to the heavens. She told what happened after she went down to register.

> The thirty-first of August in '62, the day I went into the courthouse to register, well, after I'd gotten back home, this

> man that I had worked for as a timekeeper and sharecropper for eighteen years, he said that I would just have to leave. . . . So I told him I wasn't trying to register for him, I was trying to register for myself. . . . I didn't have no other choice because for one time I wanted things to be different.

After her eviction from the plantation, Mrs. Hamer stayed with a friend in Ruleville. Ten days later, a car drove by the house and sixteen bullets were pumped into the bedroom where she slept. She was out of the house that night, and no one was hurt.

On June 9, 1963, Mrs. Hamer and five other people were returning to Greenwood from a meeting in South Carolina. The bus made a brief stop in Winona, Mississippi, and some of them went into the white waiting room. The police came and arrested all of them, including Mrs. Hamer, who had just stepped off the bus to see what was happening. They were taken to the Winona jail.

One of the group was Annell Ponder, in her twenties, black-skinned and beautiful, very quiet, who worked on voter education in Greenwood for the Southern Christian Leadership Conference. (Annell graduated from Clark College in Atlanta, and her younger sister was a student of mine at Spelman.) After they got to the jail and were separated inside, Mrs. Hamer heard Annell screaming. "I knew Annell's voice. And she was prayin' for God to forgive them. . . ."

Then they came for Mrs. Hamer. "I was carried to another cell where there was three white men and two Negro prisoners. The state trooper gave one of the Negroes the blackjack and he said . . . 'I want you to make that bitch wish she was dead. . . .' " The prisoner beat her with the blackjack, all over her body, while someone held her feet down to keep her from moving. Then the blackjack was handed to another prisoner, who continued the beating. (Negro prisoners—threatened, bribed, desperate—have often been used against other Negro prisoners, as white prisoners have been used against whites in jails all over the nation.)

The day after the arrest, a group of SNCC people, summoned by telephone, drove to Winona to see if they could help. One of them was Lawrence Guyot, a twenty-three-year-old native of Mississippi, a graduate of Tougaloo College, now a SNCC field secretary, of powerful frame, fair skin, and a voice that roars with passion at church meetings in the Delta. Guyot, trying to see the prisoners, was questioned by a state trooper, who became enraged when Guyot refused to say "Yes, sir," and "No, sir." The trooper slapped Guyot repeatedly, then turned him over to a group of Citizens Council members. They beat him until he couldn't lift his arms, hit him again and again in his face until his eyes were so swollen he couldn't open them.

Another SNCC worker in the group of visitors managed to get into the jail to see Annelle Ponder. She reported on her visit when she got back to Greenwood: "Annelle's face was swollen. . . . She could barely talk. She looked at me and was able to whisper one word: FREEDOM."

Mrs. Hamer became a field secretary for SNCC after her eviction from the plantation. Just as Moses and the other "outsiders" had become insiders, now the insiders were beginning to become outsiders to the society they had grown up in. As Mrs. Hamer put it:

> You know they said outsiders was coming in and beginning to get the people stirred up because they've always been satisfied. Well, as long as I can remember, I've never been satisfied. It was twenty of us, six girls and fourteen boys, and we just barely was making it. You know I could see the whites was going to school at a time when we would be out of school . . . and most of the time we didn't have anything to wear. I knew it was something wrong. . . . I always sensed that we was the one who always do the hard work, you know. . . .

I asked her if she was going to remain with the movement, and she responded with the words to a song: "I told them if they ever miss me from the movement and couldn't find me nowhere, come on over to the graveyard, and I'll be buried there."

Shortly after the Winona incident, a voter registration meeting held in a tiny church in the cotton-growing village of Itta Bena, just outside of Greenwood, was broken up by smoke-bombs. When forty-five Negroes marched to the town marshal's office to protest this, they were arrested; the following week, thirteen youngsters working with SNCC, some of them from Itta Bena, were arrested in Greenwood.

My wife and I were in Greenwood in August, 1963, when those fifty-eight people finally were freed on bond money supplied via the National Council of Churches. That night SNCC headquarters had the eerie quality of a field hospital after a battle. Youngsters out of jail—sixteen and seventeen years old—were sprawled here and there. Two of them lay on the narrow cots upstairs while a few of the SNCC girls dabbed their eyes with boric acid solutions; some dietary deficiency in jail had affected their eyes. One boy nursed an infected hand. Another boy's foot was swollen. He had started to lose feeling in it while in the "hot box" at Parchman Penitentiary, and had stamped on it desperately to restore circulation. Medical attention was refused them in prison.

Newspaper reports about demonstrators arrested in the Deep South have never conveyed fully the reality of a Black Belt jail. As we stood around in SNCC headquarters, three of the youngsters out of Parchman spoke of their arrest and their two months in jail. The first was Willie Rogers:

> . . . it was twenty minutes to one when the chief came out of his car and across the street in front of the courthouse. It was June 25—Tuesday. The chief said, I'm askin' you-all to move on. We said that we were up there to get our folks registered.

> . . . He said I'm askin' you to leave now. We said we came to get them registered and soon as they registered we would leave. So he started placing us under arrest one by one. . . . The judge sentenced us to four months and $200 fine for refusing to move on. . . .
>
> We stayed in the hot box two nights. It's a cell about six foot square, which they call the hot box. Long as they don't turn the heat on—with three in there—you can make it. There's no openings for light or air; there was a little crack under the door, but you couldn't see your hand before your face less you get down on your knees. When they got ready to feed you they hand the tray through a little door which they close—and then you can't eat unless you get down on your knees by the light comin' in the door—then you can see how to eat. And they had a little round hole in the floor which was a commode. . . .

Next to speak was Jesse James Glover, another teenager, who told of nine of them being put in the hot box one time, and thirteen another time.

> We were making it okay about thirty minutes with the fan off, breathing in this oxygen, letting out this carbon dioxide—and the air was evaporating on top of the building, and it got so hot the water was falling off the top of the building all around the sides like it was raining. . . . He let us out . . . we told everyone to keep quiet because we didn't want to get in the hot box again. Then a few fellows were talking to each other. He came down and told Lawrence Guyot, "I'm going to put these niggers up to this damn bar if I hear any of this racket"—so they hung MacArthur Cotton and Willie Rogers on the bars—MacArthur was singin' some Freedom songs. . . . Altogether, I was thirteen days in the hot box. . . . How did I get in the movement? I was at a mass meeting in Itta Bena. I'd been walkin' and canvassin' on my own. Bob Moses asked me, did I want to work with SNCC? I told him yes. . . .

Fred Harris spoke:

> . . . He came around and said, "You gonna move? you gonna move?" And he frightened the old people. And when we didn't move he arrested us. . . . In all I spent 160 hours in the hole—the hot box that is. . . . I'm seventeen. I got involved with the movement back in 1960, when SNCC came up. I was fourteen then. Sam Block was talking to me about the movement. I told him, yes, I'd be glad to help, and I started from there on. . . . At first my mother didn't want me to be in it. Then she realized it would be best for her and for me . . . she told me I could go ahead.

The next afternoon we drove in two cars, with Bob Moses, Stokely Carmichael, and several others, to Itta Bena. People came out of the cotton fields to meet in a dilapidated little church, welcoming back the Parchman prisoners, singing freedom songs with an overpowering spirit. One of the returned prisoners was Mother Perkins, fragile and small, seventy-five years old, who had just spent, like the rest, two months on the county prison farm for wanting to register to vote. Cars filled with white men rumbled by along the road that passed by the church door, but the meeting and the singing went on.

Bob Moses spoke, told them that there were no jobs in Chicago or Detroit for white or black, that they must stay and wrench from the State of Mississippi what they deserved as human beings. Anyone who felt the urge got up to speak. An old man rose on his cane and said slowly, thoughtfully: "All these years, going along behind my plow, I thought some day things would change. But I never dreamed I'd see it now."

In the fall of 1963, the SNCC workers concentrated in Greenwood began to spread out all over the state in the most daring political action undertaken by Mississippi Negroes since Reconstruction. With Negroes prevented—by intimidation and reprisal—from registering and voting in the regular gubernatorial election (between Paul Johnson, segregationist Democrat, and Rubel Phillips, segregationist Republican), it was decided to give them a chance to vote for a Negro governor, Aaron Henry, in an unofficial Freedom Ballot.

Henry, a forty-one-year-old pharmacist, army veteran, and NAACP leader, was from Clarksdale, Mississippi, and one of the pillars of the movement in the state. Running for Lieutenant-Governor on Henry's ticket was a twenty-seven-year-old white minister, Edwin King, chaplain at Tougaloo College. King was born in Vicksburg, Mississippi, educated at Millsaps College in Jackson, then went off to study theology at Boston University. He had been arrested four times since 1960 for various civil rights actions and was once beaten in a jail in Montgomery. The Henry-King platform stressed the subjection of poor whites as well as Negroes to the political and economic dictatorship that had so long run the state of Mississippi.

All the civil rights organizations in the Council of Federated Organizations cooperated in the campaign, and Bob Moses of SNCC directed it, with ballot boxes placed in churches and meeting places throughout the state, where adult Negroes could come and vote. In October and November, hundreds of workers canvassed the State of Mississippi, aided by visiting white students from Yale and Stanford, organized by Al Lowenstein, a young political scientist. There were jailings, beatings, and shootings, but the campaign went on.

In Rolling Forks, Mississippi, Ivanhoe Donaldson was canvassing along with Charlie Cobb. People were on their front porches, back from church, or in the back yard. As Donaldson describes one exchange:

"Good afternoon, Ma'am. Have you voted in the election yet?"

"No. What election?"

"Well, Dr. Aaron Henry, a Negro from Clarksdale, Mississippi. . . ." A pickup truck with a white man in it careened onto the lawn.

"Nigger, we aren't going to have any more of this agitation around here. Niggers 'round here don't need to vote, so you and your damned buddy get out of here. God damn it, nigger: I'll give you one minute to get out of town or I'll kill you!"

Another time, a policeman had Ivanhoe Donaldson in the back of a police car, and worked himself into a rage, pulling his pistol, cocking it, holding it near Donaldson's head, shouting: "You and the other goddamn Moses' niggers around here ain't gonna git nuthin but a bullet in the haid! Black son of a bitch, I'm gonna kill you, nigger!" Another policeman came over and suggested this was not the time or place for a killing, and finally he was let go.

Claude Weaver is a Negro student at Harvard College, very young-looking, mild-mannered, who plays the guitar and draws hilarious cartoons with charcoal (his greatest creation is "Supersnick," a humble Negro janitor named Tom who turns into "Supersnick" at will and saves his brethren from Mississippi sheriffs). Weaver joined the SNCC staff in time for the Freedom Ballot campaign. He wrote from Mississippi:

> The Delta lies vacant and barren all day; it broods in the evening and it cries all night. I get the impression that the land is cursed and suffering, groaning under the awful weight of history's sins. I can understand what Faulkner meant; it must be loved or hated . . . or both. It's hard to imagine how any music but the blues could have taken root in the black soil around me.

Weaver stayed on after the Freedom Ballot campaign. He was jailed several times, and was once threatened by a policeman with a pistol-whipping if he didn't say "Yes, sir." He wrote to a friend back home, as if he were simply offering a piece of news: "We are not afraid."

When the Freedom Ballot campaign was over, 80,000 Negroes had marked ballots for Henry and King, four times the number officially registered in the state. It showed, Bob

Moses said, that Mississippi Negroes *would* vote, in huge numbers, if given the chance. It showed that Negro and white youngsters were still not afraid, despite everything that had happened in the last two years, to move into the towns and villages and farmland of Mississippi and talk to people about what the future might be like.

For SNCC the McComb days of 1961 had been a quick and ugly rebuff. The Greenwood concentration of 1962–1963, in spite of the violence and the pain, had awakened voices and hopes in Mississippi that could not be stilled. Perhaps 1964 would be *the year* for the transformation of the state of Mississippi. SNCC now had 130 staff members throughout the South, with forty of these jail-hardened youngsters concentrated in Mississippi, spread out in different places throughout the state. One of these places, in Forrest County, was the little city of Hattiesburg.

6. Mississippi III: Hattiesburg

It was a bumpy air ride going west out of Atlanta on the twin-engined Southern Airways DC-3. The tall, very friendly air stewardess was surprised to see the airplane crowded with clergymen from the North on their way to Hattiesburg, and joked with them all the way in her deep drawl. I was the only one in the group not a member of the clergy, but when they found that I was also going to Hattiesburg to be with SNCC for Freedom Day, I was almost ordained.

Driving from the airport to SNCC headquarters, we passed a huge sign: "In the Beginning, God Made Us Holy." Some months before, a SNCC field secretary had written from Hattiesburg to the Atlanta office:

> We plan to let Guyot speak. . . . We are going to announce an interdenominational Bible study course that will be dedicated to the proposition that religion doesn't have to be bullshit. We hope to tie in an active image of the Christ, and what would he have done had he been here, now . . . you see?

The ministers probably would have approved.

Hattiesburg, a short drive from the Gulf in Southern Mississippi, had been looked on by SNCC workers with some hope, ever since Curtis Hayes and Hollis Watkins left school in the spring of 1962 to start a voter registration campaign there, at the request of their McComb cellmate, Bob Moses. CORE man Dave Dennis had done some crucial ground-breaking work there. "Hattiesburg," one of the reports to Atlanta read, "is fantastic material for a beautifully organized shift from the old to the new . . . they are ready now. . . ." Hattiesburg Negroes were not quite as poor as those in the Delta; police brutality seemed not quite as harsh there. As we drove into town, we passed the mansion of Paul Johnson, whose father had been governor of Mississippi, and who had just been elected governor himself. The radio was reporting Governor Johnson's inaugural address; it had a distinctly more moderate tone than his fierce campaign pronouncements on race.

In the rundown Negro section of Hattiesburg, on a cracked and crooked street filled with little cafes, was SNCC's Freedom House, owned by Mrs. Wood, a widow and a member of a prominent Negro family in Hattiesburg. (When John O'Neal, a SNCC worker from Southern Illinois University, arrived to work in Hattiesburg in the summer of 1963, he wrote to Moses: "Mrs. Wood received us late Wednesday night, and put a room open for us. She's a fine old warrior . . .") Outside the headquarters, a crowd of Negro youngsters milled around in the street, talking excitedly. Snatches of freedom songs rose here and there. This was Tuesday, January 21, 1964, and tomorrow was Freedom Day in Hattiesburg.

Inside the Freedom House, which was cluttered with typewriters, mimeograph machines, charts, photos, and notices, and was filled with people and an incessant noise, the first person I saw was Mrs. Hamer sitting near the doorway. Upstairs, Bob Moses greeted me and took me past the big open parlor area where a meeting was going on planning strategy for the next day. He showed me into the room where he and his wife Dona were staying; only a few weeks before he had married Dona Richards, a diminutive, attractive University of Chicago graduate with a tough, quick mind, who had come to Mississippi to work with SNCC on a special education project. It was a combination bedroom and SNCC office, with a huge mirrored closet, carved mahogany bedstead, four typewriters, a gas heater, a suitcase, a wash basin, a map of Hattiesburg, and a vase of flowers.

Other SNCC people drifted into the room, and a session on Freedom Day strategy began. It was assumed that, as in every case where a picket line was set up in Mississippi, the pickets would be arrested. So a number of decisions had to be made. Some SNCC staff people would have to go to prison to keep up the morale of those who were not so experienced in Mississippi jails—Lawrence Guyot, Donna Moses, and five or six more; others would have to stay out to run the voter registration campaign after the jailings—Jesse Harris, MacArthur Cotton, Mrs. Hamer. Bob Moses, it was decided, would join the picket line, would go to jail, and would stay there, to dramatize to the nation that the basic right of protest did not exist in Mississippi.

The meeting moved outside into the hall, so that Donna Moses could begin packing the few little things they would need in jail. A wire was sent to Attorney General Robert Kennedy:

> Tomorrow morning, hundreds of Hattiesburg's citizens will attempt to register to vote. We request the presence of federal marshals to protect them. We also request that local police interfering with constitutional rights be arrested and prosecuted. Signed, Bob Moses.

The meeting was interrupted briefly as Ella Baker and John Lewis walked in, having just arrived from Atlanta after a long and wearying train ride. Plans for the summer of '64 were put forth. A thousand or two thousand people would be brought from all over the country to work in Mississippi during the summer months, to man newly set-up community centers, to teach in "freedom schools" for Mississippi youngsters, and to work on voter registration. The National Council of Churches was going to give massive help. Both CORE and SCLC would send more people in. As the group talked, you could hear the young kids outside singing: "We will go-o-o to jail. . . . Don't need no bail. . . . No, no, no, no . . . we won't come out . . . until our people vo-o-o-te!"

That night there was a mass meeting in a church, with every seat filled, every aisle packed, the doorways jammed; it was almost impossible to get in. The lights went out, and a buzz of excitement ran through the audience; there were a thousand people, massed tight in the blackness. Then, out of the dark, one person began singing, "We shall not, we shall not be moved . . ." and everyone took it up. Someone put a flashlight up on the speakers' stand, and the meeting began that way until after a while the lights came on.

Aaron Henry, for whom Hattiesburg Negroes had turned out en masse to vote in the Freedom Ballot (3500 Negroes out of 7400 of voting age in Forrest County cast Freedom Ballots) told the crowd that it was back in 1949 that the first affidavit had been filed in Hattiesburg with the Justice Department citing discrimination against Negroes trying to register, and here it was fifteen years later and the Federal government had not been able to make good. "We don't plan to leave Hattiesburg," Henry said, "until the Justice Department takes Registrar Lynd in hand. That's why we're here."

Henry introduced John Lewis, saying about SNCC: "If there is any group that has borne more the burden of the struggle, none of us know about it." After Lewis spoke, Annelle Ponder spoke for the Southern Christian Leadership Conference, and Dave Dennis for CORE. A lawyer from the National Council of Churches, John Pratt, pointed out that the Justice Department had just secured a final decision from the Supreme Court ordering Registrar Theron Lynd to stop discriminating and to stop picking out of the 285 sections of the Mississippi constitution different ones for Negroes to interpret than were given to whites: "We're here to prod the Justice Department a bit." A rabbi spoke, one of two in the delegation of fifty ministers who were ready to picket and go to jail the next day.

Then Ella Baker spoke, holding before the crowd, as she did so often, a vision beyond the immediate: "Even if segregation is gone, we will still need to be free; we will still have to see that everyone has a job. Even if we can all vote, but if people are still hungry, we will not be free. . . . Singing alone is not enough; we need schools and learning. . . . Remember, we are not fighting for the freedom of the Negro alone, but for the freedom of the human spirit, a larger freedom that encompasses all mankind."

Lawrence Guyot, who had come after his beating in Winona and his long prison term in Parchman to direct the operation in Hattiesburg, was introduced, and a great roar went up. Everyone in the church stood and applauded as he came down the aisle; it was a spontaneous expression of the kind of love SNCC organizers receive when they have become part of a community in the Deep South. Guyot combines a pensive intellectualism with a fierce and radical activism. He stood before the audience, his large frame trembling, raised a fist high over his head, and shouted, pronouncing slowly and carefully: "Immanuel Kant. . . ." The church was hushed. ". . . Immanuel Kant asks—Do you exist?" In the front row, teen-age boys and girls stared at Guyot; a young woman was holding two babies. Guyot paused. "Kant says, every speck of earth must be treated as important!" His audience waited, somewhat awed, and he went on to get very specific about instructions for Freedom Day at the county courthouse.

When Guyot finished, someone cried out: "Freedom!" And the audience responded: "Now!" Again and again: "Freedom . . . Now!" The meeting was over, and everyone linked hands and sang "We Shall Overcome," then poured out into the darkness outside the church, still singing. It was almost midnight.

At the Freedom House, on Mobile Street, some people prepared to go to sleep; others stood around, talking. Mrs. Wood came down to the big cluttered open area where we were, anxious that we should all have a place to stay for the night. She took Mendy Samstein and me to a little room in the back and pointed out the cot she had just set up for both of us. We returned to the front and continued talking. The place began to empty as youngsters drifted out, or lay down to sleep on tables, benches, chairs, the floor. It was one in the morning; over on a long counter a half-dozen people, including Donna Moses, were lettering the picket signs to be carried seven hours later.

Lawrence Guyot sat wearily on a chair against the wall and we talked. He was born in a tiny coastal town in Mississippi, on the Gulf, named Pass Christian ("That town is the most complete mechanism of destruction I have seen"), the eldest of five brothers. His father was a cement finisher, now unemployed, his mother a housewife and a maid. When he graduated from Tougaloo College in 1963 he had already been a SNCC staff member for many months.

> Why did I join the movement? I was rebelling against everything. I still am. I think we need to change every institution we know. I came to that conclusion when I was seventeen years old. At first I thought of being a teacher, or a doctor; now I would like to get married, and do just what I'm doing now. . . . I'm not satisfied with any condition that I'm aware of in America."

Mendy and I decided to hit the sack for the night, but when we went back we found a body snoring on our cot; it looked like Norris MacNamara, free-lance photographer and audio man who decided some time in 1963 to give his talents to SNCC. We decided to let him be, and went back into the front room. At 2:00 A.M. there were still a dozen people around; the signs were still being made; we talked some more. Guyot said someone was trying to find a place for us to stay; there were four of us now looking for a place to sleep. Besides me, there were Mendy Samstein, Brandeis graduate and University of Chicago doctoral candidate in history, a faculty member at Morehouse College, now a SNCC field man in Mississippi; Oscar Chase, Yale Law school graduate, now with SNCC; and Avery Williams, a cheerful SNCC man from Alabama State College. At 3:00 A.M. we began looking for a good spot on the floor, since all the benches and tables were taken, but then someone came along with a slip of paper and an address.

A cab let us out in front of a small frame house in the Negro part of town. It was about 3:30 A.M. The street was dark, and the house was dark inside. We hesitated, then Oscar approached and knocked cautiously on the front door. A Negro man opened the door and looked at us; he was in his pajamas. Here we were, three whites and a Negro, none of whom he had ever seen. Oscar said hesitantly "They told us at headquarters. . . ." The man smiled broadly, "Come on in!" He shouted through the darkness back into his bedroom, "Hey, honey, look who's here!" The lights were on now and his wife came out: "Can I fix something for you fellows?" We said no, and apologized for getting them up. The man waved his hand: "Oh, I was going to get up soon anyway."

The man disappeared and came back in a moment dragging a mattress onto the floor near the couch. "Here, two of you can sleep on the mattress, one on the couch, and we have a little cot inside." The lights went out soon after. There was a brief murmured conversation in the dark among us, and then we were asleep.

I awoke just as dawn was filtering through the windows, and in the semi-darkness I could see the forms of the other fellows near me, still asleep. I became aware of the sound that had awakened me; at first I had thought it part of a dream, but I heard it now still, a woman's voice, pure and poignant. She was chanting softly. At first I thought it came from outside, then I realized it was coming from the bedroom of the Negro couple, that the man was gone from the house, and it was his wife, praying, intoning . . . "Oh, Lord, Jesus, Oh, let things go well today, Jesus . . . Oh, make them see, Jesus . . . Show your love today, Jesus . . . Oh, it's been a long, long time, oh, Jesus . . . Oh, Lord, Oh, Jesus . . ."

The chanting stopped. I heard Avery call from the next room: "Wake up, fellows, it's Freedom Day." A radio was turned on with dance music played loud. A light went on in the kitchen. As we dressed I looked through the open doorway into the Negro couple's bedroom and saw there was no mattress on their bed. They had led us to believe that they had brought out a spare mattress for us, but had given us theirs.

The woman came out of the kitchen and turned on the gas heater in the living room for us: "Come and get your breakfast, fellows." It was a feast—eggs and grits and bacon and hot biscuits and coffee. Her husband drove down to the Gulf every day to work on the fishing docks, and the woman was soon to be picked up in a truck and taken off to work as a maid; her daughter was a senior in high school. Her young son said: "Yesterday morning, when I woke up, the light from a police car was shining in the windows. Guess they know us." The woman, waiting outside for her ride, came in for a second to report to us what a neighbor had just told her. Downtown the streets were full of police, carrying clubs and sticks and guns, wearing helmets. She went off in the truck. We prepared to leave, and Avery Williams looked outside: "It's raining!"

At the headquarters were noise and confusion and great crowds of people—ministers, youngsters, newspapermen, SNCC staff members. We got a lift to the county courthouse, rain falling softly. The picket line was already formed, with white ministers, carrying signs, walking back and forth in front of the concrete steps leading up to the Forrest County Courthouse, employees staring out of the windows of the courthouse, a camera in a second story window focused on the scene.

About 9:30 A.M., there was the sound of marching feet on the wet pavement and two lines of policemen came down the street, heading for the courthouse, all traffic cleared in front of them. A police car swung to the curb, a loudspeaker on its roof, and then the announcement blared out into the street, harsh, hurting the ears: "This is the Hattiesburg Police Department. We're asking you to disperse. Clear the sidewalk!" There were thirty-two pickets on the line. John Lewis and I stood across the street in front of Sears Roebuck, on the sidewalk. No one made a move to leave. The marching policemen came up even with the county courthouse, in four squads, wearing yellow rain slickers, and blue or white or red helmets, carrying clubs. "First squad! Forward march!" The first line peeled off and came up on the sidewalk parallel to the picket line. "Squad halt!"

The loudspeaker rasped again: "People who wish to register, line up four at a time, and they will be accepted. All those not registering to vote move off. This is the Hattiesburg Police Department!" Fifty Negro youngsters came out of nowhere and formed a second picket line in front of the courthouse, near the line of ministers. All four squads of police had peeled off now and were facing the picket line, clubs in hand. It looked as if everything would go as predicted: an order to disperse, no one moving, everyone put under arrest. I could see Moses across the street, peering at the scene, hunched a little under the falling rain.

It was 9:40 A.M. Ten minutes had elapsed since the police had come marching in formation down the street. They were lined up now opposite the two picket lines, twenty-five helmets a few feet from the line and twenty-five more across the street. For the third time, from the police loudspeaker: "All those not registering to vote move off."

The line of black youngsters merged with the line of white ministers to form one long picket line in front of the courthouse, the messages on their signs clear even in the greyness of the day: ONE MAN, ONE VOTE; FREEDOM DAY IN HATTIESBURG. No one moved off the line. Police began clearing off the sidewalk across the street from the courthouse and we moved across to the steps of the courthouse. The picket line remained undisturbed. The scene was peaceful. There were virtually no white observers. If our senses did not deceive us, something unprecedented was taking place in the state of Mississippi: a black and white line of demonstrators was picketing a public building, allowed to do so by the police. In all of the demonstrations of the past two and one-half years, this had never happened.

Over a hundred pickets were walking now, the rain still coming down. A blond Episcopalian minister was carrying a picket sign with an inscription in Hebrew. A Negro schoolboy carried a sign: "LET MY PARENTS VOTE." Jim Forman escorted a Negro woman across the street, through the rain, up the stairs. But they wouldn't let her in the courthouse. Voter registrants were lined up on the steps outside the glass door, which was guarded on the inside by the sheriff. Only four people were being allowed inside at a time, and it took about an hour for another four to be admitted, so the rest of the people formed a line down the steps, exposed to the rain. At ten o'clock what had been a medium drizzle became a downpour. No one left the line. Bob Moses escorted a Negro man across the street and up the steps.

I walked around the back, got inside the courthouse, and made my way to the registrar's office, just inside the glass door. Television cameras were focused on Theron Lynd, the three-hundred-pound Forrest County Registrar, who was now under final injunction by the Supreme Court to stop discriminating against Negroes under penalty of going to jail. Lynd was dressed in a black suit, his grey hair cut short, a stub of a cigar in his mouth, his manner affable. At a federal court hearing in March, 1962, the Justice Department pointed out that Lynd, who had never registered a single Negro, had allowed 1,836 whites to register without filling out the application form or interpreting a section of the constitution. Until January 30, 1961, no Negro had even been permitted to fill out a form. In early January, 1964, the Supreme Court had affirmed a Fifth Circuit Court decision that Lynd was guilty of civil contempt unless he complied with court orders not to discriminate.

Two Negro women were filling out blanks at the counter, and one Negro man was there, with a big SNCC button on his overalls. Lynd ambled around, apparently trying to be helpful, as newspapermen and photographers stood nearby. I spoke to him: "Mr. Lynd, is it to be assumed that all orders of the court are being followed now?" He turned to me: "Yes, indeed. I will treat all applicants alike, just as I have always done. To us this is no special day."

I went outside. It was still raining, coming down hard. Someone said that Bob Moses had just been taken off to jail. He'd been arrested for standing on the sidewalk opposite the courthouse and refusing to move on.

Jim Forman stood just outside the glass door of the courthouse, shirt collar open under his raincoat, pipe in his right hand, gesticulating with his left hand, Negro men and women bunched around him. He was calling to the sheriff and two well-dressed official-looking men who were holding the door shut from the inside: "Sheriff, it's raining out here, and these people would like to come into the courthouse. You seem to have plenty of room inside." No reply. Forman held the arm of an old Negro woman and called again through the glass door: "Sheriff, will you be a Christian and let this old lady inside, a lady who has toiled in the fields of Forrest County many years, an old lady who now must stand out in the rain because she wants to register to vote? Is there no compassion in Forrest County for a woman seventy-one years old, whose feet are wet as she waits, who has nursed white children in her time, who can't even get a chair so she can sit down, for whom there is no room in the county courthouse?" No reply. A newspaperman gestured to me: "Forman is really putting it on, isn't he?"

It was 11:15 A.M. and still raining. Forman motioned to the people standing in line on the steps. "Maybe if we get down on our knees and pray, someone will hear us." Twenty people knelt in the rain on the courthouse steps and an old Negro man prayed aloud. Below, in the long line of people with signs moving in front of the courthouse, someone was handing out little boxes of raisins and crackerjacks to sustain the energy of those who had been marching for three hours.

At noon the courthouse closed for lunch. Through the morning twelve people had gotten inside to fill out applications. I walked back with Forman to SNCC headquarters. He said: "Maybe it seems strange to make a fuss over standing in the rain, but it's exactly in all these little things that the Negro has been made to feel inferior over the centuries. And it's important educationally. To show the Negroes in Hattiesburg that it is possible to speak up loudly and firmly to a white sheriff as an equal—something they're not accustomed to doing."

The picket line continued all afternoon. Two white girls from Mississippi Southern University in Hattiesburg stood on the courthouse steps, watching, taking notes. They were from the University radio station. They would not oppose a Negro's admission to the University, they said. Lafayette Surney, a nineteen-year-old SNCC staff member from Ruleville, Mississippi, came over, and the three of them chatted amiably, about Mississippi, civil rights, voter registration, and college.

Down on the picket line I could see the familiar form of Mrs. Hamer, moving along with her characteristic limp, holding a sign, her face wet with the rain and turned upwards, crying out her song against the sky: "Which Side Are You On?" A little later I took her picket sign from her and walked while she rested on the steps. At five the line disbanded, gathered briefly on the courthouse steps to bow in prayer, and marched back to headquarters. The policemen ended their vigil.

There was one more piece of news: Oscar Chase had been taken off to jail. His car had bumped a parked truck that morning, doing no damage, but a policeman had noted what happened, and about 4:00 P.M. he had been hustled into a police car and carted away. The charge: "leaving the scene of an accident."

It had been a day of surprises. The picketing went on all day with no mass arrests. Perhaps this was due to the desire of the newly-elected Governor Paul Johnson to play the race issue slow; perhaps it was due to the presence of clergymen, TV cameras, newspapermen; or perhaps it was simply a tribute to the tirelessness of SNCC in putting people out in the streets again and again, until police and politicians got weary of trundling them off to jail. At any rate, over a hundred Negro men and women had come to register, though few got through the courthouse door, and only a handful were eventually declared to have passed the test.

So, Freedom Day passed as a kind of quiet victory and everyone was commenting on how well things had gone. Nobody was aware, of course, that about six o'clock that evening, in his cell downtown, Oscar Chase, the SNCC man fresh out of Yale Law School, was being beaten bloody and unconscious by a fellow prisoner while policemen stood by watching.

No one knew until the next morning. I awoke at six on the narrow cot in the back of the Freedom House. Everyone around me was still asleep. Through the wall I could hear the faint sound of a typewriter and wondered who the heck was typing at six in the morning. I dressed and went into the next room. A Negro kid, about fifteen years old, was sitting at a typewriter, pecking slowly at the keys. He looked at me apologetically, seeing he had roused me: "Writing a letter to my sister."

I walked into the big front room, where in the darkness I could make out the forms of sleeping youngsters. One fellow was stretched out on a wooden table, one on the counter where the signs had been lettered, one on three chairs, using his jacket as a pillow, one leaning back in a chair, his head against the wall. Around a desk sat three teen-agers, as if holding a conference, sound asleep in their chairs. The first rays of sunlight were coming in through the windows.

I walked outside to get some breakfast, and SNCC field secretary Milton Hancock joined me at a little cafe across the street. We sat at a table, ate, and talked, and watched through a window as a man on the sidewalk unloaded a batch of fresh-caught sheepshead fish from a truck, just up from the gulf. Then someone came along to say that Oscar Chase had phoned in to headquarters that he had been beaten the night before, and he wanted to be bonded out. Two of the visiting ministers were going down to fetch him, and I went along.

The police dogs in their kennels were growling and barking as we entered the jailhouse. It was a few minutes before 8:00 A.M. The bond money was turned over. A moment later, Oscar came down the corridor, unescorted, not a soul around. A few moments before, the corridor had been full of policemen; it seemed now as if no one wanted to be around to look at him. Even the dogs had stopped growling. He was still wearing his badly worn corduroy pants, and his old boots, caked with mud. His blue workshirt was splattered with blood, and under it his T-shirt was very bloody. The right side of his face—his lips, his nose, his cheek—was swollen. His nose looked as if it were broken. Blood was caked over his eye.

We called for the police chief: "We want you to look at this man as he comes out of your jail, chief." The chief looked surprised, even concerned. He turned to Oscar, put his face close to his, "Tell them, tell them, didn't I take that fellow out of your cell when he was threatening you?" Oscar nodded. He told us the story.

The chief had removed one of the three prisoners in the cell early in the evening, when Oscar complained that he was being threatened. But shortly afterward they put in another prisoner, of even uglier disposition. And this was the one who a few hours later kicked and beat Oscar into insensibility in the presence of several policemen. He was not as drunk as the man who'd been taken out. But he was in a state of great agitation. He announced, first, that he could lick any man in the cell; there were Oscar and another prisoner. "He was very upset about the demonstration—wanted to know why the jail wasn't 'full of niggers.' " He had been a paratrooper in World War II, and told Oscar he "would rather kill a nigger lover than a Nazi or a Jap."

The third man in the cell proceeded to tell the former paratrooper that Oscar was an integrationist. Now he began a series of threatening moves. He pushed a cigarette near Oscar's face and said he would burn his eyes out. He said that first he would knock him unconscious and while he was out he would use the lighted cigarette on his eyes. Oscar called for the jailer. The jailer came. Oscar asked to be removed from the cell. The jailer didn't respond. The ex-paratrooper asked the jailer if Oscar was "one of them nigger-lovers." The jailer nodded.

What Oscar Chase remembers after that is that the prisoner said something close to "Now I know why I'm in this jail." Then:

> The next thing I can remember was lying on the floor, looking up. I could see the jailer and some other policemen looking at me and smiling. I could also see the other prisoner standing over me, kicking me. I began to get up, was knocked down again, and then heard the door of the cell open. The cops pulled me out and brought me into another cell, where I remained by myself for the rest of the night. . . . I was still bleeding a couple of hours after the incident. Watching from the door of my new cell, I saw the trusty put a pack of cigarettes and some matches under the door of my attacker's cell. Later I heard the police come in and let him out. I could hear them laughing . . .

We went from the jailhouse to the home of one of the two Negro doctors in town, and agreed to meet him at his clinic in a little while. Then we took Oscar to SNCC headquarters. Mrs. Wood kept pressing her hands together, in great distress, "Oh, my poor boy!" Jim Forman came out of his room sleepily, waking up quickly as he saw Oscar. He shook his head: "Jesus Christ!" The lawyers were summoned, and we prepared to go to the F.B.I.

There was one moment of sick humor as the incident came to a close. Four of us waited in the F.B.I. office in Hattiesburg for the interrogating agent to come in to get the facts from Oscar Chase about his beating. John Pratt, attorney with the National Council of Churches, tall, blond, slender, was impeccably dressed in a dark suit with faint stripes. Robert Lunney, of the Lawyer's Committee on Civil Rights (set up as a volunteer group to aid in civil rights cases), dark-haired and clean-cut, was attired as befit an attorney with a leading Wall Street firm. I did not quite come up to their standards, because I had left without my coat and tie, and my pants had lost their press from the rain the day before; but I was clean-shaven, and not too disreputable looking. Oscar sat in a corner, looking exactly as he had a few hours before when I saw him come down the corridor from his cell, his face swollen, his clothes bloody. The F.B.I. agent came out from the inner office and closed the door behind him. He surveyed the four of us with a quick professional eye and then asked, "Who was it got the beating?"

At four that afternoon, the Hattiesburg Municipal Court convened to hear the case of Robert Moses, on trial for obstructing traffic by standing on the sidewalk and refusing to move on when ordered to by a policeman. Many of the white ministers went to the trial, and we had agreed that we would sit in the Negro section; so far, any attempt made in Mississippi to sit integrated in a local courtroom had ended in arrest.

I entered the courtroom, sat down on the "colored" side of the aisle, and noted that there were about ten white people on that side, and an equal number of Negroes on the "white" side. Nine marshals stood against the wall. The judge entered the chamber and everyone rose. To our surprise, it was a woman, Judge Mildred W. Norris, an attractive, gracious lady who smiled and posed for the photographers as she approached the bench, then nodded for everyone to be seated. She smiled pleasantly at the spectators, paused a moment, then said sweetly, "Will the marshals please segregate the courtroom?" Everything was quiet.

The marshals moved towards us. The lady judge said: "I will ask you to please move to the side of the courtroom where you belong, or leave. If you do not, you will be held in contempt of court and placed under arrest." No one moved. The marshals came up closer. As one approached me, I raised my hand. He stopped, and said, rather uncertainly, "Do you wish to make a statement?" I replied, "Yes." The judge said, "You may make a statement." I got to my feet and said, "Your Honor, the Supreme Court of the United States has ruled that segregated seating in a courtroom is unconstitutional. Will you please abide by that ruling?" The courtroom buzzed. The judge hesitated. John Pratt, who with Bob Lunney was acting as counsel for Moses, spoke up and asked for a recess of a few minutes, and the judge granted it. The courtroom became alive with conversation again.

During the recess, no one changed seats. The judge reconvened the court, and the room was absolutely silent. She said: "We here in Mississippi have had our way of life for hundreds of years, and I obey the laws of Mississippi. I have asked that you sit segregated or leave, or be placed under arrest. We would have appreciated your complying." She paused. "But since you do not, we will allow you to remain as you are, provided you do not create a disturbance." We sat there, astonished, but silent. And the court session began.

"Defendant Robert Moses, come right up." Bob Moses stood before the bench, in his blue overall jacket, corduroy pants, white shirt with open collar, while the charge was read: ". . . with intent to provoke a breach of peace, did congregate on the sidewalk and did interfere with the passage of pedestrians and refused to move on when ordered to do so. . . ." He pleaded not guilty.

Three policemen took the stand, the first one named John Quincy Adams, and testified that Moses had obstructed pedestrian traffic by standing on the sidewalk. The courtroom was hot, and the judge, smiling slightly, picked up a cardboard sign near her and began fanning herself with it. It was one of the exhibits, a picket sign with large letters: "FREEDOM NOW!" It showed a picture of two small Negro boys, and said "GIVE THEM A FUTURE IN MISSISSIPPI." The judge continued to fan herself with the sign.

Cross-examined by Bob Lunney, Patrolman John Quincy Adams admitted no other pedestrians had complained about the sidewalk being obstructed, and that he did not see anyone who did not have free access. The second policeman was shown a picket sign by the city attorney which said, "JOIN THE FREEDOM FITE". The attorney asked, "Do you understand what a fight is?" "Yes," the patrolman replied.

At about 7:00 P.M. Bob Moses took the stand, the only witness in his defense. After a series of questions by Robert Lunney, he was turned over for cross-examination to the attorney for the city, Francis Zachary, a large man with iron grey hair, a black suit, and horn-rimmed glasses. Zachary kept Moses on the stand for over an hour in the most fierce, pounding cross-examination I had ever seen. Zachary's voice was filled alternately with anger, contempt, disgust. He walked back and forth in front of the witness, using his voice like a whip, shaking papers in front of Moses' face, and moving up close and pointing his finger, the combination of voice and gestures and incessant pointless questions adding up to an assault on the senses, an attempt to break down the witness through emotional exhaustion. Through it all, Moses, a little tired from his day in jail, sat there on the witness stand, answering in the same quiet, even voice, pointing out patiently again and again where the prosecutor had misunderstood his reply, occasionally blinking his eyes under the glare of the lights in the courtroom, looking steadily, seriously at his questioner.

ZACHARY: Let me ask you this: You knew there were 150 of you outsiders in this community demonstrating, didn't you?
MOSES: No, that is not true.
ZACHARY: That is not true?
MOSES: That is not true.
ZACHARY (angrily): At the time you were arrested, there wasn't 150 of you walking around in front of the Court House?
MOSES: You said "outsiders." There were not 150 outsiders walking around the Court House.

Or again:

ZACHARY: Where would this democracy be if everybody obeyed officers like you did?
MOSES: I think that it would be in very good shape. I . . .
ZACAHARY: Good; now, you've answered it, now let's move on. . . .

Zachary held up a list of the ministers who had come down for Freedom Day and waved it in Moses' face. He went down the list, asking about the ministers and the organizations on it.

ZACHARY: The (he paused, and stumbled over the word "Rabbinical") Rabbin-in-ical Assembly of America. Are you a member of that organization?

MOSES (gently correcting him): *Rabbinical* Assembly. No, I am not.

At one point, the prosecutor, trying to hold in his rage against the quiet calm of the witness, broke out: "Moses! Let me tell you something . . ."
Again:

ZACHARY: Why didn't you mind this officer when he gave you an order?
MOSES: I had a right to be there. . . .
ZACHARY: What law school did you graduate from?
LUNNEY: Objection.
THE COURT: I will have to overrule you.
ZACHARY (again to Moses): I want to know what you base this right on. Are you a legal student?
MOSES: I base the right on the fact of the First Amendment. . . . That is the whole point of democracy, that the citizens know what their rights are, and they don't have to go to law school to know what their rights are.

About 9:15 P.M., with the attorneys' closing remarks over, the judge denied Lunney's motion to dismiss, and declared that the court found Robert Moses guilty, sentencing him to a fine of $200 and sixty days in jail. We all filed out of the courtroom into the night, and Patrolman John Quincy Adams took Bob Moses back to his cell.

A few days later Bob Moses was out on bail, once again directing the Mississippi voter registration drive for the SNCC. Plans were being made for a big summer, with a thousand students coming into Mississippi for July and August of 1964. And, for the first time since Reconstruction, a group of Mississippi Negroes announced their candidacy for the U.S. Congress: Mrs. Fannie Hamer of Ruleville; Mrs. Victoria Gray of Hattiesburg; the Rev. John Cameron of Hattiesburg. Thus, a new native leadership was taking form, already beginning to unsettle the official hierarchy of the state by its challenge.

SNCC came out of McComb after the summer of 1961 battered and uncertain. It moved on to Greenwood and other towns in the Delta, grew in numbers, gathered thousands of supporters throughout the state. In places like Hattiesburg it took blows, but it left the town transformed, its black people —and possibly some white people—awakened. Most of all, for the Negroes of Mississippi, in the summer of 1964, as college students from all over America began to join them to help bring democracy to Mississippi and the nation, the long silence was over.

7. Southwest Georgia: The Outsider as Insider

It has been the particular contribution of SNCC to American democracy to move into long-dormant areas of the Deep South, to arouse Negroes there from quiescence to revolt, and, in so doing, to disturb the conscience of the entire nation. This is what happened in the fall of 1961 when Charles Sherrod, twenty-two, and Cordell Reagan, eighteen, veterans of the sit-ins, the Freedom Rides, and McComb, arrived by bus in Albany, Georgia, to set up a voter registration office.

Two months later, Albany was the scene of unprecedented mass arrests in the first large-scale Negro uprising since the Montgomery bus boycott. It became the prototype for demonstrations that later rocked Birmingham and dozens of other cities throughout the nation. It represented a permanent turn from the lunch counter and the bus terminal to the streets, from hit-and-run attacks by students and professional civil rights workers to populist rebellion by lower-class Negroes. And the Albany crisis revealed clearly for the first time the reluctance of the national government to protect constitutional rights in the Deep South.

Sherrod and Reagan are both of medium height, slim, brown-skinned. When they stand up in front of a church at a mass meeting they can stir a crowd to song like no one else. Sherrod is more outgoing; he smiles boyishly when he speaks, his voice is softly resonant, and he lowers it to a vibrant whisper when he wants to emphasize a point about which he feels very deeply. Reagan is quiet, intense, a thin cord of energy and emotion, with the cheekbones and countenance of a Mongol nomad. When he and Sherrod came to Albany in October, 1961, they came as outsiders, preceded by their reputations as Freedom Riders and agitators with whom it was dangerous to associate. They stayed, locked themselves into the community, and came to be loved with the kind of adoration bestowed on folk heroes.

Albany was picked for a voter registration campaign for the same reasons Mississippi was chosen: educated Negro youngsters from the border states of the South wanted to return, it seemed, to the source of their people's agony, to that area which was the heart of the slave plantation system, in order to cleanse it once and for all time. Albany was the old trading center for the slave plantation country of southwest Georgia, and though it was now becoming modern and commercial, and selling more pecans than cotton, it was surrounded by the past. In the counties around Albany blacks outnumbered whites; they worked the land and lived in shacks and didn't dare to raise a single cry against the rutted order of their lives. Around Albany were "Terrible" Terrell County, "Bad" Baker County; Sherrod added a few appellations of his own—Unmitigated Mitchell, Lamentable Lee.

In Albany itself, Negroes constituted 40 percent of the city's population of 56,000 and lived in a tightly segregated society from the cradle to the grave. From the world outside came, in the 1950's, the first tremors of change: the Supreme Court decision, the Montgomery bus boycott, Little Rock, the sit-ins and Freedom Rides, the emergence of the new black nations of Africa. But in Albany few Negroes voted, and those who spoke up did so quietly, among themselves. By early 1961, a small group of Albany Negroes decided to meet and to present complaints in a petition to the city commissioners. But the mass of the Negro population held back, remained silent. It was this screen of silence which SNCC organizers Sherrod and Reagan were determined to penetrate. Sherrod says:

> When we first came to Albany, the people were afraid, really afraid. Sometimes we'd walk down the streets and the little kids would call us Freedom Riders and the people walking in the same direction would go across the street from us, because they were afraid; they didn't want to be connected with us in any way. . . . Many of the ministers were afraid to let us use their churches, afraid that their churches would be bombed, that their homes would be stoned. There was fear in the air, and if we were to progress we knew that we must cut through that fear. We thought and we thought . . . and the students were the answer.

There was one institution of higher education in town, Albany State College for Negroes. Reagan and Sherrod began visiting the campus, talking to the students, who had begun to stir early in 1961 when marauding whites in automobiles raced through the campus, throwing eggs, firing guns, and once trying to run down a Negro girl. Protesting against this, the students had found themselves up against the conservatism of a Negro college president, dependent for his job on the Board of Regents of the State of Georgia. The Dean of Students at Albany State was a militant young woman named Irene Asbury Wright, married to an Air Force lieutenant stationed in Albany. She sided with the students, and then resigned in protest against the administration's repressive policies. Sherrod described in his own way the situation he and Reagan found when they began to organize the students:

> There is a school in Albany, Albany State College, where the minds of young men and women are not free to reason for themselves what is most important in life. They are "protected from" all seduction to think on what it means to be a black man in Albany or anywhere else in the South. . . . The campus is separated from the community by a river, a dump

> yard and a cemetery. And if any system of intelligence gets through all of that it is promptly stomped underfoot by men in administrative positions who refuse to think further than a new car, a bulging refrigerator, and an insatiable lust for more than enough of everything we call leisure. . . .

Sherrod and Reagan were joined by Charles Jones, who came out of the Charlotte, North Carolina student movement, who had been arrested five times in four states, and who now became the third SNCC field secretary assigned to Albany. They set up a SNCC office in a little rundown building not far from the Shiloh Baptist Church in the Negro section. The plaster was falling from the walls; the mimeograph machine kept breaking down; the big room was cold and damp; but they turned out leaflets and newsletters, held meetings with students, registered voters, and conducted sessions in the techniques of nonviolent direct action. The ministers were beginning to be more responsive now, and many of their sessions were held in churches, in Shiloh Baptist, or in the Rev. Ben Gay's Bethel AME Church. At the workshops they enacted scenes in which students sitting-in would be attacked by "whites," testing their capacity to remain nonviolent. The simulated attacks were so realistic that fierce emotions boiled up at the sessions; this too was a part of the training process.

As Sherrod says, ". . . we drew young people from the colleges, trade schools, and high schools, and from the street. They were searching for a meaning in life. . . . Every night we grew larger and larger. But we had not been training in nonviolence in a vacuum. November 1 was to be the date." That was the first day that the ruling of the Interstate Commerce Commission barring segregation in terminals was to go into effect. Sherrod and Reagan had themselves been jailed in Mississippi in the Freedom Ride campaign which led to that ruling. Now they prepared to test it in the segregated terminals of Albany.

On November 1 Sherrod and Reagan, who had been visiting the SNCC office in Atlanta that day, rode back on the Trailways bus to Albany with Charles Jones and Jim Forman. With them too was a friend, sitting apart from them on the bus, but prepared to act as witness to the test when they got to Albany. The friend was Salynn McCollum, a white girl from Tennessee who had attended Peabody College in Nashville, gone on the Freedom Rides, been arrested in Birmingham, and was now working in the SNCC office in Atlanta.

From the moment the bus left Atlanta, police in Atlanta and in Albany were in communication with one another. State troopers halted the bus en route and looked over the occupants. But no arrests were made. When the bus arrived in Albany, ten Albany policemen were waiting for it at the station, and the SNCC people feared they wouldn't even get into the white waiting room. It was therefore decided to postpone the test, to evade the policemen, and later get back to the terminal to carry out the original plans. Salynn darted out of the terminal and raced through the streets and back alleys in the Negro section to the home of Irene Wright.

In the meantime, Sherrod, Reagan, and Jones were talking to students in Albany about testing the ICC ruling. Later that afternoon, Salynn, in a makeshift disguise, slipped out of the Wrights' home and made her way back to the terminal. Nine students were there, sitting in the white waiting room. She watched them being ordered out by the police, and within forty-eight hours, the violation was reported to the Justice Department. It was the first in a long series of tests for the United States government in the Albany area, in which it proved ineffectual in enforcing federal law.

Albany was beginning to stir now. The Youth Council of the NAACP, the Baptist Ministers' Alliance, other Negro groups, were meeting, talking, arguing, but agreeing on one basic fact: it was time to act. On November 22, these organizations, along with SNCC, formed a coalition group called the

Albany Movement, with local osteopath Dr. William G. Anderson as president, and real estate man Slater King as vice-president. They agreed to begin an assault on all forms of segregation and discrimination in Albany. Irene Wright said: "The kids were going to do it anyway . . . they were holding their own mass meetings and making plans . . . we didn't want them to have to do it alone." With the coalescing of all forces into a united and militant movement, it meant that massive reinforcements would be ready to act when the next reconnaissance action took place.

That action came Thanksgiving weekend, November 22, 1961, three weeks after the ICC ruling. Three members of the NAACP Youth Council entered the Trailways bus terminal, went into the restaurant there, and were met by Albany Police Chief Laurie Pritchett. Pritchett called them outside and told them that if they re-entered the lunch room he would arrest them. They went back into the restaurant, and were promptly arrested. A half hour later, they were released on bond.

Later that afternoon, hundreds of Albany State students arrived at the terminal to go home for the Thanksgiving holidays. The new Dean of Students at Albany State College was stationed there, to point out the colored waiting room. Two students who had been working with SNCC, Bertha Gober of Atlanta, and Blanton Hall of Athens, went into the white waiting room, and were arrested. Rather than be freed on bond, they stayed in jail for several days. By the time they came out, the Negro community was moving into action behind the Albany Movement. A mass meeting was called, the first such meeting in the history of Albany. Sherrod describes the excitement of that evening:

> The church was packed before eight o'clock. People were everywhere, in the aisles, sitting and standing in the choir stands, hanging over the railing of the balcony, sitting in trees outside the windows. . . . When the last speaker among the students, Bertha Gober, had finished, there was nothing

> left to say. Tears filled the eyes of hard, grown men who had seen with their own eyes merciless atrocities committed. . . . Bertha told of spending Thanksgiving in jail. . . . And when we rose to sing "We Shall Overcome," nobody could imagine what kept the church on four corners. . . . I threw my head back and closed my eyes as I sang with my whole body. I remembered walking dusty roads for weeks without food. I remembered staying up all night for two and three nights in succession writing and cutting stencils and mimeographing and wondering—How long?

Bertha Gober and Blanton Hall were hardly out of jail when they received letters from the dean of Albany State College expelling them. Students marched to the president's house to protest the expulsion, and many were fired from jobs they held on campus. But things were moving now.

On December 10, 1961, came the fourth contest between the resoluteness of the Albany police in violating the ICC ruling, and the determination of the national government in enforcing it. It was a first-round knockout. The national government never even came out of its corner. That day, four SNCC people rode from Atlanta to Albany on a Central of Georgia passenger train: Jim Forman, Executive Secretary; Norma Collins, Office Manager; Bob Zellner, of SNCC's white student project; and Lenore Taitt, a volunteer worker. With them were: Bernard Lee, of SCLC; Per Laursen, a writer from Denmark; Tom Hayden, of Students for a Democratic Society, and his wife, Sandra; and Joan Browning, a white girl from Georgia. They sat integrated, ignored a conductor's request that they move, and went on to Albany. Over a hundred Negroes gathered at the railway terminal to meet them. It was a quiet Sunday afternoon, with little traffic, and few whites nearby. The police, led by Chief Pritchett, were waiting for them. The group came off the train, went into the white waiting room briefly, came out again, began to get into cars to take them downtown, and at that point were placed under arrest by Pritchett, who called out, "I told you to get off the street. You are all under arrest." In addition to the group from Atlanta, Bertha Gober was pulled out of the crowd and arrested, as were Charles Jones and an Albany State student named Willie Mae Jones. All were hustled off in a paddy wagon, charged with obstructing traffic, disorderly conduct, and failure to obey an officer, with the bond set at $200.

A witness of the scene, editor of a Negro newspaper in Albany named A. C. Searles, commented on the arrest: "There was no traffic, no disturbance, no one moving. The students had made the trip to Albany desegregated without incident. Things had gone so smoothly I think it infuriated the chief. There was a good feeling in the group. They wanted to stop this." (Months later, the Mayor of Albany told me he thought that arrest was "a mistake.")

With the eleven young people in jail, the Albany Movement began a series of actions which soon brought the city to national attention. On the day that the eleven were to be tried in city court, over four hundred high school and college students marched downtown to protest, singing as they went by the courthouse. The police, in cars with loudspeakers, ordered them to disperse, but they continued on their way. Police then herded them into an alley alongside City Hall, where they stood for two hours in a driving rain before being booked, one by one. On Wednesday morning, Slater King was arrested as he and seventy others knelt in prayer in front of the City Hall. That same evening, three hundred people marching to City Hall were arrested for parading without a permit. Chief Pritchett told reporters: "We can't tolerate the NAACP or the SNCC or any other nigger organization to take over this town with mass demonstrations."

Two nights later, Martin Luther King, Jr., invited by the Executive Committee of the Albany Movement, arrived from Atlanta with the Rev. Ralph Abernathy and told 1000 people packed into the Shiloh Baptist Church: "Don't stop now. Keep moving. Don't get weary. We will wear them down with our capacity to suffer." The following evening, King and Dr. Anderson (President of the Albany Movement) led 257 hymn-singing men, women, and youngsters toward the county courthouse, and were arrested by Chief Pritchett for parading without a permit. The total arrested now stood at 737, and with the Albany jails packed tight, prisoners were farmed out to jails in nearby counties. Never in the nation's history had so many people been imprisoned in one city for exercising the right of protest.

With the Albany crisis now in the front pages of newspapers all over the country, negotiations between the Albany Movement and city officials got under way. Verbal agreement was reached on desegregation in train and bus facilities, the release of all the demonstrators on the signing of property bonds, with the exception of the original Freedom Riders who had come down on the train from Atlanta; the calling off of further demonstrations; and a promise by the city to hear Negro complaints at the first business meeting of the new city commission. A young fellow in the SNCC office, just out of jail, asked what he thought of the agreement, smiled and said: "You curse first, then I will." It seemed a pitifully small payment for weeks of protest, for centuries of waiting.

I arrived in Albany as people were coming out of jail. They spoke of their experiences. Charles Sherrod had been taken with a group of demonstrators to "Terrible" Terrell County, escorted there by Sheriff Zeke Matthews, who announced: "There'll be no damn singin' and no damn prayin' in *my* jail." The sheriff added, "I don't want to hear nothin' about freedom!" Sherrod spoke up: "We may be in jail, but we're still human beings and still Christians." Sheriff Matthews hit him in the face, then took him into his office, where another officer hit him, cracking his lip. His mouth was full of blood. Then he was put in a cell by himself.

People sat along the wall in Shiloh Baptist Church and told about prison conditions. In the Camilla jail, eighty-eight women were in one room with twenty steel bunks and no mattresses. One woman who had been in jail for a week said: "I was in the Leesburg stockade with fifty-one other women. There was no place to sleep. The mattresses were wet and dirty. . . . They would put the food in a box, place it on the floor, and kick it into the cell." It wasn't so much the prison conditions that hurt these people deep inside, but the reason for it all. A young married woman who was a student at Albany State said: "I didn't expect to go to jail for kneeling and praying at City Hall."

Shiloh Baptist Church was packed that first night after the prisoners came out of jail. People stood up and sang Freedom Songs. In front, leading the singing, holding hands, was a line of SNCC workers, among them several who would later become known throughout the nation as the Freedom Singers: Bernice Johnson and Rutha Harris of Albany, Bertha Gober, and Cordell Reagan. In the middle of the meeting, Joan Browning, the young white girl who had been arrested with the original riders from Atlanta, walked down the aisle to the microphone. She had just been released from jail, and was out of breath. She spoke briefly in her soft Southern accent: "First time I've ever been in jail. It's a funny mixed-up feeling to hate being in a dirty place—but to be glad you're there for a good reason. . . ."

The agreement that called off the demonstrations had left the Negro community with no visible victory, except the vague promise to be heard by the City Commission. But Albany would never be the same again; a hundred years of Negro silence and white complacency had now been shattered for all time. Anyone who sat in the Shiloh Baptist Church at that prayer meeting following the settlement could tell that expectations had been raised which would not be stilled without a change in the social patterns of the city. A Negro porter on the steps of an Albany church told me: "We're just beginning. Just beginning." And Irene Wright said, as we talked: "Anybody who thinks this town is going to settle back and be the same as it was, has got to be deaf, blind, and dumb."

Sherrod reported back to Atlanta:

> ... the structure is being shaken to the very foundations.... It is no longer a matter-of-fact procedure for a Negro to respond in "yes, sirs" and "no, sirs." The people are thinking. They are becoming. In a deep southwest Georgia area, where it is generally conceded that the Negro has no rights that a white man is bound to respect, *at last*, they sing, "We Shall Overcome." There is hope!

The December, 1961, truce soon collapsed. In January, eighteen-year-old Ola Mae Quarterman sat in a front seat on an Albany city bus. The driver came up to her, poked his finger in her face, and asked if she didn't know where she was supposed to sit. She replied, "I paid my damn twenty cents and I can sit where I want." The driver called a policeman. She was jailed, and then convicted in city court of using "obscene" language. The Albany Movement responded with an intensified boycott of city buses, and the bus company was forced out of business.

Albany now began a new round of encounters between Negro demands and official intransigence. A few days after the bus incident, Sherrod and Charles Jones were arrested for sitting in the Trailways lunchroom. Shortly after that the City Commission turned down the Albany Movement's petition for a redress of grievances. And in March the trial of the original "Freedom Riders" arrested on December 10 began.

As Charles Sherrod entered the courtroom to attend that trial, he walked to the "white section" in the front, and was immediately knocked to the floor by Chief Deputy Sheriff Lamar Stewart, who then pulled him back to the rear of the courtroom. When Bob Zellner, Tom and Sandra Hayden, and Per Laursen sat down next to Sherrod in the "Negro section," deputies pounced on them and dragged them out of the courtroom. Judge Carl E. Crow, watching all of this, told newsmen, "The officers were enforcing a rule of the court."

In April there was more trouble. Dr. Anderson, Slater King, Emanuel "Bo" Jackson, and Elijah Harris, four leaders of the Albany Movement, were found guilty of "disorderly conduct" for picketing downtown as part of a general boycott of stores which did not hire Negro employees. Also, Charles Jones, Cordell Reagan, and two others were sentenced to sixty days on work gangs for refusing to leave a drugstore lunch counter where they sat requesting service. And twenty-six more people were arrested in lunch counter sit-ins.

About this time, Walter Harris, a Negro cafe operator in Albany, was shot to death by a policeman who claimed Harris attacked him with a knife while resisting arrest. Southwest Georgia had a long history of policemen killing Negroes for "resisting arrest." Twenty-nine adults and teenagers appeared in front of City Hall to protest the Harris shooting, and were arrested.

In July, 1962, national attention came to Albany again when Martin Luther King, Jr., and Ralph Abernathy, called back to stand trial for leading the parade in December, were found guilty in Recorders Court and sentenced to forty-five days. Defense Attorney Donald Hollowell asked Judge Durden for legal citations on which his decision was based. The Judge said he didn't have any, but that it was based on "general research of the law."

With King's arrest, Washington officialdom got busy as it had never done before in the Albany crisis, and somehow, through the payment of the fine by an unidentified man, King and Abernathy were released. They had wanted to stay in jail to continue dramatizing the Albany situation, but now they reluctantly left. Abernathy told a mass meeting that night: "I've been thrown out of lots of places in my day, but never before have I been thrown out of jail."

Through July and August, 1962, while a battery of civil rights lawyers brought lawsuits against the city to integrate its facilities and to stop interference with peaceful protests, the Albany Movement kept up pressure against the barriers of the old order. Youngsters in SNCC led the way, seeking access to the city library, to lunch counters, to the Trailways terminal restaurant, to the park and the swimming pool, to the bowling alley. Arrests mounted into the hundreds.

And violence increased. Mrs. Slater King, five months pregnant, and carrying a three-year old child, was knocked unconscious by a deputy sheriff as she visited some young people in the Camilla jail. (Several months later, the baby was born dead.) White SNCC worker Bill Hansen, put into Dougherty County jail for participating in a demonstration, had his jaw broken by a prison trusty. Albany's only Negro attorney, C. B. King (brother of Slater King), was given a bloody beating with a cane by Sheriff Cull Campbell of Dougherty County (who later told me: "Yeh, I knocked hell out of the son-of-a bitch, and I'll do it again. I wanted to let him know. . . . I'm a white man and he's a damn nigger"). Sixteen-year-old Shirley Gaines, arrested for seeking access to a bowling alley, was dragged down stone steps by policemen, kicked again and again in her back and side.

The pattern of Negro protest and police repression, of frustration and awakening, continued in Albany through 1963 and 1964. There were about 170 people arrested at various times in 1963 for picketing, distributing leaflets, sitting-in, attempting to use various segregated facilities. The city library was finally desegregated by court order, though the seats were removed to keep Negroes and whites from sitting together. Token integration began in the school system in early 1964, again by judicial demand. And the city removed all segregation statutes from its books and sold the swimming pool to a private corporation to avoid the constitutional prohibition against discrimination in public facilities.

Through more than three years of conflict and pain in Albany, the national government failed again and again to defend the constitutional liberties of Negroes in that city. By restricting its activity to a few ineffective court appearances the Department of Justice left the right of Albany citizens in the hands of Police Chief Pritchett, who crushed them time after time, while managing to maintain his image in the national press as a prudent keeper of order in Albany.

Through it all, Charles Sherrod was confident that important social change was taking place in Albany. "The people are beginning to talk now . . . the knowledge of meetings is growing. People are registering to vote." Five hundred Negroes were registered in Albany from the fall of 1961 to the summer of 1962, at a rate unprecedented in the history of the city. When Thomas Chatmon, a leader in the Albany Movement, ran for city commissioner, he polled 3000 votes, coming second in a field of three. In 1963, Slater King ran for mayor, and in 1964, C. B. King prepared to run for Congress.

Most important of all, the lives of thousands of Negroes in Albany had been touched and changed in some way. Especially those of the young people. The forty students who were expelled from Albany State College for being in the demonstrations would never be the same again; Bernice Johnson, and Bertha Gober, and Annette Jones came out of that experience with a fire burning inside that would never be put out. And there were many more.

The movement spread, by that invisible process in which ideas flow from individual to individual, to a sixteen-year old boy in Lee County, a few miles from Albany. He was Charles Wingfield.

> I wondered what it was like to live. . . . Countless nights I cried myself to sleep. Sometimes I could look at my mother and I could feel the pains her body was undergoing because of the hard work done each day to make ends meet. . . . Sometimes mother would see the tears falling from my eyes. . . .

> When she asked me what was wrong I told her that something stuck in my eyes or a bug was in them. I must have asked God why a thousand times but I never got an answer. Was nine of us kids in the family and we all had to work. I stayed out of school a lot of days because I couldn't let my mother go to the cotton field and try to support all of us. I picked cotton and pecans for two cents a pound. I went to the fields six in the morning and worked until seven in the afternoon. When it came time to weigh up, my heart, body and bones would be aching, burning and trembling. I stood there and looked the white men right in their eyes while they cheated me, other members of my family, and the rest of the Negroes that were working. There were times when I wanted to speak, but my fearful mother would always tell me to keep silent. The sun was awful hot and the days were long. . . . The cost of survival was high. Why I paid it I'll never know.

Charles Wingfield one day put a petition on the wall in his school, the Lee County Training School, where he was an honor student. The petition asked for better equipment for the school. He was immediately expelled. Parents at the school met and voted to boycott the school, and over 1000 students (out of an enrollment of 1300) stayed out of school to protest the expulsion. But Charles Wingfield was never re-admitted. He became a SNCC worker.

Through 1962 and 1963, the SNCC staff grew in Southwest Georgia. White and Negro students from Northern colleges, leaving school, came to work as field secretaries in the Albany area, drawn initially by compassion and kept there by courage. With Albany as a base, they moved in and out of Terrell, Lee, and other counties. The appearance of white students brought some inner turmoil to Negroes in the cotton country. One man in Lee County wrote:

> I referred to my white brothers as crackers, and I hated all of them. I wanted to build a machine that I could just wind

> my watch and it would destroy the whole human population. . . . I attended a voter registration meeting in Lee County and my whole opinion of white people was changed. I met Penny Patch and Ralph Allen and we became very close friends. They were just like a brother and a sister to me. . . . I also met Kathleen Conwell and Peggy Dammond. We spent a great deal of time working throughout Lee County. They would always tell me that I should love those who hurt me. Don't allow yourself to become bitter, they said, or life will crumble. This puzzled me. I asked myself these questions over and over again. Are these kids crazy, or is it because they are from the North and just don't know any better. How do they expect me to love those who have cheated me, robbed, killed, and beaten my people for all these hundreds of years. . . . But I found out that it is easier to love than to hate. . . .

SNCC workers going into Terrell County knew they were in dangerous territory. It had a long history of brutality against Negroes. As recently as 1958, a Negro named James Brazier had been beaten to death by local police. A year later, Brazier's widow was told by Terrell County Sheriff Zeke Matthews: "I ought to slap your damn brains out." Matthews told a reporter: "You know, Cap, there's nothing like fear to keep niggers in line." A former mayor of Dawson, James Griggs Raines, told investigators for the Civil Rights Commission: "Matthews is unfit. . . . I've seen him beat a pregnant Negro woman." (It was Matthews who struck Sherrod and told him, "There'll be no damn singin' and no damn prayin' in my jail.")

Negroes are almost two-thirds the population of Terrell County, but in 1960, only fifty-one Negroes were registered to vote; 2800 whites were registered. The first Justice Department lawsuit against voter discrimination was filed in Terrell County and resulted in an injunction forbidding discrimination in 1960, but this was ineffective; economic reprisal and the threat of violence still kept Negroes from the polls.

Even before the Albany crisis began, in November, 1961, Sherrod and Reagan began working to register voters in Terrell County. They stayed with Mrs. Carolyn Daniels, a young Negro woman who operates a beauty shop in Dawson, and whose home was to become a center for SNCC activity in Terrell. In the spring of 1962, Sherrod was jailed briefly in Terrell. That summer, a white student from Trinity College, Connecticut, Ralph Allen, began working there. He was beaten again and again; a truck tried to run him down, and a man drew a knife and threatened to kill him.

On July 25, 1962, a voter registration meeting at Mount Olive Church in Terrell County was invaded by Sheriff Matthews and a dozen other white men. About forty Negroes from the area were at the meeting; also Sherrod and Charles Jones, Ralph Allen, and Penny Patch, a nineteen-year-old Swarthmore college student. Sherrod was reading from the scriptures as the white men burst in. Sheriff Matthews told reporters: "We are a little fed up with this voter registration business . . . we want our colored people to live like they've been living for the last hundred years—peaceful and happy." Six weeks after this incident, Mount Olive Church was burned to the ground.

Arrests and beatings of SNCC workers continued in Terrell County. On December 8, 1963, shots were fired into the home of Mrs. Daniels, and a bomb was thrown into her front bedroom, wrecking the front half of the house.

SNCC people registered a handful of voters here, another handful there. But their most important accomplishment was to break through the frozen crust of the social order in Terrell County, and show to increasing numbers of Negroes there a glimpse of the future. Sherrod, speaking in Terrell, told men just out of the fields, women just come from white women's kitchens, and children without shoes:

> All our lives we've had to bow and scrape, laugh when there was nothing funny and scratch our heads and say "yes, sir."

We want to change that; we want to be men; that's what the power of the vote can do.... It's people like you, with faith in God, who are going to change this country. And we'll do it together.

Canvassing in Dawson one day, Ralph Allen was picked up by the police chief and taken to Sheriff Matthews office, where he was interrogated by a deputy. He reported the dialogue:

DEPUTY: Who sent you here? Did President Kennedy send you here? Did Bobby Kennedy send you here?
ALLEN: Indirectly. I am working on voter registration for the Student Nonviolent Coordinating Committee.
DEPUTY: What nationality are you?
ALLEN: I do not know exactly. I have never considered nationality relevant enough to find out my origins. I am a human being, and that is all that is important to me.
DEPUTY: You nigger-lovin' son of a bitch. Why do you have to come down here to register voters? . . . Lock him up.

Carver (Chico) Neblett, nineteen, a tall Negro student from Illinois, came into Terrell County, and reported back to Atlanta:

My first impression in the Deep South was fear. I almost forgot my fears . . . until a white post office worker in Dawson threatened to send Jack Chatfield home in a box. How does one get it across to the people that we are not alone, when all around them white men are killing, and getting away? . . . I tell them they can't get away with it. Then they start saying yussa and nossa, You sho is rite, boss, etc. No matter what you say, they still say yussa. Where do we go from here? . . .

But Chico Neblett had better moments:

I talked with a blind man who is extremely interested in the civil rights movement. He has been keeping up with the

> movement from the beginning. Even though this man is blind he wants to learn all the questions on the literacy test. Imagine, while many are afraid that white men will burn our houses, shoot into them, or put us off their property, a blind man, seventy years old, wants to come to our meetings.

The SNCC worker whom the Dawson post office employee threatened to send home in a box was Jack Chatfield, a roommate of Ralph Allen's at Trinity College, who lived in Vermont and had gone to military school in Virginia. In September, 1962, that threat to Chatfield was almost made good. Night riders fired into the home of Mrs. Daniels in Dawson and hit Chatfield in the arm. If he had turned slightly at the time, he would have been dead. Sometime in Jack Chatfield's second year at college, after insisting, "There is nothing but the self," he had come to believe that "There is nothing but other people."

One day Chatfield was arrested on the street in Albany by Chief Pritchett. His three days in the Albany city jail with other white prisoners tell something important about the South, something easily missed in the heat of a conflict which takes the form of race hatred, but which, as he suggests, ultimately transcends the issue of black and white:

> I explained to each one what I was doing in jail. . . . None of them seemed to comprehend. I told a number of them (including some in the neighboring cell) that I was the fellow who was shot in Dawson. But cigarettes were the issue, not integration. . . . One said, "You'll be in serious trouble if you stay down here." I said that we were already in serious trouble. . . . He said, "People hate the niggers down here." I agreed. One drunk, who hoped I would be bailed out so I could bring him cigarettes, confided that he had stayed with "colored people" for three days once in Washington, D.C. He used the word "nigger" and "colored boy" intermittently. One thing struck me in my encounter with these men . . . that people are generally totally uninvolved. One man—who in

the next cell had finally seen what I was talking about and had said, "Oh, that's that nigger-mixing business"—called me Jack when I was put in a cell with him, and never brought "nigger-mixing" up. . . . On the fourth day, from the next cell: "You still think it's worth it, Jack." Answer, "Yes." Sometime later, "I can't understand you, Jack. What you gonna get out of this?"

I learned something else: that whites are yanked in for flukey offenses; that whites are treated like dogs in jail; that whites hate whites. This appears of course to be a simple fact; but being bound up in a world like the world of the racial struggle in Southwest Georgia creates illusions—such as: things are extremely simple here, archetypes crawl about like flies, la la. You know of course the whole time that you are missing something, that there is something else in the human animal that you have missed; that things are not purely white versus Negro. . . . It is a story about human beings and there are nuances that you skip like puddles and little smatterings of humanness that you swat away like the cigarette smoke curling into your face because they mess things up. . . .

The reports coming out of Southwest Georgia to the Atlanta office were often long and eloquent, and Jim Forman smilingly said they showed a "Proustian influence." Julian Bond wrote Bob Moses in Mississippi: "Sherrod is writing like a drunk Jack Kerouac and O'Neal and Chatfield write like drunk Sherrods."

One spring day in 1963, SNCC worker James Crawford, a young Negro fellow from Albany, took a Negro woman to the county courthouse in Leesburg, Lee County, to register. Deputy Registrar Sol Yeoman approached them. Crawford reported the following conversation later to Jack Chatfield, who sat outside in a car:

YEOMAN: What do you want?
CRAWFORD: I brought this lady down to register.
YEOMAN (after giving the woman a card to fill out and send-

ing her outside in the hall): Why did you bring this lady down here?

CRAWFORD: Because she wants to be a first class citizen like y'all.

YEOMAN: Where are you from?

CRAWFORD: Albany.

YEOMAN: Who do you work for?

CRAWFORD: SNICK.

YEOMAN: What is that?

CRAWFORD: Student Nonviolent Coordinating Committee.

YEOMAN: Who are you to bring people down to register?

CRAWFORD: It's my job . . . (Yeoman then asked him if he had heard about the boy in Mississippi who was shot in the head. James told him he had not.)

YEOMAN: Suppose you get two bullets in your head right now?

CRAWFORD: I got to die anyhow.

YEOMAN: If I don't do it, I can get somebody else to do it.

No answer.

YEOMAN: Are you scared?

CRAWFORD: No.

YEOMAN: Suppose somebody came in that door and shoot you in the back of the head right now. What would you do?

CRAWFORD: I couldn't do nothing. If they shoot me in the back of the head there are people coming from all over the world.

YEOMAN: What people?

CRAWFORD: The people I work for.

The Negro woman filling out the card was trembling. She put "Sumter County" where she should have written "Smithville" and James told her to write "Smithville." Yeoman got angry, and said to the woman, "Now you're through." As they left the courthouse, James turned and said to Yeoman: "I'll be back Saturday. That's what I'm here for—to die or to live."

Jack Chatfield and James Crawford took the woman home; then their car broke down, but finally they got a truck to pull them into Smithville to the home of Robert Burney, who had a phone. As they called Sherrod in Albany to tell him what happened, a black Ford with four white men in it carrying guns pulled up to the house. Then an Oldsmobile pulled up. A Negro man in the house loaded his shotgun. The man who owned the house asked the SNCC people to leave, tears in his eyes. It was getting dark. Chatfield and the other SNCC workers started across a field, then saw Sherrod's car pulling up to the house. They raced back, got in, and Sherrod drove off. The Oldsmobile came behind, rammed them once. A Negro girl sitting near Chatfield began to cry hysterically. The Oldsmobile followed them a few minutes longer, then left. Writing his report on this incident, Chatfield concluded tersely: "A nice evening. Six people had applied for registration."

The small band of Northerners and Southerners, black and white, who formed the SNCC task force in Southwest Georgia from 1961 to 1964, were *educating* in the ultimate meaning of that word, bringing out from deep inside the Negro people of that area the muffled cries, the dreams so long kept to themselves. And in doing this they lifted, just a little, the membrane of fear that enclosed the Georgia countryside. Peggy Dammond, a Boston University student, tells of the sense of release at a gathering in Lee County: "Tears that had long since been clotted in dry throats gushed forth when another neighbor raised his hand at meeting to tell he'd been down to the courthouse to register, and next week all his family was going to be there."

Penny Patch, the girl from Swarthmore, spent one frightening autumn night in 1962 in the Albany Freedom House with Faith Holsaert, a girl from Barnard College. They were alone, and at midnight they heard a bottle broken outside, footsteps around the back yard, breathing outside the window near the bed. They phoned, and a friend came and took them somewhere else to sleep. Things always looked different the next day, and Penny wrote once to Atlanta: "It is now five o'clock in the morning, and the cocks are crowing. You know,

Southwest Georgia is very, very beautiful. It just needs a little bit of fixing."

She compresses the problem: "I come up on a porch and an ancient lady, full of dignity in *her* world, says 'Yes, mam,' and offers me her chair. An enraged white face shouts curses out of the car window. Jack Chatfield walks up to a house and the lady on the porch shakes visibly. The voter registration team is greeted with fear at the door. 'I didn't know that colored people could vote!' . . . And people ask why we are down here. . . ."

And Peggy Dammond compresses the pride: "In the South, courage is a quiet thing. It may be born in a candle-lit farmhouse far back on a cornfield late one night over a pot of greens. Or one morning a man might wake up and decide to go down to the courthouse to register and because he doesn't have a car he might walk the nine miles into town."

The SNCC workers came and went, left part of themselves in Georgia, and took part of the red earth back with them. Sherrod remained. "I remembered thinking about home, a thousand miles away, and fun—games, dancing, movies. . . ." He stayed through it all for two and one-half years, until people in Albany, old and young and little children, and people in Lee County and Terrell County followed him like a Pied Piper of Freedom. Sherrod's favorite refuge was the home of Mama Dollie.

> Mama Dollie was speaking to me as I sat close to the heater in a little old house way back in the woods of Lee County, only eight country miles away from Shady Grove Baptist Church, burned down during the summer.
>
> This was "Mama." Standing fine—fine, strong, resembling a proud Indian woman worn with the years but unbowed. . . . In spite of bomb scares, shootings, threats, we walked along lonely roads. . . . Mama was always there.
>
> When we came to Southwest Georgia in October, 1961, we

offered before the people our minds and bodies. That was all we had. Three months later, nearly a thousand bodies and minds were being offered before us. . . .

There is an indoctrination. . . . Negroes don't stick together. . . . White is right. . . . Jail is a hammer. . . . But we broke the hammer of jail with another maxim: "A jail is just another house," and with this lever we broke the other two. Eyes have been opened; men have become alive. Albany is the center; watch it!

Memories will flash back. The days in December when we met in an old tent in Sasser where two churches burned, where we met in the rain, where we huddled together to keep warm. We will remember our headquarters in Albany, a three-room house where thirteen of us gathered for staff meetings and strategy sessions. We will never forget the all-night sessions in which we made bare our artificial defenses and shared our fears and joys and hopes and suffocations. . . .

We stand together, black and white. Southwest Georgia is unknown now, but one day somebody will do as Mama Dollie said one day in Lee County: "Now, boy, you go to writing and write up a new day."

8. Alabama: Freedom Day in Selma

On the night of June 11, 1963, the Rev. Bernard Lafayette, ready to park at his home, was approached by a man who told him that his car had stalled across the street and he needed a push. "How much will you charge me for a push?" the man asked. "Nothing," replied Lafayette, and lined up his car behind the other one. It was a scene that has taken place a thousand times in a thousand American towns. But this was different: the town was Selma, Alabama; Bernard Lafayette was a former Freedom Rider and a field secretary for SNCC; the man asking for help was white. When Lafayette bent to see if the bumpers matched, he was clubbed on the head, and he fell to the pavement, blood spurting over his clothes. Then he was hit twice more on the head, and the man drove off. He got to a doctor, who sewed up his wound with six stitches, and the next day he was back at his job, registering voters in Selma.

Selma has an unreal air about it. It is as if a movie producer had reconstructed a pre-Civil War Southern town—the decaying buildings, the muddy streets, the little cafes, and the huge red brick Hotel Albert, modelled after a medieval Venetian palace. A mule draws a wagonload of cotton down the street. But cotton is just hanging on. At one time, 627,000 acres in the area grew cotton. Now it's down to 27,000 acres.

You walk into the Silver Moon Cafe. On the shelves facing you there are bottles of whiskey and boxes of corn flakes. At your feet, running the length of the counter, is a tin channel spittoon. Past a swinging door you can make out the murky interior of the Negro section of the cafe. In the white section, in a booth, sits a Mexican family, eating in silence (eighty-five Mexicans were brought in this year to pick cotton; they pick more cotton for less money than Negroes do, say the local whites). Two women sit at a table, drinking beer, looking up to curse the strangers sitting at the counter. You recall what *Newsweek* writer Karl Fleming was told in another Alabama city: "We killed two-year old Indian babes to get this country and you want to give it to the niggers."

Selma was a slave market before the Civil War. In one three-story house, still standing, four or five hundred Negroes were kept at one time to be exhibited and sold. The town became a military depot for the Confederacy. At the turn of the century, it was a lynching town. By the 1950's, the lynching had stopped, but the threat of it remained. Selma became the birthplace of the Citizens Council in Alabama, wrapped tight in the rules of race.

A little south of the geographic center of Alabama, Selma is about fifty miles due west of Montgomery, and downstream from it on the Alabama River. It is the seat of Dallas County, where, in 1961, 57 percent of the population was Negro, but only about 1 percent of the eligible Negroes were registered to vote, while 64 percent of the eligible whites were registered. The median income for Negroes is about $28 a week. With several new government buildings in the center of town, Selma has a trace of the twentieth century; but beyond it the Alabama countryside is an unpenetrated social jungle. In neighboring Wilcox County, for instance, where Negroes are 78 percent of the population, not one of them is registered to vote; their median income is about $20 a week.

Bruce Boynton is a Negro attorney, now in Chattanooga, who grew up in Selma. (His mother, Mrs. Amelia Boynton, still lives there, a rock to whom the new freedom movement is anchored, a 1964 candidate for the U.S. Senate.) Mr. Boynton says:

> A Negro boy growing up in Selma lives a life that other Americans cannot easily understand. When he wakes up in the morning he looks outside the window and it is dusty, hot, wet, the street mired in mud. He is aware that his mother is away all the time, at work. He is aware of the jobs his mother and father have, how little they make, how much more the white folks make. Coming home from school he sees the sign on the bus directing him to the back. One of his first ideas is: I must get out of this town.

In February of 1963, Bernard Lafayette and his wife Colia came to Selma to begin a voter registration drive for SNCC. It was slow, hard going. One of the first consequences was that thirty-two schoolteachers who tried to register to vote were fired. Arrests mounted, for minor or imaginary traffic offenses, for picketing at the county courthouse, for simply being seen downtown or riding in an automobile. Worth Long, a SNCC man, was beaten by a deputy sheriff in the county jail. John Lewis was arrested for leading a picket line at the courthouse. A nineteen-year-old girl was knocked off a stool in a store and prodded with a electric pole as she lay on the floor unconscious.

Between September 15 and October 2, 1963, over three hundred people were arrested in Selma in connection with voter registration activities. The Federal government filed suit, but its mild efforts left the constitutional liberties of Selma citizens in the hands of Sheriff Jim Clark. Clark augmented his regular force of deputies with several hundred ordinary citizens, armed them with clubs and cattle prods, and stated that he was convinced that all this voting activity was part of a world communist conspiracy. In May, when Jim Forman came to Selma to address the first mass meeting at the Tabernacle Baptist Church, the posse surrounded the church. Those inside waited, long after the meeting was over, until they felt it safe to go home.

"Do you know any white man in Selma—just one even—who is sympathetic with your cause?" I asked three young Selma fellows as we talked in Mrs. Boynton's home. "Not one," they said. "Well, maybe one," one of them added. There was a Jewish storekeeper for whom his mother worked, and the man would sit and talk with the boy in the back of the store, telling him, "Keep up the good work." Later that night, I saw a list of Citizens Council members who signed a proclamation in the local paper; the storekeeper's name was near the top of the list. There are over a hundred Jews in Selma, many of them businessmen, many of them—through conviction or through fear—members of the Citizens Council.

The only white man who openly helped the Negro movement was Father Maurice Ouillet, a thirty-seven-year-old Catholic priest in charge of St. Edmonds Mission in Selma. Father Ouillet was called in once by a group of white leaders of the city and advised to leave town for his own protection, told he might be killed. He received abusive phone calls. Once, he told *Texas Observer* editor Ronnie Dugger, as he visited demonstrators at the jail, someone called him a "adjective, adjective nigger-lover."

With John Lewis and seven others still in jail in October, 1963, with Sheriff Clark's posse armed and on the prowl, with people afraid to go down to the courthouse, SNCC decided on a large-scale offensive. They had discovered elsewhere that fear decreased with numbers. It was decided to set October 7 as the day to bring hundreds to the county courthouse to register. As Freedom Day approached, mass meetings were held every night, and the churches were packed.

On October 5, Dick Gregory came to Selma. His wife, Lillian, had been jailed in Selma while demonstrating. He spoke to a crowded church meeting that evening. It was an incredible performance. With armed deputies ringing the church outside, and three local officials sitting in the audience taking notes, Gregory lashed out at white Southern society with a steely wit and a passion that sent his Negro listeners into delighted applause again and again. Never in the history of this area had a black man stood like this on a public platform, ridiculing and denouncing white officials to their faces. It was a historic coming of age for Selma, Alabama. It was also something of a miracle that Gregory was able to leave town alive. The local newspaper said that a "wildly applauding crowd" listened that night to "the most scathing attack unleashed here in current racial demonstrations."

Gregory told the audience that the Southern white man had nothing he could call his own, no real identity, except "segregated drinking fountains, segregated toilets, and the right to call me nigger." He added, "And when the white man is threatened with losing his *toilet,* he's ready to kill!" He wished, Gregory said, that the whole Negro race would disappear overnight. "They would go crazy looking for us!" The crowd roared and applauded. Gregory lowered his voice, and he was suddenly serious: "But it looks like we got to do it the hard way, and stay down here, and educate them."

He called the Southern police officials "peons, the idiots who do all the dirty work, the dogs who do all the biting." He went on for over two hours in that vein; essentially it was a lesson in economics and sociology, streaked with humor. "The white man starts all the wars, then he talks about you cuttin' somebody. . . . They talk about our education. But the most important thing is to teach people how to live. . . ."

Later, Jim Forman spoke to the crowd, making the last preparations for Freedom Day. "All right, let's go through the phone book. You'll know who's Negro, because they won't have Mr. or Mrs. in front of their names! You got to get on the phone tonight and call these people and tell them to come down to the courthouse tomorrow, that it's Freedom Day. You take a boloney sandwich and a glass of cool water and go down there and stay all day. Now get on that phone tonight. Who'll take the letter "A"? . . ."

The Selma Freedom Chorus sang, the most beautiful singing I had heard since the mass meetings in Albany; among them there were some really small children, some teen-agers, a boy at the piano. There was a big sign up on the platform, "DO YOU WANT TO BE FREE." After the singing, everyone went home, through the doors out into the street, where two cars with white men inside had been sitting all evening in the darkness outside the church.

Some of us waited that night at Mrs. Boynton's for James Baldwin to arrive. He was flying into Birmingham; some SNCC fellows would pick him up there and drive him to Selma. He was coming to observe Freedom Day. While waiting, we sat around in the kitchen and talked. Jim Forman expertly scrambled eggs in a frying pan with one hand, gesturing with the other to make a point. It was after midnight when Baldwin came in, his brother David with him. Everyone sat in the living room and waited for him to say something. He smiled broadly: "You fellows talk. I'm new here. I'm trying to find out what's happening." Forman started off; there was a fast exchange of information and opinions, then everyone said goodnight. It was getting close to Freedom Day.

I made notes, almost minute by minute, that October 7, 1963:

9:30 A.M. It was sunny and pleasant in downtown Selma. I asked a Negro man on the corner the way to the county courthouse. He told me, looking at me just a little longer than a Negro looks at a white man in the South. The courthouse is green stone, quite modern looking compared to the rest of Selma. There was already a line of Negroes outside the door, on the steps of the courthouse, then running alongside the building, broken briefly to make room for people going in and out of an alley which ran along the courthouse, then continuing for another seventy-five feet. I counted over a hundred people in line. On the steps of the courthouse and down in the street stood a dozen or so deputy sheriffs and members of Sheriff Clark's special posse. They wore green helmets or white helmets, guns at their hips, long clubs. One young deputy, black-haired, with very long sideburns, swung a club as long as a baseball bat. A few newspapermen were already on the scene. The editor of the *Selma Times-Journal*, Arthur Capell, quiet, thin, dark-haired, said: "Those people on line will never get registered. There are three members of the Board inside, and they spend quite some time on each registrant. There's never been more than thirty or forty registered in one day." The office would close at 4:30 P.M., and I realized now those people were going to wait on line eight hours, knowing they would not get inside the courthouse. I looked down the line. Middle-aged Negro men and women, some old folks, a few young ones, dressed not in their Sunday best, but neatly, standing close together in line.

In Alabama, as in Mississippi, one doesn't simply register to vote; one *applies* to register. This meant filling out a long form with twenty-one questions. *Question 15*: "Name some of the duties and obligations of citizenship." *Question 15A*: "Do you regard those duties and obligations as having priority over the duties and obligations you owe to any other secular organization when they are in conflict?" Then the registrar would ask oral questions, such as, "Summarize the Constitution of the United States." Three weeks later there would be a postcard: passed or failed. Another quaint thing about registration procedure in Dallas County was that applications were accepted only on the first and third Mondays of each month. Registering at the rate of thirty a day, even if all were passed, it would take ten years for Negroes to make up the 7000 plurality held by white registrants in Dallas County.

9:45 A.M. The line now extended around the corner. I saw Sheriff Jim Clark for the first time, a six-footer with a big stomach, on his green helmet a gold medallion with an eagle, a big gold star on his shirt, the Confederate flag stamped on his helmet, an open collar, epaulets on his shoulders. Gun at his hip.

10:00 A.M. More posse members were arriving and taking up positions near the line. It was clear they hadn't expected so many Negroes to show up, so that they had to keep calling for reinforcements. I walked down the line counting—about twenty-five inside the door and on the steps, then one hundred down to the corner, then fifty around the corner—total, 175. It was clear and sunny. Cameramen from NBC and CBS were arriving. I noticed a scaffold up one story on the county courthouse; two young white men in painter's overalls were on the scaffold, puttying windows, suspended eerily over the events below.

10:15 A.M. The line of Negroes growing. Never in the history of Selma had so many Negroes showed up to register to vote. More members of the posse took up positions near the line; now there was an unbroken line of helmeted men in khakis or fatigues, carrying guns at their hips, clubs in their hands.

I wondered if Prathia Hall would show up at the courthouse. She was a field secretary for SNCC, a pleasant, very intelligent young woman from Philadelphia, with a reputation for fervent oratory at mass meetings. She had gained her experience in the movement the preceding year in Terrell County, Georgia. Now she was directing the voter registration campaign in Selma. She'd been absent from the mass meeting Saturday night: word was out that a warrant had been issued for her arrest. Yesterday, Sunday, I had spoken to her at Mrs. Boynton's house and was going to interview her at length, but we delayed it so she could get some rest (our talk was not to take place, for she was arrested the next day).

10:25 A.M. Jim Forman was coming down the street.

Walking alongside him was James Baldwin, in an open collar sportshirt and tan windbreaker, and next to him his brother David. I talked with one of the two Justice Department lawyers here to observe Freedom Day. I looked up and saw the American flag waving overhead; now I realized the new stone building directly across the street from the county courthouse was the federal building. Inside was the federal court; also, the social security office, the draft board, and the local offices of the F.B.I. I asked the Justice Department man, "How many lawyers are there now with the Civil Rights Division of the Justice Department?" "About forty," he said.

I went down the line again, counting, walking between the members of the posse and the Negroes on line. I counted over two hundred. Among them were about ten white people. It was voter registration day for everyone, and the line was integrated. Someone told me that the Citizens Council had put on a special drive to get white people to register today.

The Baldwin brothers walked with Jim Forman as he went down the line, saying hello, encouraging people to stay. "Now you just sit here," Forman said as he walked along, "just sit here and get some sunshine." Two posse men followed him. When Forman stopped, one of them said: "Get goin'! You're blockin' the sidewalk."

10:40 A.M. More posse arriving. Two posse members stood near me, munching peanuts. There were enough now to have them a few feet apart all along the line and around the corner. Nothing in the Deep South was more dangerous to public order, it seemed, than a line of Negro citizens trying to register to vote. Across the street was a police car with two loudspeakers on top. Two young police officers in white helmets were near it. Aside from the dozen or so news photographers and reporters, there were very few white people around—just a handful of onlookers standing at the corner.

11:00 A.M. More people joining the line. I counted again,

thinking once more that these people coming on to the line knew they would never enter the courthouse that day. There were twenty on the steps and inside, fifty in the first section up to the alley, one hundred twenty in the second section down to the corner, one hundred around the corner—290 people altogether.

11:15 A.M. Jim Forman spoke to Bruce Gordon about its getting near lunch time. Bruce is a SNCC field secretary, originally from New York. I had talked with him when I arrived in Selma Saturday afternoon, at the First Baptist Church, and he was dressed now as then—he wore jeans and a T-shirt; a pack of cigarettes was stuck inside the shoulder of the T-shirt. He is slim, very dark, with a big head of curly hair, very articulate—a former actor and set man. "My father never taught hate. . . . He encouraged me to go into the movement, said it's better to fail grandly than to succeed at piddling little things. . . . I got out of the Army in March, '62, got to Atlanta in June, got with SNCC. . . . Julian said to me, 'how would you like a job with SNCC for ten dollars a week?' I said, 'Yes. . . .' I haven't seen that money yet." He laughed. "I had a scholarship at Clark College for this fall, a job with Lockheed for $110 a week, and a chance to play a good role with an overseas troupe which is doing *Jamaica* in Europe in November. But I threw it all over for the movement. I was in Savannah for a while. Now I'm here." (The next day someone told me that Bruce had led a demonstration against police headquarters in Savannah, and had spent fifty-five days in jail.)

Forman told Bruce to get three big slabs of boloney and about ten to twelve loaves of bread, to feed the people on line.

11:20 A.M. Forman, Gordon, and I were talking near the side entrance of the County Courthouse, around the corner—no line there. Sheriff Clark came over, his eyes vacant, his voice rising: "All right, clear out of here, you're blocking the sidewalk!"

11:30 A.M. On the corner, in front of the courthouse door, a man with sound equipment spoke to James Baldwin. Baldwin's eyes looked enormous, fiery. He waved towards the line of helmeted troopers: "The federal government is not doing what it is supposed to do. . . ."

11:40 A.M. Nobody up to this point could find a Negro who had come out of the courthouse who had actually gone through the registration procedure. But now a small group gathered around a Negro woman on the corner. "Yes, I went through, just finished. I believe twelve have gone through." Twelve, in three hours. And over three hundred people on line.

11:45 A.M. The two white men were still on the scaffold above the scene, calmly puttying windows.

11:50 A.M. Jim Forman told us Sheriff Clark and two deputies had just been to Mrs. Boynton's and arrested Prathia Hall. The charge was "contributing to the delinquency of a minor." Clark had just returned from this little mission, for he now appeared behind Forman. His mood was ugly. He poked his club again and again into Forman's side. "Get on! Get on!" Forman moved down the line towards the end. Ten Negro men were joining the line. We kept going, completely around the corner, Clark now far behind.

11:55 A.M. Forman mused about the problem of getting water to the people on line. The sun was beating down. I was in front of the courthouse door, the posse thicker now. I looked across the street to the federal building and saw there on the steps—standing so still that for a weird moment they looked like statues—two SNCC fellows, holding signs that faced the registration line. One, in overalls and a fedora, had a sign saying, "REGISTER TO VOTE."

I moved across the street to get a better look. As I did so, Sheriff Clark and three helmeted deputies came walking fast across the street. They went past two Justice Department attorneys and two F.B.I. men up the steps of the federal building and grabbed hold of the two SNCC fellows. Clark called out: "You're under arrest for unlawful assembly!" A small knot of white men on the corner were yelling: "Get 'em, Big Jim! Get 'em!" The deputies pulled the two fellows down the steps of the federal building and pushed them into a police car. One of the white men on the corner yelled, "You forgot one, Big Jim!" I looked around and saw a lone SNCC man around the corner, on the steps to the other entrance into the federal building, holding a Voter Registration sign. Clark mounted the steps, and reached the lone sign-carrier: "You're under arrest for unlawful assembly!" He too was pulled into the police car.

I had seen other instances of federal invisibility in Deep South crises, but this was too much. I turned to the Justice Department man near me. "Is that a *federal* building?" I asked. "Yes," he said, and turned away. The police car with the three SNCC men sped off.

12:10 P.M. Jim Forman walked over to Mrs. Boynton's office three blocks away to phone the Atlanta SNCC office about the arrests, and I walked with him. On the way, we intercepted six young SNCC fellows on the way to the county courthouse. Forman waved them back. "We need all of you today. We can't afford to have any of you arrested." In the office, before phoning, he sat down for a moment, reached into his overalls and pulled out his ulcer pills. In January, he had had to have surgery on a badly bleeding ulcer, requiring five blood transfusions. "How often do you take those?" I asked. He smiled. "Every two hours. But now, with what we have here, every twenty minutes." He told me that last night he had wired the Justice Department for federal marshals, sure there would be trouble. The Justice Department had not replied.

12:15 P.M. J. L. Chestnut, the one Negro lawyer in town, a slim, youthful man, came by. Forman said to him: "We've got to get Prathia out of jail *today*. We need her, man."

In the little room behind Mrs. Boynton's front office, James Baldwin sat with his brother David. A bottle of Ballantine Scotch was on the table in front of him and a few paper cups of water. He was writing in his notebook. Forman and the fellows in the office began discussing how to get the people on line fed. Many of them had been there since early in the morning with no food, no water. Someone suggested that there was a Community Center two blocks from the courthouse where food might be set up. People could leave the line in groups, get fed at the center, then return. They considered this idea for a while until someone said that it would be bad psychologically for people to leave the line; some might not return. Jim agreed. Food would either have to be brought to the line, or people would come across the street to a food station and then return.

In the front office, a young Negro woman, fair-skinned, her hair tinted lightly with red, was sitting at a desk going over the registration form with an old bent Negro woman who might have been seventy. She read off the questions, and with each one, asked, "Do you understand, mother?" The woman nodded her head calmly each time.

Word came back that the registrars had stopped registering for the lunch period. They would start again at two. Forman said, "We've got to keep those people in line." Again, the question of food and drink was discussed. More word from the courthouse: a caravan of automobiles with state troopers had arrived at the county courthouse. People counted 350 Negroes on the registration line.

I walked back alone to the courthouse. The state troopers' autos were lined up along the curb from one end of the street to the other—eleven long automobiles, searchlights mounted on top. The troopers themselves had now taken posts all along the registration line—about forty of them—with blue helmets, clubs, guns. A few of them, apparently in command, were bunched near the courthouse entrance. Their commander, Colonel Al Lingo, the veteran bully of Birmingham and the Freedom Walk, the man who had made infamous the use of electric prods in civil rights demonstrations, was not around. Taking his place was a hefty trooper with gold leaf insignia on his shoulders, Major Joe Smelley. I got up close to the troopers near the door. Several of them were holding cattle prods, squarish sticks with prongs at the end, the juice supplied by a battery and activated by a touch of the finger, burning the skin wherever it touched.

1:30 P.M. I stood across the street near the federal building and talked to one of the Justice Department attorneys, a young Negro lawyer in the Civil Rights Division. He shook his head sadly. "I've become jaded. A young Negro fellow comes up to me with his face cut and tells me a policeman did it, and I shrug my shoulders. Sure, I think these local officials are breaking the law. But someone up there in Washington doesn't think so."

1:40 P.M. Jim Forman conferred briefly with a representative of the Department of Justice. The problem was the same: how to get the people fed. The word had gotten through the line that the troopers would not let anyone leave and return to the line. Joe Smelley stood there, near the head of the line, surrounded by a coterie of blue helmets, a cigar in his mouth. The sun was warmer; the hunger on the line was greater; Jim Forman's anger was increasing; the Justice Department lawyers were more nervous. Tension was building up on that normally quiet corner, now a blur of painted helmets and armed men. A SNCC car was parked in front of the federal building and in it were the sandwiches. The only problem was: how to get them to the people on line without breaking up the line.

1:45 P.M. A Negro lawyer, visiting Selma this day from Detroit, made no effort to contain his fury, as he spoke to me about the impotence of the federal government on that corner in Selma, Alabama: four F.B.I. men, two Justice Department lawyers, an American flag overhead, a great carved stone eagle on the corner near the federal building. The lawyer's language was neither academic nor legal. He pointed to the young, dark-haired F.B.I. man ten feet away and shook his head. "He's a real hot number, isn't he! Boy, whenever anyone tells me about the F.B.I. . . ." His own words seemed to build his anger, because he suddenly walked over to the F.B.I. man and said, "Say, you see any violations today?" The F.B.I. man took his eye from the camera he was holding. He looked surprised, mildly annoyed. He didn't say anything. The Negro lawyer persisted: "I asked you if you saw any violations of federal law today?" The F.B.I. man said "No comment," and walked away.

1:50 P.M. It was fairly clear by now that the sheriff, his posse, and the state troopers were determined that the people on line would not be fed or approached in any way. At this moment, a little old white man walked down the line of Negroes, unconcerned, and immune. He was selling newspapers, and doing very well; after all, he was the line's only direct contact with the outside world.

1:55 P.M. Word kept coming to Jim Forman, "People won't leave the line to get something to eat. They're afraid they won't be able to get back!"

Forman and Mrs. Boynton walked across the street from the federal building to the courthouse entrance to talk to Sheriff Jim Clark. The Sheriff seemed to be in a rage. The conversation went something like this (I was a few feet away and scribbled as fast as I could):

FORMAN: We'd like to bring food to these people on line. They've been waiting all day.

CLARK: They will not be molested in any way.

Mrs. Boynton: Does giving them food mean molesting them?

Clark: They will not be molested in any way. If you do, you'll be arrested.

Forman: We'd like to talk to them; they're standing on line to register to vote, and we'd like to explain registration procedure to them.

Clark: They will not be molested in any way, and that includes talking to them.

2:00 p.m. A fragile thread was stretched taut, and everyone watched. Forman and Mrs. Boynton went back across the street. As they did, I heard aloud, creaking noise and looked up; it was the scaffold that had been suspended above the scene with the two window puttiers; it was coming down now. I looked closer at the windows of the courthouse and saw the faces of county employees jammed up against them.

I spoke briefly with Danny Lyon, the photographer who had been following "the movement" all over the South and taking pictures of it, a curly-haired fellow with a thick mustache, high-spirited, unafraid. We mused over the emblem on the door of the county courthouse. It said, "Dallas County, Alabama," and showed what looked like a figure bearing a set of scales. The scales were tipped sharply. "Justice?" Danny asked, smiling. A posse man near us was showing his electric cattle prod to a companion.

2:05 p.m. I spoke to the senior Justice Department attorney: "Is there any reason why a representative of the Justice Department can't go over and talk to the state troopers and say these people are entitled to food and water?" He was perturbed by the question. There was a long pause. Then he said, "I won't do it." He paused again. "I believe they do have the right to receive food and water. But I won't do it."

2:10 p.m. Forman was calling newsmen and photographers together to witness the next scene. All were gathered in the alley alongside the Federal Building, around a shopping cart which contained the uneaten sandwiches and the keg of water. Mrs. Boynton said: "We're determined to reach these people on line with food." Two SNCC field secretaries stood before the shopping cart and filled their arms with food. One of them was Avery Williams, Alabama-born. Another was Chico Neblett from Carbondale, Illinois. Both had left college to work for SNCC.

Chico gave his wallet to Forman, a final small gesture of acceptance of going to jail. He said to Avery, "Let's go, man." They walked down to the corner (a SNCC man never jaywalks in the South!) with all eyes on the street focused on them. They crossed at the corner. A group of us—photographers, newsmen, others—crossed the street at the same time. It was 2:20 P.M. As Chico and Avery came close to the line, the fat trooper with the cigar and the blue helmet, Major Smelley, barked at them, "Move on!" They kept going towards the line of registrants. He called out, "Get 'em!" The next thing I saw was Chico Neblett on the ground, troopers all around him. They poked at him with clubs and sticks. I heard him cry out and saw his body jump convulsively again and again; they were jabbing him with the cattle prods. Photographers were taking pictures, and the Major yelled, "Get in front of those cameramen!" Four troopers lifted Chico by his arms and legs, carried him to the corner, threw him into the green arrest truck that stood at the curb.

Now the troopers and posse men turned on the group of us who had followed all this; they pushed and shoved, ripped a photographer's shirt. A young reporter for the *Montgomery Advertiser,* himself a native of Selma, had his camera smacked by a state trooper using his billyclub. Then the trooper pinned the reporter against a parked truck and ripped his shirt. When he walked to the sidewalk, a posse man back-handed him across the mouth.

We moved back across the street to the federal building.

The Justice Department attorney was at the public telephone on the corner, making a call. He looked troubled. The green arrest truck pulled away. Chico and Avery waved. The Justice Department attorney took the name of the photographer who had been hit; several of us went into the F.B.I. office and swore out statements on what had happened.

3:30 P.M. Four of us sat on the steps of the federal building and talked: the young Negro attorney from Detroit, James Baldwin, the white attorney from the Justice Department, and myself. The Detroit attorney said, "Those cops could have massacred all those three hundred Negroes on line, and still nothing would have been done." Baldwin was angry, upset. The Justice Department man was defensive. He asked Baldwin what he was working on now. Answer: a play. What was the title? *Blues for Mister Charlie,* Baldwin replied.

3:40 P.M. Still no food and no water for the people waiting. I walked down the street, checking the number of people, to see if the arrests and the excitement had diminished the line. It was longer than before.

3:55 P.M. Baldwin was talking to a newspaperman, "It *cannot* be true, it is *impossible* that the federal government cannot do anything."

A police loudspeaker boomed out into the street: "All you people who don't have business here get on. White and colored folks, move on." We gathered on the steps of the federal building, not sure it would prove a refuge. Jim Forman joined us.

4:30 P.M. The courthouse closed its doors. The line was breaking up. The Detroit lawyer watched men and women walk slowly away. His voice trembled, "Those people should be given medals." We made our way back to SNCC headquarters.

That night, there was a mass meeting at the church called for 8:00 P.M. At 7:00 P.M. fifteen people were there. I spoke to an old man. He was a veteran of World War I, seventy-three years old, had lived in Selma all his life. I asked him if, in his recollection, there had ever been any activity by Selma Negroes like this? He shook his head. "Nothing like this ever happened to Selma. Nothing, until SNCC came here."

At five minutes of eight, the church was packed, every seat taken, people standing along the walls. Father Ouillet and another Catholic priest sat in the audience. The Negro attorney from the Justice Department sat there also. The kids in the chorus were up front, singing: "Oh, that light of free-ee-dom, I'm gonna let it shine!" A chandelier hung way up in the domed ceiling, a circle of twenty-five bare light bulbs glowing. A Negro minister started the meeting with prayer, the local newspaper editor, a white man, bowing his head as the minister intoned: "Bless this wicked city in which we live, oh Lord, have mercy on us!"

Forman spoke. The emotion of the day was still inside him: part of it triumph because 350 Negroes had stood on line from morning to evening in full view of the armed men who ruled Dallas County; part of it bitterness that those people, defending the United States Constitution against Sheriff Jim Clark and his posse, had to do it alone. "We ought to be happy today," Forman told the crowd, "because we did something great. . . ." Everyone applauded. Forman went on: "Jim Clark never saw that many niggers down there!" The audience laughed with him. "Yeah, there was Jim Clark, rubbin' his head and his big fat belly; he was shuffling today like *we* used to!" The crowd roared, needing release. When Forman finished, the Freedom Chorus sang: "If you miss me, can't find me nowhere, just come on over to the county jail, I'll be sittin' over there."

David Baldwin spoke, his voice choked: "Until you come down here, you don't believe it. . . . I'm not going to lie and say I wish I was going to stay longer. . . . It's an evil town." Just before he spoke, the Freedom Chorus sang the African folk song "Kumbaya," with their own words. One of the stanzas was: "Selma needs you, Lord, Kumbaya! Selma needs you, Lord, Kumbaya! Selma needs you, Lord, Kumbaya! Oh Lord, Kumbaya!"

Then James Baldwin stood at the rostrum, his huge eyes burning into the crowd: "The sheriff and his deputies . . . these ignorant people . . . were created by the good white people on the hill—and in Washington—and they've created a monster they can't control. . . . It's not an act of God. It is deliberately done, deliberately created by the American Republic."

The meeting closed as always, with everyone linking arms and singing "We Shall Overcome," youngsters and old people and young women with babies in their arms, the SNCC people, the Catholic priests, the speakers on the platform. Over on the other side of the church I could see the young Negro attorney for the Justice Department, his arms crossed like everyone else, singing.

9. The White Man in the Movement

Beyond the picketing and the demonstrations, the furor over the right to vote and to be seated in a restaurant, there rises that ultimate question, answered negatively by the Muslims, worried over by liberals, exploded in the center of the intellectuals' parlor talk by James Baldwin: Can white people and black people truly live together as friends in the United States?

It is characteristic of the young people in the Student Nonviolent Coordinating Committee that they should not speak their answer, but *show* it—and that they should do this not in the cushioned atmosphere of Northern tolerance, but in the violence-ridden towns of the rural South. White and black youngsters in SNCC—in Dawson, Georgia; Selma, Alabama; Greenwood, Mississippi; Pine Bluff, Arkansas; Danville, Virginia—walk the streets together, share the same sleeping quarters, the same food, the same dangers, join in the same songs through prison corridors where iron bars separate them. Never in the history of the United States has there been a movement where the lives, day by day, of Negro and white people are so entwined physically, intellectually, emotionally.

The reality behind this statement is somewhat more complex. There have been tensions and troubles, anti-white and black nationalist feelings among Negroes in SNCC, resentment expressed against white kids rushing into the movement, personal piques and gripes and explosions, and, in one setting of high nervous tension, a fistfight. But these are the aches of progress, the inevitable and welcome signs that people are meeting for the first time, and that through a transition which brings occasional bursts of hostility, people are learning to live with one another. The tensions are a counterpoint to the old "peace" of separation and subordination; therefore jarring, full of surprises and passions. Among these passions, there rises again and again that feeling between one person and another that can only be described as love. And in the deep and complex relationships among people in SNCC, we have perhaps the blurred vision of what awaits the nation and the world when the artifice of race no longer stands in the way of human contact.

The first white field secretary in SNCC was a Southerner —Bob Zellner, born and raised in Southern Alabama where his father, a Methodist preacher with scant means, moved from one small town to another (the list looks like a KKK itinerary: Slocum, Roxley, Daphne, East Bruton, Mobile). In fact, his father once was a member of the KKK and a fundamentalist preacher. But while Bob was a child, the Reverend Zellner went through the emotional and intellectual transformation that made him an iconoclast in the church and a rebel in Alabama. Without the support of his father and mother, Bob doubts that he could have survived the series of rebellions against Southern white orthodoxy that finally brought him into SNCC, one of its most-jailed, most-beaten, and most-respected members.

I first saw Bob Zellner one day in December, 1961, when I waited outside the Dougherty County jail for the emergence of the Freedom Riders whose imprisonment had led to the mass demonstrations in Albany. He came out through the gate with the rest; he was bearded and somewhat unkempt after ten days in that miserable jail. As he walked over to join the others a policeman grabbed him. It seemed that he alone had an additional charge against him, which would delay his release. As the policeman pushed and dragged him off, Bob waved and smiled to his friends, and there was something in that gesture which stirred me to a good deal of thought that night.

Bob Zellner has light brown hair, an athletic build, an easy grin. Vaguely aware, in high school, of his father's growing heretical views on race, he argued with friends for Autherine Lucy's right to attend the University of Alabama without being really sure why he felt that way. But it was during his last two years at Huntingdon College in Montgomery, where he was an outstanding student, that he made the decisive turn. He came into conflict with the college administration over the firing of a teacher whom he admired. Around this time also he was reading in the newspapers about the sit-ins, and found himself identifying with the Negro students waiting for long hours at the lunch counters.

When he took a course on Race Relations in the winter of 1960, instead of doing his research in the library he decided to investigate the problem first-hand. He visited the Rev. Ralph Abernathy in Montgomery, brought college friends to court hearings and to mass meetings at Negro churches, and began to attract the attention of both the state of Alabama and the college administration. He and several friends attended a nonviolent workshop conducted by SNCC people in Montgomery. Police surrounded the place, and they had to escape through a back exit. With the college administration aroused, Bob and the others were threatened with expulsion. Nevertheless he graduated that June, perhaps because he had won several of the school's highest academic awards, perhaps because he and his parents had put up a vigorous battle to defend his right to act as he did.

Bob now discovered that there were other Southern white people who thought as he did, and this strengthened him. Anne Braden had come to interview him for *The Southern Patriot*, an integrationist newspaper put out by the Southern Conference Education Fund. Then they corresponded with one another. Through Clifford and Virginia Durr and other

Montgomery liberals Bob began to learn about various contemporary political issues. After his graduation he spent part of the summer at the interracial Highlander Folk School in Tennessee, then applied for a Southern Conference Education Fund grant to work with white students in the South for SNCC. On September 11, 1961, he arrived in Atlanta to start work.

His job in SNCC did not turn out exactly as expected. As he later reported:

> At first I thought my work would mainly be a quiet sort—simply meeting and talking with students about what was going on. But I soon realized the impossibility of explaining what was going on unless I myself became an integral part of it, and of course my personality make-up and psychology also tended to draw me into the area of action. So I did get into action, first in McComb, rather suddenly. . . .

In McComb on October 4, 1961 to attend a SNCC planning session, Zellner learned of the murder of Herbert Lee and the arrest of teenager Brenda Travis. At noon, he heard singing outside the SNCC office; students were assembling to march downtown in the first street demonstration to take place in Mississippi. Everyone around him was moving to take part in the march, Bob Moses, Chuck McDew, and a hundred high school kids, and Bob was suddenly faced with a hard choice: to take part might seriously hurt his "quiet sort of work" among white Southern students, yet he wanted to declare, both to these Negro youngsters and to himself, his place in this movement. As the line began to move down the street from the office, he ran outside and joined it.

He was the only white person in the long line of youngsters, who walked silently through town to the main highway. Then, with the sun beginning to set, they came back through McComb to the City Hall, where they found the streets crowded with white people, jeering and shouting, and large numbers of automobiles, and policemen all around. Someone in the crowd shouted out Bob's name and threatened to kill him.

The demonstrators walked up the steps of the City Hall, but the crowd was pressing all around so that they could not move forward or back. Men came out of the crowd, surrounded Zellner, and began clutching at him. Bob Moses and Chuck McDew tried to shield him with their bodies, but they and the other SNCC people at the head of the line were dragged off by the police, one by one, into the City Hall. Then the McComb Chief of Police held Zellner fast while the men began to beat him and to pull him into the crowd. He clutched at the railing, and tried to crawl up the steps. While the policemen watched, he was punched and kicked, his face scratched, his eyes gouged, and while on the ground he was kicked repeatedly in the head until he passed out. He regained consciousness in the police station, was pushed outside into an automobile, driven by the Police Chief fifteen miles to Magnolia, and let out.

For Bob Zellner, that experience had the effect of welding him to the movement by a feeling so deep that it was akin to a religious experience. For the Negro youngsters in McComb, the sight of Bob Zellner walking with them into the mob and being beaten was a jolt to their general distrust of white people, an opening wedge for a new understanding about the tyranny of race.

Four months later, Bob Zellner and Chuck McDew (the football player turned SNCC organizer, the Christian turned Jew, the black man turned Everyman) found themselves in East Baton Rouge jail, Louisiana, through an altogether bizarre set of events, facing possible ten-year sentences on criminal anarchy charges.

They had been visiting SNCC projects in the Delta and stopped in Baton Rouge to visit Dion Diamond, the Freedom Rider who had left Howard University to work for SNCC, had been arrested twenty-one times in civil rights demonstrations in Virginia and Maryland, and was now in the Baton Rouge jail. Diamond was arrested this time while trying to organize Negro students at Southern University in Baton Rouge; among the charges against him was one of criminal anarchy. McDew and Zellner went to the jailhouse to bring him some cigarettes, chewing gum, books, and a copy of *The Nation* (*The Ugly American* and *Scottsboro Boy* were confiscated, but *The Nation* was let in) and were promptly arrested. They weren't told immediately what the charges were, but an officer told McDew that one of them was "possible vagrancy." McDew was put into an isolation cell, and Zellner into a cell block with about sixty-five men.

The following morning, policemen brought newspapers into Zellner's cell block. In the headlines was a story about two Communists who had been caught trying to smuggle obscene literature on race-mixing into the jail. Their names were given and it was said that they were being charged with criminal anarchy, that they were trying to overthrow the government of the State of Louisiana. Bob was wearing a wristband which all prisoners wore, with his name and date of arrest; one of the men grabbed his wrist, saw his name, and then there was a commotion in the cell. Zellner was surrounded, forced into a corner, punched in the mouth, spat on, threatened with death. Day after day the ordeal continued, with the policemen egging on the prisoners. When he dozed off, ice water was thrown on him to force him to wake up. The men approached him with sharpened spoons and razor blades, and told they were going to pin him to his mattress and castrate him. Meanwhile, the policemen stood outside the cell, watching, cursing him.

Finally he got word to his lawyers, who interceded, and he was removed to an isolated cell called "the hole." They pushed him into a 5 × 7 cubicle, dark, hot, and stench-filled. All this time he had not known what happened to Chuck

McDew after they were arrested. Suddenly he heard a voice calling in a loud whisper "Bob, Bob, is that you?" He looked through the tiny opening in the steel door, and could see McDew's face reflected in a piece of metal on the stone wall facing his cell. Bob now realized that McDew was in the next cubicle, and was so happy that he began to cry.

They talked for a while, exchanging stories of their experiences in jail. Then they sang. The police pounded on the door for them to stop, but they sang: "Woke Up This Morning With My Mind on Freedom." The heat was turned up in their cells, and for seven days they remained in those tiny hot holes, at times so weak from the heat that they could not raise their heads.

Chuck McDew's days in "the hole" were something of a nightmare. When he was first put in, he found two psychotics in the cells near him; it seemed that Louisiana kept mental cases in jail until their transfer to state institutions for the insane. One of these was a fifty-year-old white woman who screamed and moaned continually, who banged her head against the bars, tore off her clothes, and repeatedly tried to hang herself. With the heat turned high in McDew's cell, he would lie on his cot at night and sweat; he lost thirteen pounds. The cot was as narrow as a bench, and too short for him, and he would wake up to night to find his feet dangling in the open toilet bowl that was near his cot. The guards would leave the lights on for days, then turn them off for long periods, so the only way he knew the time of day was by the meal schedule.

Right-wing groups conducted tours of the prison to see McDew. High school students and others would be escorted past the cells, and McDew would be pointed out as "that nigger Communist" and "nigger anarchist" and they would peer at him through the little hole. One time two high school girls on a tour strayed near the end of the procession, came over to the window, and whispered, "Say something Communist." Chuck then said, "*Kish mir in tuchas,*" which in

Yiddish means, "Kiss my ass." Delighted, they walked away.

After four weeks in jail, McDew and Zellner were formally arraigned, the charge being that they

> . . . with force of arms, in the Parish of East Baton Rouge, feloniously did . . . advocate in public and in private opposition to the Government of the State of Louisiana by unlawful means and are members of the Student Non-Violent Coordinating Committee, an organization which is known to the offenders to advocate, teach and practice opposition to the Government of the State of Louisiana by unlawful means.

Their bail had been set at $7000 each, and Diamond's bail was $13,000, but legal efforts finally succeeded in reducing the bail and they were released. Diamond stayed in jail fifty-eight days, and went through a very difficult emotional ordeal. He was determined, nevertheless, to stay in jail as a protest against the first use of excessive bail to stifle SNCC's activity. Ultimately the charges against Zellner and McDew were dropped, but two years later Dion Diamond had to return to spend sixty days in jail in Baton Rouge on the original charge of disorderly conduct.

No one can measure the consequences of that experience for Zellner, a white Southerner, and McDew, a black man, locked together, physically and emotionally, in the East Baton Rouge jail. And no one can gauge the consequences for all of American society, which in some future hour will show the effects of the increasing association of people who never before knew one another intimately. What we are seeing in the McDews and the Zellners is the faint but growing evidence of a new relationship between Negro and white in the United States. And what we also see is the kind of anguish the nation must endure before this comes to pass.

In the spring of 1963, a white Baltimore postman, William L. Moore, headed for Mississippi with signs protesting racial discrimination, was murdered on an Alabama highway. That incident led to Bob Zellner's next major job as a field secretary for SNCC.

The day after Moore's body was found on the road near Attalla, Alabama, a poll was made by telephone of the SNCC Executive Committee, and they agreed to continue his walk to Jackson, Mississippi. The following day, April 25, 1963, SNCC sent a wire to Alabama Governor George C. Wallace, informing him of the walk, and asking him: "Will the State of Alabama provide protection for our walkers?" Wallace had denounced the murder and even offered a reward for apprehension of the killer, but he replied: "Your proposed actions, calculated to cause unrest, disorder, and a breach of the peace in the state of Alabama, will not be condoned or tolerated. Laws of the State of Alabama will be strictly enforced."

Then SNCC sent a wire to President Kennedy, who had expressed his shock and condemnation of the murder, asking: "Will the Federal Government provide protection for our walkers?" There was no response.

The murdered man had been a member of the Baltimore chapter of CORE, and they too were planning to continue his walk. It was decided that SNCC and CORE should undertake it jointly, with an interracial group of ten, five from each organization. The CORE men were Winston Lockett (who had been working in Lebanon, Tennessee), Richard Haley (program director), Bob Gore (publicity director), Zev Aelony (later to be one of the four jailed in Americus, Ga.), and Eric Weinberger (who had been working with sharecroppers in Tennessee).

The five from SNCC were Sam Shirah (a twenty-year-old white Alabaman who was working with white Southern college students), Bill Hansen (also white, a veteran SNCC staffer), Jesse Harris (from Mississippi), Chico Neblett, and Bob Zellner. It was agreed that the ten would start out on May 1 from Chattanooga, equipped with boots and camping equipment, and would walk on Moore's route, continuing all the way to Jackson, Mississippi. As they prepared to set out, Jesse Harris received a letter from his friend and fellow Mississippian Willie Peacock:

> *Hello Crazy,*
>
> I'm sitting in the SNCC and I look down the list of names of people going on the walk and I see your name down there along with a few other crazies. I don't know exactly what it took for you guys to go on such a walk; some call it guts and some call it courageousness, but they are all worn out terms.... At any rate, I feel that I can share your fears when you are walking along the highway. As for the other fellows from SNCC I somehow knew they would be along on the walk if anybody did.
>
> The best parts of me are with you guys, which is my heart and mind. May all of your children be conceived in freedom for which you seek....
>
> *Willie Peacock*

As the walkers left the Greyhound Bus Terminal (from which Moore had begun his trek) in Chattanooga about 8:00 A.M. the morning of May 1, followed by a caravan of reporters in cars, there were a few well-wishers, a few catcalls. Sam Shirah, in the lead, wore the sign William Moore had carried, with its messages, "EAT AT JOE'S, BOTH BLACK AND WHITE" and "EQUAL RIGHTS FOR ALL (MISSISSIPPI OR BUST)". Out of Chattanooga, going up a mountainside high above the Tennessee River, the day sunny and cool, Sam Shirah began to sing softly: "Ain't gonna let nobody turn me 'round!" Chattanooga police and Tennessee patrolmen guarded the line, and there was no trouble, although once a handful of gravel was thrown from a passing car.

By nightfall they had walked ten miles, crossing the border into Georgia, where they stopped to spend the night at the Calvary Baptist Church in the isolated mountain town of Hooker. White people in cars and trucks raced up and down the gravel road alongside the church, gunning their engines, raising clouds of dust. In Tennessee, the police had formed a protective cordon around them. Here in Georgia, there were no police to be seen. Two white SNCC girls, Texan Casey Hayden and New Yorker Dotty Miller, stayed with the group, running errands of various kinds.

Following are excerpts from a diary kept by Bill Hansen that first night, May 1, and the next day:

8:30 P.M. Cars have been gathering in front of the church for almost an hour now. There seem to be in the neighborhood of thirty-five whites, most of them young. They are about fifty yards from the church. Eric Weinberger is out there talking to them now. . . . The walkers are a little wary of the situation but we are all rather calm at this point. Zellner and Chico are asleep. Eric just came in. He said they don't seem to be visibly hostile, but that could change.

8:45 P.M. All the newsmen are still with us (Time-Life, AP, and West Germany). Bob Gore is playing the piano . . . the rest of us are just sitting around talking. It's getting rather chilly and we only have one bucket of coal but we've started a fire anyway.

10:00 P.M. We turned out all the lights and prepared to go to sleep. About a half hour later cars with headlights on pulled into the yard. They stayed for quite a while, but I went to sleep and don't know what time they left.

7:10 A.M. We woke up and was it cold, especially after sleeping on the church floor all night. The Freedom Canteen (a truck supplied by the NAACP) brought us coffee and donuts for breakfast.

8:15 A.M. We got underway for the second day. It's rather chilly this morning. We had to wash in an ice cold spring outside the church.

8:15–9:35 A.M. The terrain is one hill after another. Winston Lockett of CORE is carrying the sign and leading the line this morning. Alabama cars are becoming very numerous. . . . There definitely is trouble ahead—it seems there is a mob waiting at the Alabama line. A car with Alabama plates threw a firecracker at us. No one was hurt. A Cadillac with Georgia plates came across to our side of the road at about sixty-five m.p.h. and tried to run us down. It missed Eric, Jesse, Sam, Chico and myself by about three or four inches. Sometimes the cars of whites from Alabama stop and gather by the side of the road in groups and yell obscenities at us as we walk by.

10:45 A.M. My feet are hurting terrifically and my legs are aching from my hips to the end of my big toes. I've taken off my boots and changed to sneakers because of a big blister on my heel. . . .

11:05 A.M. We started into Trenton, Georgia. Very large crowds are gathered all along U.S. 11. . . . The Georgia Highway Patrol and the Dade County Sheriff have been with us intermittently since a few minutes after we started.

12 noon. Eric has been limping for the past hour now.

2:30 P.M. No one is really paying attention to anything anymore except the feet of the person in front. My legs ache everywhere and from indications so does everyone else's. Up and down—up and down these mountains.

4 P.M. We have finally stopped for the day. Everyone is completely shot. We are 6.8 miles from the Alabama line. Newsmen who have driven to the border tell us a couple of hundred people await our arrival along with Al Lingo and the Alabama State Police.

That second day, rocks and bottles and eggs were hurled at them all day long. They stopped at Rising Fawn, Georgia, but there was no housing there, so they spent that night in the homes of various Negro families in Rome, Georgia. The next day, May 3, they found the highway clogged with hundreds of people; the mob walked beside and behind them, lobbing missiles of various kinds. They were walking on the left side of the road, while about forty newspapermen went along parallel with them on the right side. Two Georgia highway patrolmen were in back of the walkers to "protect" them, but they were not very effective. At noon, a white man came up to Winston Lockett and struck him in the neck, bruising it badly. One newspaperman was kicked, another shoved, a newspaperwoman threatened. (Later, Bob Zellner had high praise for the courage of reporters Claude Sitton of the *New York Times*, and Carl Fleming of *Newsweek*, who stuck with them from beginning to end.)

At a stop shortly before they reached the border Sam Shirah wired Governor Wallace asking that he let the group pass. Wallace had been a member of the church in Clayton, Alabama of which Shirah's father was pastor, and had taught a Sunday school class there of which Sam was a member. Meanwhile, as the walkers approached Alabama, Attorney Fred Gray in Montgomery was desperately trying to get a federal court to issue an injunction against Alabama Public Safety Director Al Lingo to prevent the arrest of the walkers.

At 3:30 P.M. on May 3 they reached the Georgia-Alabama line. Planes were circling overhead. Down at the bottom of the hill and around a curve was the state line and a fence. Behind the fence over a thousand white people were massed, with Alabama policemen standing in front of them, shoulder to shoulder. Traffic was stopped, and six or seven patrol cars stood alongside the road. Al Lingo, short, stocky, surrounded by Alabama State Troopers, ordered them to disperse. Sam Shirah walked straight ahead, the rest following, and Lingo called for their arrest. The troopers rushed at them. Bob Zellner lay down and was dragged along the ground and into a police car. Eric Weinberger fell to the ground, and the troopers used three-foot cattle prods on him, giving him repeated electric shocks, then four of them picked him up and threw him into a car. As the troopers jabbed away with their prods (Claude Sitton reported in *The Times*), an elderly toothless white man shouted from the roadside: "Stick him again! Stick him again!"

The prisoners were jailed on a charge of breaching the peace, then sent to Fort Kilbie, where they were kept in Death Row. For Bill Hansen, it was his twentieth arrest. After thirty-one days in jail, they were convicted of breach of peace and fined $200. Eric Weinberger, emaciated, was barely able to walk into the courtroom; he had fasted all thirty-one days. This was the end of the Freedom Walk. Some day, its participants promised, it would be resumed.

In June of 1963, with trouble brewing in Danville, Virginia, local Negro leaders there called SNCC for help and Bob Zellner came, along with Avon Rollins, a young Negro field secretary who was to make Danville his home base for the next year. It turned out to be an ugly summer in Danville, reaching its climax on June 10, when police repeatedly attacked Negroes marching to city hall, using billyclubs and water hoses, clubbing men and women who, bloody and drenched with water, staggered back to the church headquarters and then to the hospital.

Bob Zellner was arrested that day. Two weeks later, as he and two other SNCC workers were talking at the High Street Baptist Church, police kicked down the door of the church, rushed in, and arrested them, charging them with "inciting the colored population to acts of violence and war against the white population." Attorney Len Holt, a Negro lawyer from Norfolk who had handled most of the civil rights cases in Danville that summer, was also indicted.

The summer ended in Danville with police rule still a fact, with the wall of racism still standing. But the first assault had taken place. And, beyond this, another important thing had happened: the presence of Bob Zellner and other white workers affected Danville that summer as Zellner and others like him have affected so many towns in the Deep South since the sit-ins began in 1960. The point was made vividly to Negroes that compassion as much as cruelty crossed race lines. And the point was made to Southern whites that, try as they might to obliterate the image, *someone* like them, someone with *white* skin and from the South, had a different view of the way people should live together on earth. Those points, reiterated again and again these past few years every time whites and Negroes have gone together on sit-ins, on Freedom Rides, on picket lines, on Freedom Walks, constitute one of the truly splendid achievements of the current civil rights revolt.

In Southwest Georgia, Sherrod stuck to this viewpoint from the beginning. He brought white students, male and female, into Albany, and even into Lee and Terrell Counties, to work alongside young Negroes in voter registration and other activities. He knew there would be serious difficulties; he also knew that such difficulties would have to be endured, sweated out, worn down with patient effort through a thousand failures.

For a white person to find his way past the tangled veils of fear and suspicion that shroud the memories of Black Belt Negroes requires a rare combination of wisdom and luck. It can be done and it has been done, in Southwest Georgia and elsewhere. But it is not easy. With young people, black and white, it is easiest; with old people, it is much harder. Perhaps the best approach is boldness in moving into situations where interracial contact will take place, and then patience in letting them develop.

Peter deLissovoy, a white Harvard student who went to Albany to work for SNCC and stayed far beyond his term, gave (in *The Harvard Crimson,* November 12, 1963) a devastating portrait of the white college girl down in Terrell County for SNCC, with long hair, silver earrings, and sandals, bouncing confidently along a Georgia road to a sharecropper's shack, exhorting the awed and worried Negro who opened the door to register, and insisting that he call her by her first name. There were such people in SNCC, very close to that caricature. They came and went. As deLissovoy wrote:

> Whiteness is the problem of a tenacious if sometimes comical little minority within the American Negro Movement. It is not an insurmountable problem, as the cynics would insist, but it is difficult, tree-like in its old deep roots and twisting ramifications, and, if not faced honestly and quickly by the afflicted, it can be crippling.

As he said, it is not an insurmountable problem. Bob Zellner surmounted it. So did deLissovoy himself. So did Dotty Zellner, and Casey Hayden, and Bill Hansen, and Sam Shirah, and many others in the movement. And in this group must be counted the white person whom I first saw, neat and Ivy League-ish, at a civil rights conference at Sarah Lawrence College, and whom I saw the second time, dirty and unshaven, just out of Terrell County, Georgia. This was Ralph Allen.

On September 13, 1963, a letter was smuggled out of the Sumter County jail in Americus, Georgia. It was written by Ralph Allen, who had been there for thirty-seven days on a charge which could bring a sentence of death. In it, he described the evening of his arrest, August 8, when he attended a mass meeting of the Sumter County Movement . . . and then walked downtown to find Negroes lining the streets and singing.

> As I approached the intersection I saw the police arrest Don Harris . . . (a Negro, football captain at the Fieldston School, graduate of Rutgers University, now with SNCC) Police then began to wade into the crowd of demonstrators with clubs,

> driving them back down the street with me, while someone in plain clothes stood at the intersection firing a pistol in the air. . . . Then the city marshal charged me from across the street and hit me a couple of times on the back and shoulders. . . . I then noticed another white SNCC worker, John Perdew, as the marshal attacked him. After beating Perdew up . . . he came after me and hit me twice on the head with a billyclub. . . . Then he said, "When I say run, you'd better run, you nigger-lovin' son-of-a-bitch. . . ." My head was streaming blood. . . . Don, John, and I were charged with "inciting an insurrection," a capital offense.

The following night, 150 Americus Negroes marched towards the city hall to protest the arrests, walking slowly in twos across a lot to avoid blocking traffic. Police appeared, armed with guns, clubs, and cattle prods, and began bludgeoning anyone they could reach. Two sixteen-year-old boys and one sixty-seven-year-old man were knocked bleeding to the ground. James Williams, a young father of two children, who had not been in the demonstration but was simply walking nearby, was attacked by police, who clubbed him repeatedly on his head and kicked him, leaving him with a broken leg. Twenty girls, many of them eleven, twelve, and thirteen years old, were kept for weeks in the Leesburg stockade with nothing to sleep on but the floor, no mattresses or blankets or covering of any kind.

A week later, thirty-five people were arrested when they went to pray at the police station. Among them was white CORE worker Zev Aelony, a veteran of the Freedom Walk, who was also charged with "inciting to insurrection." For the next four months Aelony, Perdew, Harris, and Allen were kept in jail in Americus, with no bail permitted and a death penalty hanging over them. Finally, a three-judge federal court ruled unconstitutional the Georgia statute under which they were held, and they were released.

While the four men were in the Americus jail, some of the

young Negroes in Sumter County corresponded with them. One Americus girl wrote to Ralph Allen:

> White boy, only a fool
> Would leave his heaven
> on earth just to fight
> For undeserving Negroes.

He replied, and their exchange suggests the poignant, troubled feelings of Negroes and whites as they abandon the mystique of race.

> I do not understand, Gloria. It's no heaven on earth I left.... Depends on what you mean by heaven. If you mean a place where everyone has so much money they have no sensitivity—no love, no sympathy, and no hopes beyond their own narrow little worlds.... But to me the conceited, loud, self-centered All-American free white and twenty-one college boy stinks. I know, I was one. But something happened to make me human, something that I don't yet understand.... There's a poem by E. E. Cummings which reads:
>
> What of a much of a which of a wind
> Should give the truth to summer's lie,
> Bloodies with dizzying tears fall down.
>
> Well, Gloria, that is what I hope we can do. I hope we can upset people enough to make them human....
>
> One last thing. I love four people: my mother, a girl in New York named ———, another named ———, and a minister named Charles Sherrod. ———, ———, and Sherrod are all black. If I did not have my friends, I would be very much alone. And I don't want to eat in anyone's restaurant alone, to go to nobody's movie alone, to swim in nobody's pool alone. You dig?...

Race, which should mean nothing more than the insignificant fact of physical difference, has been invested by history and circumstance, by accident and by design, with a thousand mysteries which we now, at this stage of history, must pull apart one by one. It is a delicate operation, in which mistakes are easily made, where there are no primers on behavior, where perhaps the only absolute requirements are honesty in seeking the truth, and an affection for those others who seek it too.

While no one can point out *the* path, it may be possible to note some common mistakes. It is a mistake to think that one can forget completely about race, can pretend that the structure of artifice has not been erected and does not have to be dealt with in some way. It is also a mistake to think that one must not *try*, as often as possible, to forget about race. It is a mistake to ignore the fact of Negro sensitivity; it is also a mistake always to play up this sensitivity.

It is a mistake for a white person to play at being black. Sam Shirah's advice to other whites in the movement was: "You can't be black, so don't try." It is easy to romanticize the Negro, simply because in this period of our history, *he* is carrying the torch of American idealism. But one should ponder the fact that the new integrated world will have unjust and power-hungry people of both races, that the problems of freedom and justice cross the color line. Our dilemma is that we must somehow build a raceless society with the tools of a race-conscious world.

The key to a solution of the dilemma is contact—continued and massive contact among people of different races. Inside SNCC, people have been able to create marvelously warm friendships, because there is a magical social effect that comes from people living, working, sacrificing together. Friendships, and love affairs, have crossed race lines in SNCC. At least two interracial marriages have taken place among SNCC staff members: Chuck McDew married a white Sarah Lawrence girl; Bill Hansen married a Negro girl from Arkansas A & M College in Pine Bluff. (The Attorney General of

Arkansas, where Mr. and Mrs. Hansen are now working in the movement, called their marriage "a deliberate, direct disservice to the white and colored people of our state.")

The complexity of it all is perhaps revealed in a brief exchange which took place at a SNCC meeting between James Baldwin and Ella Baker. Someone had asked Baldwin about the role of whites in the movement. He replied, "A white man is a white man only if he says he is—but you haven't *got* to be white." Then Ella Baker added, "The place of the Negro is not as a Negro, but as a human being." And Baldwin said, "That's right."

Later, Ella Baker returned to that idea and, noting Baldwin's exhortation that whites coming into the movement should forget they're white, said, "We too must forget we're Negro." Responding to what she detected as a rising mood of something akin to black nationalism among some SNCC workers, she said:

> I can understand that as we grow in our own strength and as we flex our muscles of leadership . . . we can begin to feel that the other fellow should come through *us*. But this is not the way to create a new world. . . . We need to penetrate the mystery of life and perfect the mastery of life, and the latter requires understanding that human beings are human beings.

In November, 1963, the SNCC staff in Mississippi met in Greenville for three days of planning and discussion. There were some representatives there from CORE and SCLC; about forty of the forty-five people at the meeting were from SNCC. On Friday, the first day of the session, before Bob Moses had arrived, there was a lively discussion on the role of whites in the movement, and several suggestions for restricting their role. On Saturday evening, with Bob Moses chairing, the discussion started at 7:00 P.M. and ended at midnight and, as it turned out, a good deal of this talk centered on the role of whites. The exchange was candid and open, and revealed in a remarkable way the complexity of feeling among those there (roughly thirty-five Negroes and seven whites) trying desperately to escape the bind of race, while at the same time tyrannized in varying degrees by it.

The discussion was precipitated by two facts: The first was that proposals were being made at this meeting to bring one or two thousand students from other parts of the United States to Mississippi in the summer of 1964 in a determined effort to break through the shell of absolutist rule in the state. The second was that the coming of sizable numbers of white students to Mississippi to help with the Aaron Henry Freedom Ballot in October had led to much grumbling among Negro staff members that some of the white students had rushed into leadership positions, they had come quickly, gotten publicity, and left.

Four or five of the Negro staff members now urged that the role of whites be limited. For whites to talk to Mississippi Negroes about voter registration, they said, only reinforced the Southern Negro's tendency to believe that whites *were* superior. Whites tended to take over leadership roles in the movement, thus preventing Southern Negroes from being trained to lead. Why didn't whites just work in the white Southern community? One man noted that in Africa the new nations were training black Africans to take over all important government positions. Another told of meeting a Black Muslim in Atlanta who warned him that whites were taking over the movement. "I had this feeling inside. I felt what he said was true."

This was countered by other Negroes at the meeting. Lawrence Guyot said the coming of whites to Mississippi would have a powerful and a good effect, "a lot of Negroes in Mississippi meeting a lot of white people, on a human individual to human individual relationship." Another said: "This thing has got to be a colorless movement. We all have these little feelings . . . we all have these little reactions—'workin' for the white man. Okay. Then we start thinking. And that's why we're here. This is a colorless group and it's got to remain this way." Mrs. Hamer said: "If we're trying to break down this barrier of segregation, we can't segregate ourselves."

Several of the people, young Negro fellows in the field, discussed their inner turmoil on the question. "I think one way and act another way. It's not rational. But these feelings are there." Another: "These feelings are inside the Negro. Now we may feel we are all brothers. But these feelings in the Negro community cannot be ignored. . . . We must take the reality out there, that race has corrupted America tremendously. We want to change that. But in the meantime, we cannot act out in society the way we act in here."

A teenage Negro from Itta Bena, Mississippi, disagreed: "I think that when the white people come down here into the Negro areas, I think this makes the people from Mississippi understand better, see? Makes people change their minds."

One interesting thing was that the whites and Negroes at the meeting were split among themselves about the role of whites in the movement, with complex divisions of opinion inside both groups.

Bob Moses argued against the idea of judging on the basis of color who should come to Mississippi to work. "My feeling has been that the type of person you have is much more important than whether he's white or not." He was careful, he said, to bring to Mississippi the kind of white worker who could "break down the depersonalization of people," those whom Negroes would learn to know as human beings in all their qualities, good and bad. He was concerned, he said, that the Mississippi movement should become integrated "because otherwise we'll grow up and have a racist movement."

It was important, Moses said, to break down the idea that Negroes could get things completely by themselves. "And the only way you can break that down is to have white people working alongside of you, so then it changes the whole complexion of what you're doing, so it isn't any longer Negro fighting white, it's a question of rational people against irrational people."

Yes, someone interjected, but shouldn't there be *something* in American society where Negroes could lead? "I always thought," Moses said quietly, "that the one thing we can do for the country that no one else can do is to be above the race issue."

It was midnight now. Everyone was very tired. The meeting was called to a close. Everyone stood up, and locked hands, every single person there in the circle, and sang, "We Shall Overcome," stanza after stanza. I had heard the song sung many times at various meetings with deep passion, but never quite like this. I felt that people were gripping each other's hands tighter than usual. When they came to the stanzas "We shall brothers be" and "Black and white together," the voices somehow grew louder, more intense. People looked at one another. A few broke hands and applauded. The song came to an end, and the people at the meeting, talking in low voices, moved out together into the darkness.

10. "I Want To Know: Which Side Is the Federal Government On?"

When 200,000 people gathered in the historic March on Washington, D.C., in August, 1963, and listened near the huge Lincoln Memorial to the speeches made by leaders of the civil rights organizations, they did not know that one of those speeches, at the last moment, had been altered. It was the one delivered by John Lewis, chairman of the Student Nonviolent Coordinating Committee. His prepared text was objected to by Catholic Archbishop O'Boyle of Washington and other leaders of the March persuaded him to moderate it, though Lewis did this with misgivings. Even so, the speech was a study in controlled anger. But some of its most trenchant passages had been removed, just before it was delivered.

Why was Lewis' speech toned down? Why did national leaders of civil rights, of labor, of the church, put such coercive pressure on him, in a movement sacrificing so much for freedom? The exact cause is not certain—but one reasonable hypothesis is that John Lewis, instead of confining his attack to generalized and customary targets—the Southern racists and opponents of Civil Rights legislation—was lashing out immoderately at the federal government itself, charging the Kennedy Administration with failure to fulfill its responsibility to Negroes in the South.

Until the moment Lewis began to speak, the Administration had been successful in directing the indignation of those 200,000 people at everyone but itself. The bitterness of Lewis' attack must have startled his liberal listeners, who looked on President Kennedy as a friend of civil rights, who were impressed by the Administration's sponsorship of a new Civil Rights Bill, and by its endorsement of the great March.

But John Lewis, twenty-three years old, born on an Alabama farm, veteran of the Nashville sit-ins, beaten in the Freedom Rides, jailed twenty times, and now national chairman of SNCC, represented a point of view rarely heard in Washington. He was speaking that day for the SNCC people on the front lines in Mississippi, Alabama, and Southwest Georgia, for the Negroes of the Black Belt, for people who had endured the unendurable and had been left on their own by the national government. John Lewis knew that while the President and the Attorney General spoke out on civil rights in Washington, D.C., their voices were scarcely whispers in the towns and hamlets of the Deep South; that while Negroes were shot and beaten in Mississippi and Alabama, the federal government scrupulously maintained a policy of minimum interference.

From the time the civil rights movement became a revolt, in the spring of 1960, SNCC has been the most persistent critic of national policy on civil rights. There are two reasons for this.

One is that, more than any other civil rights group, SNCC works deep in the Black Belt, in outlaw territory, in a kind of no man's land where the most terrible attacks on human dignity take place while the rest of the nation looks elsewhere. Only when such attacks reach a crescendo and receive national publicity, as in the prolonged Birmingham crisis of 1963, do the public and the government take notice; when the crisis is over the attention recedes, and five million Negroes are left alone again, every hour of every day. And when this happens, the SNCC workers remain with them.

The second reason for SNCC's alienation from the Washington establishment is that SNCC holds a view of federal constitutional authority which is different from that of the Department of Justice. The legal reasoning of SNCC is as follows: The United States Constitution says that Americans have the right to speak freely, to distribute literature, to assemble peacefully, to petition the government for a redress of grievances (First Amendment), and that no state or local official may deprive anyone of these rights (Fourteenth Amendment), or subject any person to discrimination or abuse because of his color. These constitutional provisions are "the supreme law of the land" (Article VI). The President of the United States, according to Article II of the Constitution, has the responsibility to see "that the laws be faithfully executed." But on countless occasions these past few years, state and local officials have violated the constitutional rights of Negroes and whites in the Deep South, and the Executive Branch of the government has not taken any effective action to stop this. The President of the United States, then, and specifically the Department of Justice, which is the law enforcement arm of the Administration, have not been fulfilling their responsibilities under the Constitution.

Though SNCC's interpretation of the powers of the government is simple and blunt, it is supported by some of the leading experts on constitutional law in the nation. There is little dispute on the facts. In literally thousands of instances these past few years, Southern policemen and local officials have trampled on the Constitution with no interference, as if they were a law unto themselves, as if they were not in the United States, as if the Constitution did not apply to them, as if the power of the federal government was non-existent. They have done this openly, in many cases under the eyes of federal officials, and have remained untouched by the law.

This book is filled with the details of such instances: the violence in McComb; the murder of Herbert Lee; the beating after beating, cruelty upon cruelty, in Hinds County jail, in Winona jail, in Parchman jail; the murders and attempted murders throughout the state of Mississippi; the use of electric prods on helpless prisoners by sheriffs and deputy sheriffs in various places; the caning of C. B. King; the kicking and beating of the pregnant Mrs. Slater King; the beating of Bill Hansen; the shooting of Charlie Ware; the breaking of James Williams' leg; the wave of shootings and bombings in Southwest Georgia; the clubbing of women and children in Danville; the jailing under the most unbearable conditions of women and old people and small children. And beyond this, the putting into jail of thousands of innocent people throughout the South who had done nothing but speak out peacefully to air their grievances. In fact, these people were only trying to accomplish by themselves what the national government had failed to do for them: to establish the rule of the Constitution in the Deep South.

The ordinary citizen of the United States might claim ignorance of what is happening in the Deep South—as many ordinary Germans claimed not to know of the death camps. But the national government cannot say it is ignorant. Hundreds upon hundreds of affidavits have been filed with the Department of Justice, crying out for redress of grievances, with no results. Phone calls have been made again and again to the F.B.I. or the Justice Department from civil rights workers in desperate need of immediate protection, but have gone unheeded. Requests for protection, made in advance of anticipated trouble, have been consistently refused. Justice Department attorneys have watched and done nothing (as in Selma) while local police arrested citizens who were standing peacefully on federal property. Men from the F.B.I. have stood by and watched (as in McComb) while policemen gave bloody beatings to citizens who were breaking no law, while (as on the Freedom Walk) state patrolmen administered electrical shocks to men who had committed no crime.

Every time a policeman willfully commits an act of brutality against a citizen, deprives him of the equal protection of the laws, of freedom of speech or peaceful assembly, or any other constitutional right, he is violating a federal law. That is the Enforcement Act of 1870 which supplemented a Civil Rights Act of 1866, and is written into the statute books as Section 242, Title 18, of the U.S. Code. The statute reads:

> Whoever, under color of any law, statute, ordinance, regulation, or custom, willfully subjects, or causes to be subjected, any inhabitant of any State, Territory, or District to the deprivation of any rights, privileges, or immunities secured or protected by the Constitution and laws of the United States . . . shall be fined not more than $1000 or imprisoned not more than one year, or both.

Despite hundreds of violations of this act, only in a few instances have Department of Justice attorneys initiated prosecution under it. One of their arguments is that they are reluctant to prosecute because all-white juries in the South will not convict a policeman accused of beating a Negro. This amounts to a virtual admission by the national government that it is powerless to execute its own laws. A barrage of prosecutions, even if they did not result in a verdict of guilty, might have a healthy deterrent effect. The Department might begin to think imaginatively of judicial devices to get Negroes on Southern juries, or even to remove cases to federal courts in other jurisdictions.

The Justice Department is full of arguments against using Section 242, but none of them stand up under close examination. They point to the difficulty of even getting an indictment. But since the crime is a misdemeanor an indictment is not necessary; the trial can take place simply by the filing of "an information." They point to the interpretation of Section 242 in the Screws Case, in which a Baker County, Georgia, sheriff beat a Negro to death, and where the Supreme Court ordered a retrial. But that was in 1945, almost twenty years ago; we are living in a new time, we have a new Supreme Court, and there is an excellent chance of getting new interpretations of this statute, *if only the Department of Justice would try.*

Section 242 can also be used in cases where violence is done by private persons with the connivance or approval of law enforcement authorities so that all those instances where beatings have taken place in Southern prisons, in the presence of policemen, could lead to prosecution. But the Department of Justice has taken no action on these cases.

Another statute which the Justice Department could use is Section 241, Title 18, which makes it a crime punishable by as much as $5000 or ten years in jail if "two or more persons conspire to injure, oppress, threaten, or intimidate any citizen in the free exercise or enjoyment of any right or privilege secured to him by the Constitution or laws of the United States." This could be a powerful weapon against not only public officials but private parties who act to deprive the Negro or anyone else of constitutional rights. But it has not been employed.

Sections 241 and 242 enable prosecution of those who have already broken the law, and this usually takes place long after the damage is done. But there is nothing to prevent either the F.B.I. or federal marshals, if they are on the scene while the violation is taking place (as they have been many times), from arresting the violator *on the spot.* Section 3052, Title 18, of the U.S. Administrative Code was amended in 1951 to give F.B.I. agents the same power which United States marshals have, to make arrests without warrants "for any offense against the United States committed in their presence." Curiously enough, the F.B.I., which makes arrests in kidnapping cases, bank robberies, drug cases, espionage cases, etc., does not make arrests on the spot in civil rights cases. It would appear that not only are Negroes second-class citizens, but that civil rights law is second-class law.

For instance, when Sheriff Jim Clark marched across the street in Selma towards the federal building where two SNCC workers were standing on the steps with voter registration signs, one of the Justice Department attorneys or one of the F.B.I. men who were standing right there should have stepped in the way, and informed Sheriff Clark that standing on the steps of the federal building was a constitutional right, and that interference with this would constitute a crime. If the Sheriff persisted, he should have been taken into custody immediately. Thus far, no Southern official—whether Governor Barnett of Mississippi or Governor Wallace of Alabama or Registrar Lynd of Forrest County—has defied the federal authorities *when faced with the possibility of arrest.*

The Federal Bureau of Investigation has proved to be incapable of dealing with the civil rights crisis of the 1960's, and absolutely ineffective in defending American citizens against intimidation and violence in the Deep South. Time and again SNCC people have found that F.B.I. agents were cold, unresponsive, and at times hostile.

The Civil Rights Commission, in its 1960 report, *Justice,* pointed out that the F.B.I. is often tied closely to local policemen because of their association in the solution of ordinary crimes. The Commission suggested that perhaps another agency might be used to enforce civil rights law. Moreover, SNCC workers have found that F.B.I. men in the South often share the segregationist views of the people around them; this is reflected in the lack of enthusiasm which F.B.I. men show in handling civil rights cases. Mrs. Fannie Hamer once told an F.B.I. agent, "If I get to heaven and I see you there, I will tell St. Peter to send me on back to Mississippi!"

But the real problem goes beyond the F.B.I., to the Department of Justice, the Attorney General of the United States and up to the President of the United States. What the president could do is create a special force of federal agents in the Deep South (and in other parts of the country when they are needed; violations of constitutional rights take place in the North as well). These agents would have one specific function:

to defend the constitutional rights of any person against private or official action.

They would be present at all demonstrations; they would be subject to immediate calls for help; they would have the power to intercede whenever there was good reason to believe that a local official was violating someone's rights. And while they would be trained to use persuasion and mediation, they would have the power also to make on-the-spot arrests in the event of a violation of federal law. In addition, every local police station in the country might have a "hot line" direct to the regional federal agents' office, so that a person arrested could get help immediately if needed.

The Department of Justice has been reluctant to use its full powers to protect persons in the Deep South from invasion of their constitutional rights. Early in 1963, a letter was sent by John Pemberton of the American Civil Liberties Union to Mr. Burke Marshall, head of the Civil Rights Division of the Department of Justice, asking why the Department had refused to supply marshals or F.B.I. men requested for protection by persons involved in civil rights work. Marshall replied:

> . . . in regard to your query as to why the Department does not supply federal protection when requested, it is appropriate to observe that the responsibility for preservation of law and order, and the protection of citizens against unlawful conduct on the part of others, is the responsibility of local authorities.

What this statement amounts to is a withdrawal of the national government from its responsibility to enforce its own laws. If local officials respected federal law, then the national government could leave the field to them. But because in the Deep South—and often elsewhere—local officials have repeatedly and flagrantly violated federal law, it is the responsibility of the President, as directed by Article II, Section 3 of the Constitution, to see "that the laws be faithfully executed."

Another high official of the Justice Department, Deputy Attorney General Nicholas Katzenbach, told a Boston College audience in April, 1964, that civil rights workers would have to depend on state and local officials to protect their rights, that "to do anything else would be making major changes in the federal system." Civil rights groups, he said, "through despair or ignorance of the federal system seek to invoke the power of the federal government to enforce personal rights."

Oddly enough, the civil rights workers would seem to have a clearer comprehension of the federal system than Mr. Katzenbach who, along with Mr. Marshall, keeps citing the delicate balance between state and nation in our federal system as an excuse for unchecked police tyranny. The truth is that the President and the Department of Justice have not been observing the constitutional requirements of that balance. When the Fourteenth Amendment was passed, a hundred years ago, it made explicit what was implied by the loss of half a million lives in the Civil War; that henceforth state and local governments could not deal with their inhabitants unrestrained by national power.

The purpose of the Fourteenth Amendment and of the Civil Rights Acts passed at the end of the Civil War was precisely to make sure that local officials could not deprive persons of their rights and to put such rights within the protection of *federal* authority. What happened then was that Northern politicians and Southern politicians got together in 1877 and put a definite end to Reconstruction by the Compromise of that year, agreeing, in effect, that the national government would from that time on leave the Negro in the hands of the white South.

As C. Vann Woodward put it in his book *Reunion and Reaction,* the Compromise of 1877 "did assure the dominant whites political autonomy and non-intervention in matters of race policy. . . ." The Compromise, which amounted to an abdication of the government's responsibility to enforce the

Constitution, has been observed by every American President for a hundred years. What SNCC and other civil rights groups are asking is that some President finally show the political courage in Washington that Negroes and their white supporters are showing in the Deep South and repudiate the 1877 Compromise for all time.

In Marshall's letter to Pemberton, he noted that "this Department has utilized necessary force to suppress disorders so general in nature as to render ineffectual the efforts of local authorities to protect citizens exercising federal rights." He was referring, apparently, to the dispatch of troops at times of intense crisis: by Eisenhower to Little Rock in 1957, and by Kennedy to Oxford, Mississippi, in 1961.

The response of the federal government to the civil rights crisis has been on two levels. It has initiated over forty suits in federal court designed to end voting discrimination in the South. These suits have been too few, too weak, too late, and ineffective in ending voting discrimination. The second type of action has been that referred to above—the dispatch of troops in major crises. What has been missing, however, is a third kind of action, and the most important of all: day-to-day protection of Negroes against infringement of their liberties by the establishment of a permanent federal presence in the Deep South in the form of special agents, as we have pointed out above. (The small number of prosecutions under Section 242 initiated by the Department of Justice does not meet the problem.)

The President already has the authority to create such a force, using the same statute which empowers him to send troops to trouble spots. That is Section 333, Title 10, of the U.S. Code, which says:

> The President, by using the militia or the armed forces, or both, *or by any other means* (my emphasis), shall take such measures as he considers necessary to suppress, in a State, any . . . domestic violence, unlawful combination, or con-

> spiracy, if it . . . opposes or obstructs the execution of the laws of the United States or impedes the course of justice under those laws. . . .

It is precisely because the day-to-day protection is missing, and because the legal action brought by the Department of Justice is so ineffectual, that major crises occur which then require the use of troops.

The creation of a federal presence in the South will act as a deterrent to official lawlessness. Policemen, deputy sheriffs, and local officials must know that they will be immediately locked up in a federal penitentiary upon evidence that they have violated federal law in actions against citizens. *Habeas corpus* and due process will be accorded them, but they will face what thousands of innocent people have endured up to now: the burden of raising bail money, of physically getting out of jail, of waiting for slow judicial processes to take effect.

There is no purity of choice before the nation. Either we put up with jailing and brutality for tens of thousands of Negroes and whites who have done nothing but ask for rights asserted in our Constitution, or we put into jail—*without* brutality—enough local policemen and state officials to make clear what the federal system really is.

In liberal circles there is genuine trepidation about the creation of such a federal power. But there was similar concern when the New Deal was born, with its stringent federal regulation of economic activity, until people realized that the absence of central power may simply leave the citizen victim to the greater tyranny of local or private power. It was the storm of economic crisis in the 1930's that blew out of sight Jeffersonian caution in regard to federal power in economic activity. The nation learned that there is no *necessary* lessening of individual freedom with stronger central authority, so long as such authority is specifically confined to a limited field of action. With governmental power so overwhelming in our time, perhaps one tactic of defense for the otherwise helpless citizen is to exercise a kind of political judo, and turn the force of the state back upon itself.

Along with the establishment of a day-to-day federal presence in the South, what is needed is a bold use of the injunctive power by the Department of Justice. Injunctions could be extremely potent devices for protecting constitutional rights in the South. For one thing, they act to *deter* and *prevent* violations before they occur, because they are court orders, secured in advance, directing that local officials should not engage in certain activities. Also, if a policeman or sheriff or registrar or governor violated the injunction, he could be tried by the judge alone *without* the use of a biased Southern white jury.

In civil contempt cases, in which a person is jailed until he begins to comply with the court order (for instance, a registrar might be jailed until he registered Negroes in his county), no jury trial is required. And, as the Supreme Court ruled in the spring of 1964 in the case of Governor Ross Barnett, even in criminal contempt, where the person is jailed for a definite period, he is not ordinarily entitled to a jury trial. Besides, it is written into law that when *the government* gets an injunction, no trial by jury is necessary.

For instance, the government could go into the federal courts and secure injunctions to prevent policemen or any other officials from interfering with the right of free speech, or the right to distribute leaflets, or the right to picket peacefully, or the right to hold a peaceful demonstration, or the right to register to vote without intimidation. This would immediately place all state and local officials on notice that they would be sent to jail if they engaged in such activities. And with federal marshals or other agents at all trouble spots, immediate arrests could be made in the event of violations.

This most powerful device has been shunned by the

Department of Justice. It has advanced the very conservative and narrow legal argument that it needs specific authorization in the form of a statute from Congress before it can go into court to ask for such injunctions. Indeed, its view is so conservative that one suspects the Justice Department does not *want* to have and to use such powers.

There is an important Supreme Court decision, the Debs Case, which has never been overturned, and which specifically asserts the authority of the national government to ask for injunctions in *any* case of constitutional rights being violated, whether or not Congress has passed a specific statute on it. As Jack Greenberg has written in his classic study, *Race Relations and American Law*:

> While proposed legislation would give the Attorney General the right to seek injunctions on behalf of civil rights other than voting... he probably, even without explicit statutory authority, may use this procedure in nonvoting cases, as indicated by *In re Debs* (1895), something, however, he has never attempted.

Why, one might ask, has the Attorney General "never attempted" this course?

In the Debs case, the government secured an injunction against a railroad strike, though Congress had passed no statute giving it a right to ask for an injunction in such a case. But the Supreme Court said such an injunction could be issued because: "Every government, entrusted by the very terms of its being with powers and duties to be exercised and discharged for the general welfare, has a right to apply to its own courts for any proper assistance . . . whenever the wrongs complained of . . . are in respect of matters which by the Constitution are entrusted to the care of the nation. . . ."

The Supreme Court went on in the Debs Case to make an important statement. An Attorney General determined enough, or a President bold enough, could use that statement as a basis for any action to defend the Constitutional rights of Americans wherever they are threatened. The Court said:

> The entire strength of the nation may be used to enforce in any part of the land the full and free exercise of all national powers and the security of all rights entrusted by the Constitution to its care.

Using this decision, the government could ask the federal courts for a sweeping set of injunctions to guard the rights of Americans in the Deep South. In the end, whether the government interprets its own powers narrowly or broadly depends to a great extent on the degree of its compassion for the victims of injustice.

A group of SNCC workers in Mississippi, along with white Mississippi lawyer William Higgs, in an unprecedented and imaginative legal action, have sought a court order to force the Department of Justice to take strong protective action in that state. That suit, officially called *Moses* v. *Kennedy* (Robert Moses v. Robert Kennedy), was turned down in the District of Columbia federal court, but is being carried to a higher court.

There is an additional problem which the civil rights movement in the South faces. Any action for injunctions or any move in the federal courts to restore constitutional rights to citizens can be swiftly blocked as long as judges with strongly-entrenched segregationist beliefs sit on federal courts. Here is one area where the President has great power to change the status quo, since he is authorized by the Constitution to appoint federal judges. Unfortunately, the appointments made by President Kennedy, in precisely those years when the civil rights struggle reached its height and court decisions were so crucial, were a great disservice to the cause of racial equality. As the Southern Regional Council suggested, if the President could not secure Senate approval for his appointments, he could leave the seats vacant to dramatize the issue.

Kennedy was just not bold enough to break the tradition of getting the approval of Southern segregationist Senators in the appointment of federal judges; thus, again and again, he appointed racists to sit on federal courts in the South.

In Georgia, he appointed J. Robert Elliott, an old member of the Talmadge machine. Elliott once said, before he became a judge (as reported in the *New York Times*): "I don't want these pinks, radicals and black voters to outvote those who are trying to preserve our segregationist laws and other traditions." But more important, as soon as he came to the bench, he acted to deprive the Albany Movement of its rights of peaceful protest, and to deny repeatedly its requests to enjoin interference with peaceful constitutional activities.

In Mississippi, Kennedy appointed William Cox to the federal bench, at the suggestion of Senator James Eastland. Cox consistently refused to rule that discrimination was being used against Negroes in Mississippi. In one case, in March, 1963, he said (the *New York Times* reported): ". . . I am not interested in whether the registrar is going to give a registration test to a bunch of niggers on a voter drive."

In Alabama, Kennedy appointed Clarence W. Allgood, who ruled that it was legal for the Birmingham school board to expel 1100 Negro children from schools because they joined desegregation demonstrations.

In Louisiana, he appointed E. Gordon West, who reluctantly ordered an East Baton Rouge school board to present a desegregation plan, but wrote (as reported in The *Boston Globe*): "I personally regard the 1954 holding of the United States Supreme Court in the now famous Brown case as one of the truly regrettable decisions of all times." Another Kennedy appointee in Louisiana, Frank Ellis, joined West in holding constitutional a Louisiana law requiring that the race of candidates be put on the ballot in elections.

Furthermore, Attorney General Robert Kennedy publicly defended, in the spring of 1963, the Administration's appointment of Southern segregationists to federal judgeships. He said: "I'm very proud of the judges that have been appointed. We looked into all of them for questions of integrity and whether they would uphold the law of the land."

If it were not for the Fifth Circuit Court of Appeals, which can review decisions by lower courts in these states, there would be real trouble enforcing the Fourteenth Amendment. But the fact that a civil rights attorney must wait so often until a case gets through the district court and up to the Fifth Circuit results in crucial loss of time, while the lives and liberties of people are in peril. It is essential that the President of the United States begin appointing judges in the South who will support the "equal protection" requirement of the Constitution of the United States.

It is the executive branch of the government—the President, the Attorney General, the Civil Rights Division of the Department of Justice—which has now the main responsibility for establishing the rule of law in the Deep South. The legislative branch did its job in 1866 when it passed the Fourteenth Amendment. The Supreme Court has made it completely clear by now what the Fourteenth Amendment means—that it makes illegal any kind of official action to support segregation and that it also protects the rights of free speech and peaceable assembly, as well as other First Amendment rights. From now on, the real job rests with the Executive.

Early in his administration, President Kennedy denied the need for a civil rights bill, saying that executive orders could do effectively what had to be done. He proved to be slow and cautious however, in this field, as his moderate and much-delayed order on housing showed. Kennedy delayed almost two years in signing this order, and then did not extend its coverage to all federally connected housing, as the Civil

Rights Commission had asked. He also refrained from making comments on the moral issues involved in racial inequality. It took the severe violence in Birmingham in the spring of 1963 to arouse the President to an excellent, forthright statement on racism as a moral blight on the nation. Then, curiously, instead of being roused to sweeping executive action, he flung the responsibility at Congress, by putting a new Civil Rights Act into the works. After his tragic assassination, President Lyndon Johnson continued to put Congressional action, rather than executive responsibility, as the main issue before the nation, and the Civil Rights Act of 1964 became the focus of national attention.

What remained hidden from the American people was the fact that the *already existing civil rights legislation was not being effectively enforced,* that important Supreme Court decisions were not being followed by strong presidential action. The Civil Rights Acts of 1957 and 1960, for instance, were specifically designed to end discrimination against Negroes in voting. They did not succeed, because the President and the Justice Department confined their enforcement actions to slow, cautious lawsuits. In that one area where the Attorney General *did* have specific statutory authorization, in voting, he did not act vigorously to enforce the law. Vivid evidence of that was given on Freedom Day in Selma, October 7, 1963, when a corps of F.B.I. men and Justice Department lawyers watched local policemen pull SNCC workers down the steps of a federal building and jab others with electric prod poles because they were bringing food to Negroes waiting in line to register.

Additional proof that the crucial problem is *enforcement* comes from the fact that the legislative basis for preventing discrimination on railroads and in railway terminals goes back to the Interstate Commerce Act of 1887, that the courts made the point very clear in the 1940's and 1950's, and that a specific I.C.C. regulation went into effect November 1, 1961.

Yet, from the very first day that regulation existed, and continuing into 1962, 1963, and 1964, the executive branch of government proved unable or unwilling to enforce the law effectively (the brutal beating of the group in Winona, Mississippi in 1963 after they had used the white waiting room was only one extreme instance of this).

A dispatch from Canton, Mississippi, datelined February 29, 1964, by Claude Sitton of the *New York Times*, pointed up the inability of the law alone, unaccompanied by strong executive action, to guarantee voting rights to Negroes. Sitton quoted Dr. Leslie Dunbar, head of the Southern Regional Council, as saying: "The reality is that, to the Negro in Mississippi, the law is still the law as enforced by the sheriff, not the law that comes out of Washington."

Sitton wrote about the Civil Rights Act of 1964: "The basic objection raised to the new legislation is that the task of eliminating discriminatory practices would still be left to the Federal courts. Thus it represents no departure from the underlying principle of the Civil Rights Acts of 1957 and 1960." He went on to report a white citizen of Canton as saying that Negroes would continue to be barred from voting despite the new Act "unless Kennedy comes down here with some Federal marshals."

There are advantages to having a new Civil Rights Act spell out clearly what needs to be done in certain areas of discrimination, and once it is passed it creates even *more* principles whose enforcement can be publicly demanded. No one of equalitarian views is *opposed* to a Civil Rights Act. But it should not be used as an easy out for any administration which, pressed to take action, points to its accomplishment in getting something through Congress, while the provisions languish in the law books for lack of effective enforcement. The tremendous publicity given in 1963 and 1964 to the Civil Rights Act had one unfortunate effect: it diverted the attention of the public from the fact that the crucial problem in civil rights is not one of legislative enactment but of executive enforcement.

There is another serious disadvantage to proposing still another Civil Rights Act, and that stems from part of our judicial heritage. Constitutional tradition is that the president of the United States has almost limitless authority to act to enforce the Constitution and protect the welfare of Americans, even in the absence of specific legislation, provided Congress has not specifically barred such acts or rejected them as legislative proposals.

For instance, the Attorney General, on the basis of sound constitutional doctrine, already has the power to sue in court to defend any citizen's constitutional rights against attack. But if Congress discusses a provision to give him this specific power in police brutality cases, and if it then *rejects* the provision, it would be easy for Southern officials to argue in court that the Attorney General's power in this regard does not exist. Yale Law School Professor Alexander Bickel has pointed out, for instance, that the housing provision in the new Civil Rights Bill, because of what it excludes, actually weakens a power that the President had before the bill was proposed.

After first arguing with civil rights workers that the Justice Department simply did not have the statutory authority to go into court to protect them against police brutality, the Kennedy Administration omitted such a provision from its proposed Civil Rights Bill. When a subcommittee of the House inserted this authority into the bill, Attorney General Robert Kennedy went before it, in October of 1963, to argue *against* its inclusion, and it was removed.

One of the passages in John Lewis' March on Washington speech was: "There's not one thing in the bill that will protect our people from police brutality. This bill will not protect young children and old women from police dogs and fire hoses for engaging in peaceful demonstrations. . . ." There is strong support for injunctions in the letter which Professor Charles Black of Yale Law School wrote, in 1963, to Senator Jacob Javits of New York. Black said he believed that *without* new legislation the administration already had the authority to use the courts against police brutality and other violations of constitutional rights. He added:

> I do not know why the Justice Department will not try this course. A cynic might suspect that what they are afraid of is that the Supreme Court would sustain the thesis that a government may invoke the equity process of its own courts to enjoin massive and widespread violations of its fundamental law—and that having been held to such a power, the administration would then be expected to use it.

In the spring of 1963, a group of distinguished lawyers and other social scientists gathered at Notre Dame University to discuss civil rights. Their conclusions, which did not command national attention to the extent they deserved, are particularly pertinent to the problems we have discussed in this chapter. In the field of voting discrimination they said:

> . . . the Notre Dame Conference strongly believes that additional legislation is not a sufficient remedy. The problem is neither nation-wide nor region-wide. The condition which requires federal attention is the lawlessness that exists in a relatively small number of outlaw communities of the Deep South. This condition does not pose an issue of federalism. Federalism is a system of divided power among governments, and governments are instruments whose whole purpose is to establish an order of law. In these outlaw communities where citizenship rights are flagrantly destroyed, there is no law to respect. We have here, in short, a problem of enforcement. . . .

Referring to those "outlaw communities" of the South where Negroes are denied their voting rights, the Notre Dame Conference said:

> New and more refined legislative remedies are not required to reach this blatant disregard of rights. To contain and dis-

> arm lawlessness, a clear federal presence is required at the first outbreak. We think the Attorney General has the power, in the face of determined lawlessness supported by an acquiescent or conspiratorial community, to send federal marshals and agents of the Federal Bureau of Investigation for on-the-spot protection of the exercise of federal rights . . . and to make arrests for violations.

Martin Luther King, Jr., writing in *The Nation* in the spring of 1964, also pointed to the need for Executive action, and urged the use of federal marshals to enforce the law. In the stories of the old West, he pointed out, which are still shown on movie screens and on television, the marshal who came into a lawless territory and brought justice to it was a hero, and can be that again. He contrasted the sacrifices made by the Negro and the response of the national government:

> Negroes have marshaled extraordinary courage to employ nonviolent direct action; they have been left—by the most powerful federal government in the world—almost solely to their own resources. . . . We are nearing the year 2000 and our national power almost defies description. Yet it cannot enforce elementary law even in a dusty rural Southern village.

Northern liberals who are afraid to use federal power in the Deep South for fear it will result in Civil War give little credit to the good sense of the white Southerner. Given a definite rule of law, the average white Southerner will obey it. Only a tiny minority can be led to use violence to maintain the old system in the South. The vast majority, as has been shown in hundreds of instances of desegregation in the South, will perhaps grumble, but will adapt to the new order of things. The few who attempt forceful resistance can be contained by a firm use of federal power—not federal troops sent in military array in a time of high tension, but a permanent, cool, firm federal presence using a combination of persuasion and threat of prison to make clear that all citizens are equal before the law.

Probably the most shameful act of the Department of Justice in the recent history of civil rights crises was its prosecution of nine civil rights workers in Albany, Georgia, in late 1963, following the picketing of a white grocer's store. As John Lewis said, in his March on Washington speech:

> In Albany, Georgia, nine of our leaders have been indicted not by Dixiecrats but by the Federal Government for peaceful protest. But what did the Federal Government do when Albany's Deputy Sheriff beat Attorney C. B. King and left him half-dead? What did the Federal Government do when local police officials kicked and assaulted the pregnant wife of Slater King, and she lost her baby?

The vigor and relentlessness with which the Justice Department pursued this prosecution was a startling contrast to its inaction in defending Albany Negroes against brutality and illegal arrest. More than thirty F.B.I. agents were used; there had never been that many in evidence during the mass arrests in Albany.

The Albany indictments were based on the fact that civil rights workers in Albany had picketed the store of a white man who had served on a federal jury. That jury, all white, had just dismissed a civil suit brought by Negro Charlie Ware against Sheriff Warren Johnson of Baker County, after the sheriff shot him through the neck while Ware was in his custody. The picketing was to punish the grocer for his vote on the jury, said the federal government. Hence they charged Dr. William Anderson and two other members of the Albany Movement with conspiring to obstruct justice by that picketing. They charged five other leaders of the Albany Movement, including Slater King and Eliza Jackson, for denying they were at a meeting in their lawyer's office to discuss the grand jury hearings. And they indicted Antioch College student

Joni Rabinowitz for perjury for saying she was not at the picket line, did not see the picketing, did not know about the picketing.

Eventually all the defendants who were tried were found guilty except Dr. Anderson, whose trial resulted in a hung jury. They were sentenced to various jail terms and fines, but in the fall of 1963 the convictions were being appealed and the Department of Justice was becoming more and more embarrassed at the expressions of indignation by many Americans.

For an administration avowedly dedicated to the cause of equality before the law, the Department of Justice behaved strangely in the Albany cases. When defense attorneys argued at pre-trial hearings that their clients were not likely to get fair trials from all-white juries in Georgia, the Department of Justice—which had in many instances explained its reluctance to prosecute brutal Southern policemen on the ground that all-white juries would not judge the issue fairly—now insisted that these trials would be fair. And when each jury was selected, the government of the United States by peremptory challenge got rid of the only Negroes drawn from the panel, thus ending with an all-white jury.

Civil rights lawyer William M. Kunstler called the trials "a bone thrown to the segregationists" by the Administration. And in a critical analysis of the government's action, Attorney Shad Polier of the American Jewish Congress called it all "a misuse of the power of the Federal Government to pander to local prejudice." John Lewis' delivered remarks at the Washington march omitted this sentence which was in the original speech: "It seems to me that the Albany indictment is part of a conspiracy on the part of the Federal Government and local politicians in the interest of expediency." That was a harsh way of putting it, but it was very close to the truth.

The reluctance of the national government to protect constitutional rights in the Deep South has created a crisis for SNCC's faith in nonviolence. Nonviolence was successful in the sit-ins of 1960 and continued to be effective in places such as Charlotte, Nashville, Atlanta, Richmond, Memphis, and areas of the border and upper South where Negroes could exercise some political influence by voting, and where fundamental rights of free expression existed. But—and this was first revealed clearly when the Freedom Rides to Montgomery and Jackson exploded in sharp violence—there are areas in the Deep South which are, as Leslie Dunbar has said, "outlaw communities." In Mississippi, Alabama, Louisiana, Southwest Georgia, and Southern Virginia, the basic rights to vote, to assemble freely, to petition the government, to distribute leaflets, or to picket peacefully do not exist. They constitute what Professor James Silver has called his state of Mississippi: "a closed society."

The use of ordinary methods of nonviolent direct action in these outlaw communities is met in the same way a totalitarian state crushes opposition—by open brutality, overwhelming force. That the city of Jackson, Mississippi can create the "Thompson Tank," an armored car with machine guns to carry a dozen armed policemen for the purpose of halting civil rights demonstrations, is evidence of the problem. In situations like this, there is increased talk among Negroes of "self-defense"; Malcolm X's exhortation to Negroes to arm themselves and shoot back when attacked is hard to counter in the light of the murder of Medgar Evers, the bombing in Birmingham, the endless instances of brutality by police. As Dick Gregory has said, any other group of people in the world who would take arms and rise up against the tyranny of their government would be hailed as "Freedom Fighters." But Negroes are expected to adhere to nonviolence.

There is one powerful justification for asking Negroes in the Deep South to stick to nonviolence in the face of the terrible measures used against them by private and official forces in the Black Belt; that is, that they live in a nation where the power of the federal government can disarm and neutralize those who would take away their constitutional liberties. *But thus far the federal government has not done this.* Hence there is a renewed debate among Negroes and in civil rights groups about nonviolence.

Despite all this, the Student Nonviolent Coordinating Committee sticks officially, as its members do individually, to the belief that direct action, without violence, is both morally right and practically effective. But the inaction of the Federal Government, and the pressure of those Negroes who believe in armed resistance, make it increasingly difficult to sustain the argument for nonviolence. One effect, perhaps, of the growing frustration is that demonstrative activity, while trying to remain nonviolent, may become more extensive and more bold. Another effect is that individual members of SNCC, despite their professions, may become tempted to forsake their principles in the face of extreme provocation.

In a crucial sense, therefore, the future of nonviolent direct action as a technique for effective yet peaceful social change rests with the President of the United States. If he continues to maintain the Compromise of 1877 and leave the police states of the Deep South to violate constitutional rights with impunity, the nonviolent approach may fall. By vigorous and imaginative action, he can save it.

There are two ways in which the President of the United States may come finally to repudiate the Compromise and establish the rule of law throughout the land. One is for him to become persuaded that this is a great contribution he can make to American democracy. The other way is awful to contemplate: it is that stepped-up activity by civil rights workers in the hard-core areas of the South and growing demonstrations by Southern Negroes who are finally bursting their bonds will be met by brutal suppression in Alabama and Mississippi, perhaps in Louisiana and Arkansas, and there will be major outbreaks requiring strong federal intervention.

In the summer of 1964 this set of alternatives seemed to be drawing near: a thousand students from all over the country were planning, in a program directed by Bob Moses and the Council of Federated Organizations, to spend the summer in Mississippi, establishing schools, setting up community centers, registering voters. They would join a reinforced group of staff members of SNCC, SCLC, CORE and the NAACP. And meanwhile, the state of Mississippi was mobilizing its police forces to act as it had before, on an even larger scale.

No President in our recent history is in a better position to make the big break with the past than is Lyndon Johnson, who can talk to the South as a Southerner, who has declared fervently many times his belief that racism should disappear from American life.

When John Lewis spoke in Washington, his altered speech omitted this sentence: "I want to know: which side is the Federal Government on?" The question is put at the head of this chapter because it is an honest question, and because it has not yet been answered forthrightly by the actions of the government of the United States. Perhaps President Lyndon Johnson, finally, in a historic decision, will answer that question once and for all.

11. The Revolution Beyond Race

There are many things to criticize in SNCC. Though it has fashioned a formidable apparatus since that day when Jim Forman walked into a deserted, windowless cubby and found a month's mail strewn on the floor, it is still not scrupulously well-organized; letters may go unanswered, phone calls go unreturned, meetings start late or never or without agendas. It is so quick to act that it often does not stop and plan actions carefully to get the most value from them. It does not take enough time to work out long-range strategy. It is not groomed in the niceties of public relations, and visitors to the Atlanta office sometimes complain of an indifferent reception. It exasperates its friends almost as often as it harasses its enemies.

But the young people in SNCC have two crucial qualities which override everything else. First, they are as compassionate and as brave as human beings with human failings can be, and they form a ragged, incorruptible front line in the struggle to abolish racism in the United States. And second, they nurture a vision of a revolution beyond race, against other forms of injustice, challenging the entire value-system of the nation and of smug middle-class society everywhere.

This vision beyond race is dimly and unevenly perceived by the people in SNCC, and there is much uncertainty about the specifics. Perhaps I am speaking of an emotional force more than anything else, born in that terrible and special anguish with which youth discovers evil in the world. But the emotion is informed by a rough intelligence that comes somewhat from reading, more from thinking, and most from living inside the marrow of the nation's shame. SNCC's radicalism has the advantage of being free from dogma and tradition, uncluttered by clichés, seeing the world afresh with the eyes of a new generation.

Because of this, perhaps, there has been a nervousness in high places ever since the Negro revolt began—an anxiety over how far it would go and sporadic moves to contain it before it becomes dangerous. This does not come out of a conspiratorial plot by hobgoblins of reaction; it springs with more or less spontaneity out of the historic American tendency towards moderation whenever there is a forward thrust of social change. And it comes from liberals as often as from conservatives. The compass needle of the civil rights movement flutters, and every once in a while it settles in a direction which awakens tremors in the pilots themselves.

The anxiety in those who read John Lewis' original speech the day of the Washington March is an example of this. Omitted in the altered version of Lewis' speech was the following passage:

> We all recognize the fact that if any radical social, political and economic changes are to take place in our society, the people, the masses must bring them about. In the struggle we must seek more than mere civil rights; we must work for the community of love, peace, and true brotherhood. Our minds, souls, and hearts cannot rest until freedom and justice exist for *all the people.*

Lewis was not speaking only of sandwiches in a lunch counter or even of the right of black men and women to vote and hold office in Mississippi. He was speaking of something more than sit-ins, Freedom Rides, and the problem of black and white. For the current crisis in race has exposed all sorts of fundamental issues in American society, almost as the search for a solitary tumor may lay open to examination all of a patient's vital organs.

I want to take note of some of these issues, because it seems to me that, in the end, whether SNCC will continue as a vital force in American life will depend on whether it thrusts and points beyond race, probing the entire fabric of society to point to injustice of all kinds, constituting itself as a permanent, restless prod to the conscience of the nation.

There is, for instance, the problem of politics and power in the United States, with implications for political systems everywhere. We have learned something, these past few years, about the inadequacy of our regular political structure to bring about desirable social change in a situation of urgency. Political scientists have worried for some time about the sluggishness of our political system, but the outburst of Negro demonstrations dramatized this problem as nothing else has been able to do. When people turn in desperation to marches and parades, picketing, sit-ins, mass meetings, and Freedom Rides, this suggests that the normal channels of government are inadequate for the expression of their grievances, and that the mechanism for solution is rusty.

If there are any doubts about this rustiness, one has only to look at Congress today. Its ineffectualness goes beyond civil rights to poverty and waste in the American economy, to antiquated approaches in the field of foreign policy. It seems the hardest thing in the world to get the supreme legislative body of the world's most powerful nation to move. Congress spends huge amounts of time on petty subjects; rushes past matters of life-and-death importance; filibusters and delays on the most clear-cut matters of human rights. Each day it appears more obviously as a swamp in which vital legislation is dutifully set down, only to be drowned in parliamentary mud or lost in a verbal mist.

There are many structural defects in Congress: the duplication of work by both houses, the seniority system in committees, the filibuster in the Senate, the dictatorship of the

House Rules Committee, the under-representation of urban areas, of the poor, of Negroes, of radicals. We are a complex and heterogeneous nation, but our "representatives" fall mostly inside a narrow band of middle-class business and professional men who balk at bold social reform.

Yet the real problem is greater. For an even more accurate representation of the population would still leave a basic flaw, one that is unavoidably part of representative government everywhere, all the time. This is the permanent paradox of politics: that delegates—whether Congressmen supposed to represent a district, or trade union officials speaking for laboring men, or Communist Party members purporting to represent the working class—develop interests of their own the moment they step out of their constituency into office. The environment of a man changes the moment he becomes a representative; the forces acting upon him become different; now, competing with the far-off calls of his constituents, which become weaker as they draw less response, is the more urgent call from within of ambition and power.

When James Madison was trying to convince New Yorkers to ratify the Constitution, in Federalist Paper # 10, he praised the representative system of government as a way of filtering out the grievances and moderating the demands of the masses. Rousseau also saw this, disliked it, and so wanted to establish some form of direct democracy, where the "general will" of the people might rule, without intermediaries. Beyond the level of the town meeting, however, in the complex nations of today, such continuous direct rule becomes impossible. Yet we have recently been shown an approximate solution: this is for people to retain always, and to use constantly, the power of demonstration—or what SNCC calls "direct action" —to bring the demands of aggrieved people before the leaders of government, with a minimum of turmoil and a maximum of insistence.

Representative government dilutes demand. This becomes especially onerous in a time that requires drastic reappraisals in economic policy, civil rights, and foreign relations. At such a time, the system set up by our forefathers and sweetened mildly over the years becomes a drag on national progress. Problems today have the kind of urgency that cannot be handled by writing a letter to one's Congressman. In a time when world destruction can proceed with the push of a button, one cannot wait to communicate with government by voting in the next election.

What the civil rights movement has revealed is that it is necessary for a people concerned with liberty, even if they live in an approximately democratic state, to create a political power which resides *outside* the regular political establishment. While outside, removed from the enticements of office and close to those sources of human distress which created it, this power can use a thousand different devices to persuade and pressure the official structure into recognizing its needs.

Direct action, we are beginning to suspect, will need to be kept as a perpetual form of popular expression, because *any* political system breeds ambition, any political leadership develops a primary aim of self-perpetuation. Today, in the presence of the giant state everywhere in the world, nonviolent direct action may be the only alternative to both the bloody futility of civil war, and the ineptitude of parliamentary procedure. It may, in fact, be the last true resort of democracy, which in this way would constantly renew itself with transfusions of indignation.

But how nonviolent is "nonviolent direct action"? When SNCC was formed at the Raleigh Conference in April, 1960, it adopted a credo which still stands as the official expression of its views:

> We affirm the philosophical or religious ideal of nonviolence as the foundation of our purpose, the presupposition of our

> faith, and the manner of our action. . . . Love is the central motif of nonviolence. . . . Such love goes to the extreme; it remains loving and forgiving even in the midst of hostility. It matches the capacity of evil to inflict suffering with an even more enduring capacity to absorb evil, all the while persisting in love.
>
> By appealing to conscience and standing on the moral nature of human existence, nonviolence nurtures the atmosphere in which reconciliation and justice become actual possibilities.

Today, SNCC's view of nonviolence is more complicated than that simple statement of faith in the power of love. Although there are some in the organization who would hold to that original credo without qualification, most SNCC people, in different degree and with a great individuality of response, would probably deny that love, conscience, and morality alone could end segregation.

The actions of SNCC in the last four years have in themselves fashioned a more complex attitude towards nonviolence than is shown in the Raleigh resolution. Not that SNCC has adopted violence, or has even considered adopting violent tactics. But between the use of violence and complete reliance on moral suasion, there is a vast range of possibilities within which the thoughts and actions of SNCC people fluctuate.

For one thing, demonstrations inescapably take the risk of violence. This violence is almost always directed at the demonstrators, either by police with clubs and cattle prods, or by white fanatics using guns, bombs, and a variety of other weapons of assault. (The only exception to this one-way violence has been the occasional rock or bottle throwing by Negroes not in SNCC during high-tension situations of the past few years.) While the SNCC people are never perpetrators of this violence, but the victims of it, there is no getting away from the fact that if demonstrative activity is undertaken, violence is always a possible result.

Newspapermen have on one or two occasions claimed that SNCC people were turning to violence, but the most evidence that could be put together was that John Lewis was once seen to twist his body vigorously in the grip of policemen, and on another occasion a SNCC girl, in the midst of rough handling by police, lost her temper and kicked a policeman.

Despite the purism of the Raleigh resolution, it has become quite clear that the desegregation of restaurants and other public accommodations usually comes from touching the proprietor's pocketbook, not his conscience. An argument could be made that sit-ins, boycotts, etc., appeal to the conscience of the public, and that this has an effect on the situation. Still, it seems in most cases to be pressure, rather than love, that opens a public facility to Negroes. True, this is not violence, but we seem here to be operating in that large middle ground between pure force and pure moral appeal, and this is the real meaning of nonviolent direct action for the civil rights movement.

The recent calls by Malcolm X and others for Negroes to use self-defense, and even retaliation, against acts of violence by whites, have not found approval by the SNCC organization. Yet individual SNCC members have sometimes expressed sympathy for this position. A more moderate attitude was expressed with near-unanimity in an informal discussion among SNCC leaders early in 1964: that they would not stop a Negro farmer in Mississippi from arming himself to defend his home against attack.

It should be recalled that the Raleigh statement of SNCC was made on the basis of experience in Nashville, Atlanta, and other border and upper-South areas. The plunge into Alabama, Mississippi, and Southwest Georgia, first in the Freedom Rides and then in the prolonged voter registration campaign, disclosed a different kind of situation, where the usual techniques of nonviolent direct action were simply crushed by police power. The devices that had proved effective elsewhere met with a variety of reprisals from brutal beatings to murder. These experiences have led SNCC to ask the national government to intervene in the Deep South, using not love but the power of arrest and imprisonment to stop brutality and violence against civil rights workers by police and private persons.

We see, therefore, that experience itself has brought certain qualifications to the pure notion of "nonviolence": that the search for justice must continue even if it draws violence against the seeker; that economic and other pressures may be more decisive than moral suasion to bring about social change; that SNCC cannot oppose the use of self-defense by other people whose lives are in danger; that the power of the national government needs to be used with vigor to clear the way for nonviolent demonstrative activity in the Deep South.

Members of SNCC—and indeed of the whole civil rights movement—have faced in action that dilemma which confounds man in society: that he cannot always have both peace and justice. To insist on perfect tranquility with an absolute rejection of violence may mean surrendering the right to change an unjust social order. On the other hand, to seek justice *at any cost* may result in bloodshed so great that its evil overshadows everything else and splatters the goal beyond recognition. The problem is to weigh carefully the alternatives, so as to achieve the maximum of social progress with a minimum of pain. Society has been guilty of much quick and careless weighing in the past: on the one hand, it has conducted the most horrible of wars for goals that were dubious to begin with or were soon lost in the clamor of victory; on the other hand, it has permitted the most monstrous injustices which it might have eliminated with a bit of trouble.

Every new situation brings a new weighing of alternatives. If the national government should *not* use its overwhelming power to bring the rule of the United States Constitution to Mississippi, and if unmitigated violence continues there against local Negroes and civil rights workers, it may take a new set of daring and imaginative tactics to deal with terror in the Black Belt.

SNCC's stress on nonviolence—even if couched in absolutist language which does not correspond with reality, and does not take into consideration the weighing process involved—is healthy. It is a reminder to a violent world that man has been too quick to reach for the sword in the past, that we have a devilish capacity to invent the noblest of reasons for mass slaughter. At the same time, SNCC's insistence on the use of pressure—the willingness to depart in a small way from an absolutist position in order to make important changes in society—is a valuable counter to complacency.

There is another issue, beyond the race question, which is illumined by the civil rights struggle: the problem of free expression in the United States. We have always assumed, because the First Amendment contains guarantees for freedom of speech and press and peaceful assembly, that these are an iron-bound fact of national life. But those who have subjected the Bill of Rights to severe test have often ended up in concentration camps or jails: the pacifists during World War I, the Japanese during World War II, the Jehovah's Witnesses in small towns all over the country, the Communists during the Cold War. Radicals and extremists were so small a minority that they could be safely put away without any nationwide burst of outrage. The rest of the country remained free mainly because it remained silent, or, when it spoke, stayed within acceptable limits.

Restrictions on free expression go beyond the closed societies of the Black Belt. The spread of civil rights protests all over the nation revealed that police forces everywhere stand as a permanent obstacle to the rights of petition and peaceful assembly. We are now learning that what is true in the South is also true, to a lesser extent, all over the country, that the guarantees of the Bill of Rights are often in the hands of the policeman, and that the national government offers the individual no effective protection against local abuse of the Constitution.

We have learned also, in the past few years, a good deal about jails, judges, and justice. Not since Dorothea Dix investigated the jails of Massachusetts over a hundred years ago has there been such an opportunity to study penal conditions. With students, ministers, college professors, and distinguished society ladies taken off to prison in civil rights demonstrations, we may now listen, as we never listened to the pleas of ordinary, unknown prisoners. Thousands of involuntary inspectors have become aware suddenly that police brutality, jailhouse beatings, detention without hearing or trial, have been a permanent feature of our system of justice. Out of it all we may learn that jails are cruel and simplistic means of solving complex social problems.

All of these people, through the civil rights demonstrations, have learned about bail bonds, trial procedures, and the absolute power of the judge over everyone in his courtroom. Danny Mitchell, a CORE worker in the South who continued his activity when he returned to Syracuse University, wrote to me in the fall of 1963:

> Yesterday, we went to court for the first session of our trial. I stood in the back of the courtroom and watched a tall, white-haired judge enter. He sat under a sign reading: "IN GOD WE TRUST." My immediate reaction was that here was a man, educated in the law, living in a nice quiet section of town, who probably never walked through the Fifteenth Ward (the dismal swamp adjacent to the University). He, like so many others, lived in a Romance. And there he sat . . . playing God!

It is also possible now to make a national issue over the fact that the rich get a different kind of justice than the poor; that for lack of $20 a man may stay in prison for months on some petty charge; that not only color, but also wealth, determines whether a man goes free or to jail.

It was inevitable that at some point the civil rights movement, like any other militant American reform movement of modern times, would need to confront charges of Communism or exhortations to act cautiously in order to avoid charges of Communism. The direct accusations come in flagrant form from members of Southern officialdom who, like Sheriff Jim Clark in Selma, see the whole movement as a gigantic international Communist conspiracy. Or they come from middle-of-the-road Americans who are concerned about civil rights but worried lest these rights become a springboard for Communist activity. Sometimes they come from civil rights organizations themselves, whose leaders may scrupulously inspect their own and neighboring groups to make sure no Communists, or former Communists, or near-Communists, or suspected Communists, exist to provide targets for the racist enemy.

The approach thus far shown by SNCC, though it is complex and varies from one person to another, seems to be that individuals within SNCC will be judged on the basis of their contribution to the movement, and not on their political ideas. Bob Moses, speaking at a SNCC conference in the fall of 1963, addressed himself to an article by Theodore White in *Life,* in which White, without citing evidence, referred accusingly to a "penetration" of SNCC "by unidentified elements." Moses said:

> I think we have to, as an organization, come to the point where in policy and in public we take an absolute stand on the right of people to associate with whom they choose.... It seems to me that . . .we have to throw what little weight we have on the side of free association and on the side of autonomy within our group to pick and choose those people whom

> we will work with, on relevant criteria, and one of the criteria which is not relevant is their past political associations. And what we have to decide then is if the people who are genuinely concerned with what we are about to do . . . if we put our cards on the table and we discuss openly what it is that we're about then I don't see how it is that these people can somehow subvert what we're doing.

In January, 1963, a writer in the *Manchester Guardian* noted an attempt by Southern segregationists to get the House Committee on Un-American Activities to investigate SNCC. "Deviously and subtly," he wrote, "the idea is being sown in the receptive minds of some senators, that there *must* be some Reds in *so* militant an organization." The students themselves, he reported, "held a frank discussion of their political commitments during their rally in Nashville. They concluded that the organization had none, and that the Communists could make no use of it as long as they were true to their aims."

There is no evidence that there are indeed Communists in SNCC. The organization is rather a heterogeneous collection of young people with various ideas, many of them radical, but not tied to a political organization or a frozen dogma. Theirs is a healthy and independent radicalism. As Sherrod said, in one very candid discussion of the problem: "I'm going head-on into this stuff. I don't care who the heck it is—if he's willing to come down on the front lines and bring his body along with me to die— then he's welcome!"

In the course of that discussion, one SNCC worker said other organizations have criteria for exclusion, and one of them should be membership in the Communist Party. One or two other people agreed, saying it was a practical problem of survival of the organization. But most of the people in the discussion agreed with the SNCC worker who said: "I don't feel that we as a minority group fighting for the right to freely speak and think can take such a position."

With the criterion of *relevancy,* perhaps the SNCC

people will move far beyond race to a libertarian frontier which few reform movements in this country have approached. And that is to break down the idea of categorizing people, of depersonalizing them by reducing them to no more than members in a group. This requires a profound concern for every person to be treated as an individual, regardless of race, or nation, or whatever. For such arbitrary groupings can only approximate—and sometimes seriously distort—the qualities of a single human being.

It was not the Negro revolt that brought *poverty* to national attention. The statistics on unemployment, the conditions in Appalachia, the cries of distress from here and there, the studies of Michael Harrington and Leon Keyserling—these had their own impact, and ordinarily would bring some moderate economic reform, for such is the American tradition. What the civil rights movement has done is to bring into question whether perhaps we need a fundamental restructuring of the economic system in the United States, a change beyond Fair Deals and New Deals and other temporary aids.

Part of the impetus for radical thinking about economics comes simply from the fact that the reforms of the past have not affected the Negro's position at the bottom of the economic barrel. He still gets one-half of the average white person's wage throughout the country, and only one-third of what the white gets in the South. As poor as anyone else is, the Negro is always poorer. Hence there is a bitterness, an anger, that generates demands for more than mild reform. Frank Smith of SNCC talks about its helping to bring about "revolutionary" changes in society: "You know why we became SNCC? We were barefoot, hungry, dirty—and we were mad!"

The Negro in the Deep South, battling for the right to vote and looking North, where his people *can* vote, and are still poor, begins to wonder: can we end the Negro's poverty without some radical overhaul of the economy—without ending poverty for everyone? It is one thing, as Bayard Rustin has pointed out, to ask for a table in a cafeteria, or a seat on a bus; there are enough of those to go around. But North as well as South, when one asks for jobs, or decent homes, or new schools, it is not a matter of gaining access; there are *not* enough of those to go around. The only way the Negro can acquire a reasonable measure of *these* resources is for the entire nation to make them available for all deprived people—black and white. "Until there is a planned economy," Rustin has told SNCC people, "these problems cannot be solved."

The paradox is blunt. This country is tremendously wealthy in its natural resources; it has more than enough of certain things (automobiles, highways, office buildings, speed-boats, all the appurtenances of wealth) and not enough of other things (schools, hospitals, food, housing, medical care). The problem is not production, but rational organization and equitable distribution. And this seems to require national economic planning on the basis of public need rather than private profit. SNCC people at an economic conference in Washington on Thanksgiving weekend, 1963, applauded enthusiastically when AFL-CIO official Jack Conway spoke of "democratic central planning" and said that the expectations of America's poor could not be met "without a profound reorganization of our politics, our government, and our economy."

Martin Luther King, Jr., in some of his lesser known sermons (as Staughton Lynd has brought to our attention), has been sharply critical of the American economic arrangement, of "our unswerving devotion to monopolistic capitalism." King notes, as have so many of the younger civil rights leaders, the maldistribution of wealth in the United States:

> Our nation's productive machinery constantly brings forth such an abundance of food that we must build larger barns and spend more than a million dollars daily to store our surplus. . . . What can we do? Again the answer is simple: We can store our surplus food free of charge in the shriveled

stomachs of the millions of God's children who go to bed hungry at night.

The sit-ins stimulated, among other things, a rethinking about the sanctity of "private property"; the debate over the public accommodations section of the Civil Rights Bill has called the issue to widespread attention. The implications go far beyond race, to a fundamental fact about the national economy: that the slogan "private property" has long disguised the fact that so-called *private* enterprises drastically affect the public interest, and the public therefore has a right to make certain demands upon them.

A restaurant, the Negro revolt has reminded us, may be privately owned, but it is publicly used. It is private in one way, public in another. The Negro is not intruding on that aspect of it which is private—he is not demanding admission to ownership. He is insistent that in that aspect of it which is public he has certain fundamental rights.

Does this not go also for the manufacture of vital goods—like drugs for instance, where the sanctity of "private" property has enabled manufacturers to make incredible profits (as the Kefauver Committee hearings showed a few years ago)—out of people's desperate medical needs? Is television a *private* matter because private businesses own the television stations and advertise their products? Is the design of automobiles a purely *private* matter when the refusal of manufacturers to eliminate certain structural features contributes to the loss of thousands of lives a year?

In other words, it is just possible that the civil rights movement may lead us to re-examine our concern for "private" property, and to redefine what is private and what is public.

Early in 1964, a distinguished group of public figures (Gerard Piel, Linus Pauling, Norman Thomas, Robert Heilbroner, W. H. Ferry, and twenty-nine others) drew up a memorandum entitled *The Triple Revolution,* which they addressed to President Lyndon Johnson and to the nation. In it they wrote:

> The demand of the civil rights movement cannot be fulfilled within the present context of society. . . . There is an urgent need for a fundamental change in the mechanisms employed to insure consumer rights. . . . We urge, therefore, that society, through its appropriate legal and governmental institutions, undertake an unqualified commitment to provide every individual and every family with an adequate income as a matter of right. . . . The unqualified right to an income would take the place of the patchwork of welfare measures—from unemployment insurance to relief—designed to ensure that no citizen or resident of the U.S. actually starves.

They were asking for democratic planning of the economy, for a guaranteed minimum income for every American. Public need, they said, should replace private profit as the major stimulus to production, as the chief determinant of what kinds of things society decided to create. At this point in American life the young militants of the Negro revolt are probably closest to pressing for such a program with the same kind of energy and imagination that have gone into the civil rights upsurge.

Almost as soon as SNCC came into being, the first signs of an upheaval in the American college became apparent. Until the sit-in movement, college students in the United States were the silent generation, the unconcerned, the cynical, the ambition-ridden, the imbibers of middle-class pretense. With the formation of SNCC came the first break from this, small in the numbers immediately affected, but large in the psychological impact on others. In the beginning, it was a handful who left school. As Forman put it: "Sixteen cats in 1961 decided it would be good if a small group devoted itself full time to the movement." By 1963, hundreds of young people began to leave colleges in various parts of the country, for a summer, a semester, a year, or permanently, to work in the Deep South.

These departures from the academic community are not only the result of a new-found commitment to a specific cause; they represent a revolt against the whole value-structure of American education today—a new, profound seeking for life's meaning. A nineteen-year-old white student from California, ready to join SNCC in the South, wrote:

> A relatively short time ago I began to awake after at least an eighteen-year sleep. . . . I have said *no* to almost all of my past. . . . One influencing factor has been my reading. . . . Perhaps what profoundly influenced me, what made me make a decision . . . was the present Negro revolt. I could have so easily and tragically slipped through life and never really experienced life. I needed the Negro revolt to make me reflect, question, examine, probe a little deeper—in fact a great deal deeper . . . as the student or citizen begins to become conscious that he is immediately at odds with society instead of becoming a packaged good citizen.
>
> Certainly . . . the University is not much different than a giant marketplace of mediocrity, an extension of a corrupt, warped, illusion-ridden, over-commercial, superficial society, which categorizes in neat semester packages "knowledge"; whose basic purpose seems to be turning out students to be good citizens—dead, unconscious automatons in our hysterically consuming society. It gives pat answers where there is ambiguity, certainty where there is uncertainty. . . . I want to work in the South as this seems to be the most radical (to the core), crucial, and important place to begin to try and enlarge the freedom of humanity. The problem is a door open to me and cries out for me to come through.

The young people who leave college to join the movement have not deserted education. In an important sense, they are getting the best education in the country today. Those students who stay in college, beleaguered by transcripts, grades, credits, and graduate record exams, are the ones whose education is limited. Once the student is out "in the field," the contrast becomes even sharper. For a young person going through the intense learning experience of a direct clash with the entrenched social structure, to sit in a classroom seems pallid and unrewarding.

But the issue is not as clear-cut as that. Once out in the field, the student *misses* intense reading, intellectual discussions, the classroom exchange (perhaps the campus becomes romanticized when one is trying to find a comfortable position on an iron cot in Greenville, Mississippi). Knowing that the college is divorced from the reality of social struggle, and also that the struggle itself does not quite feed his intellectual appetites, each student solves his problem in his own way. He or she may totally withdraw from college, or regretfully return after a year or two in the field, or go through a painful mental tug-of-war, zigzagging back and forth from the movement to the campus, unable to decide.

The few hundred students—white and Negro—who have rebelled against the social neutrality of the American college system by deserting it, either temporarily or permanently, represent, I believe, only the visible part of an iceberg of discontent which chills the millions of other students who remain in school. These others don't express their dissatisfaction by joining the civil rights movement. Some of them simply bury their feelings in the folderol of fraternities or sororities; others find excuses for leaving school; others go through the ritual and graduate, but they couldn't care less.

Most of those troubled students don't even know why they are dissatisfied. But it may very well be that, deep in the consciousness of a number of them, is the thought that higher education is divorced from the life-or-death problems of this century, that colleges play with social issues, examine them at a distance, talk endlessly about them, but never *live* with them.

Among the five million white students in the nation, the effect of the civil rights drama has been complex: many react as they do to their classes, with a combination of boredom and annoyance, impatient to get out in the real world of credit cards, a comfortable income, and a shrewd marriage. For many others, the movement has had the faint scent of forbidden fruit, enticing, but distant and unknowable.

But for a handful, the heavens suddenly lit up and the stars changed their positions; these few were catapulted, by the emotional force of the movement and the passion of their own response, out of the safe world of college education and into a new sphere of danger, commitment and promise. With each month, more and more white students become involved, either partially, on their campuses, or totally, hurling themselves into the most tense trouble areas of the Deep South.

SNCC itself is making attempts to meet the dilemma of field work versus academic education. For one thing, it is beginning to turn its attention again—after several years of neglect—to the college campuses from which it sprang in 1960, to salt these campuses with its own veterans, to make of them permanent sources from which the civil rights movement can be freshened with new recruits.

In a parallel move, SNCC is attempting one of the most exciting ventures in contemporary education. With financial help from foundations, and cooperation from a few Southern Negro colleges, it is trying to develop a series of work-study programs, in which a small group of college students will leave the campus for a year to work in the movement, combining this with lectures and discussions, constituting itself a kind of seminar-in-the-field.

Also, the hundred and fifty or so SNCC staff members may soon be able to continue their studies by an internal educational program designed specifically for field people, combining short periods at educational centers with reading assignments the year round. All of this, hopefully, may begin to cause some turbulence in the ordered atmosphere of the academic world, and to set many of us to thinking, not only about society, but about the proper role of education in it.

To move beyond race means to accept the fact that black men are as capable of inhumanity and power-seeking and injustice as are white men, that, in a rational division on the basis of the just and the unjust, Negroes and whites would fall on both sides of the line. People in SNCC discovered this quickly, because as soon as they began demonstrating, they ran into entrenched conservatism, first in a number of the Negro colleges, then in Negro communities. And in unhesitatingly battling the old Negro leadership, at the same time that they were rebelling against the white power-holders in the South, they pointed the way to a race-less society.

The Negro college is a fascinating paradox. On the one hand, it has produced many of the new leaders of the civil rights crusade; on the other hand, it has done this unwittingly, and with varying degrees of resistance. The militant students coming out of the Negro colleges have had to vault over the century-long traditions of conservatism and obsequiousness which pervade many of these campuses.

It would be wrong to generalize, for in a few of the Negro colleges the presidents are forward-looking and have supported the movement vigorously. But too many still match the unforgettable picture given in the opening chapters of Ralph Ellison's *The Invisible Man.* Staughton Lynd and Bobbi Yancy have described it, in the magazine *Dissent*, as follows:

> The setting and the cast will be found all over the South: the beautiful fragrant campus with its imposing buildings; the patronizing white trustee, anxious to feel sure that his

> money is well spent; the Negro college president, unctuous in chapel, overbearing to students, deferential to donors; finally the student, eager to succeed on the terms agreed to by parents, teachers, and the mass media, but obscurely aware that some larger possibility is being forfeited.

The expulsion of students at Southern University, the intimidation of students and the dismissal of faculty at Spelman College, the faculty firings at Benedict and Allen Colleges, the repression at Alabama State—these brought the more active students into immediate conflict with Negro college presidents, and provided early instruction on the mythology of race. Saunders Redding, who had gone through the experience himself, spoke of "presidential contempt" for the students at Negro colleges, and how this led students to believe in "the infallibility of the dictatorship principle." What has happened these last few years is that these students have raised a simultaneous rebellion against dictatorship in both races.

As black and white students mingle in the movement and compare experiences they learn, somewhat to their surprise, that both white and Negro colleges suffer from the same disabilities: pallid middle-class ambitions connected with money and prestige, a condescendingly paternal attitude towards students by administrators and faculty standing on their piles of degrees, the hierarchy of authority which puts huge power in the hands of college administrators, the consequent restrictions on the academic freedom of both faculty and students. That these qualities are exaggerated in Southern Negro colleges (and in Southern white colleges) is due to the fact, easily overlooked, that they are products of a segregated society.

As the rebelling students left college and began working with the Negro community, they found that once again they were engaged in a double battle, which carried them beyond the race question. Perhaps SNCC, being the youngest and most militant of the organizations, having come into conflict most often with the Negro Establishment itself, is therefore in a particularly good position to demolish the frauds and foibles of race-consciousness.

That quality in SNCC which may be of the most profound importance to the rest of America is the one most difficult to define. For one thing, it is a renunciation, without the pretense of martyrdom, of the fraud and glitter of a distorted prosperity. It is also a recapturing from some time and place long forgotten of an emotional approach to life, aiming, beyond politics and economics, simply to remove the barriers that prevent human beings from making contact with one another.

The most obvious contribution of SNCC has been to move boldly into the center of danger and, while taking blows, enduring pain and poverty, leaving family and friends behind, to force the nation to look at itself. Among civil rights organizations, it has remained unique in its youth, its willingness to immerse itself in the black communities of the Deep South, its distance from the circles of official power.

Different from the old abolitionists in its predominantly Negro character, its greater reliance on action than words, its working from within the source of the evil rather than berating it from the outside, SNCC retains the essence of what made for greatness in Garrison, Phillips, and their contemporaries. This is the recognition that agitation, however it offends one's friends and creates temporary strife, is indispensable to social progress as a way of breaking through an otherwise frozen status quo.

Perhaps SNCC's most important achievement has been its role as a stimulant to Negroes—young and old—in the Black Belt, who have been encouraged to break through the long years of surface quiescence and create a new local leadership in dozens of communities of the Deep South. Thus, not only are expectations created which, once awakened, will not die, but the basis for fulfilling these expectations is taking root.

It might be useful now to ask some questions about the future of SNCC:

One of them is whether SNCC can, without losing its spontaneity, its fervor, its unconcern with respectability, develop more sophisticated tactics as situations change. True, even unplanned demonstrations with muddied objectives have a healthy effect in simply bringing the indignation of the aggrieved to the attention of the comfortable. But also, by pouring out huge sacrifices for small victories, they can drain the Negro community. Demonstrative activities in the future should be more carefully worked out, coordinated with legal moves and with negotiations, in order to get the most from them. Wit and muscle need to be joined so as to make the maximum of progress with the minimum of pain. Pressure may be needed to break impasses, but SNCC's commitment to *winning over people* remains valid as that ultimate goal, without which progress cannot be fastened into permanence.

It will be interesting to see how successful SNCC will be in adjusting its tactics to correspond to the different situations and stages in the civil rights struggle. There is first the absolutely silent Negro community which needs to be awakened; here, the SNCC youngsters have done marvelous work. With the awakening, there begins a series of pushes against the closed door, by demonstrative activity of all kinds, bringing economic, political, and moral pressure against the old order to break down both legal and extra-legal segregation. This has been done with much success in some states: in Nashville, Atlanta, Charlotte, Memphis, Louisville, etc. In other areas this hasn't worked, because the door is not simply closed —it is locked, and the movement has battered itself bloody trying to budge it. This has been SNCC's experience in Mississippi, Alabama, and Southwest Georgia; it led SNCC, hoping to limit the sacrifice, to ask that the key of federal power be used to open the locked door. So far, the federal government has been reluctant not only to use the key, but also to admit that it possesses one.

What SNCC has not yet had to face on a large scale is what happens when the door, whether locked by the police statism of the Deep South, or closed by the segregationists of the Upper South, is finally opened. Then, as CORE and other groups have found in the cities of the north, one moves finally into the previously barred room only to find that most of the furniture is occupied and the only place to sit is on the floor. And SNCC will soon encounter this, because more and more Atlanta and Nashville will become like New York and Chicago (as will Jackson, Mississippi, one day). And at that point its radicalism, which easily expiates itself as heroism in the battle-spots of the Deep South, will face profound questions of social strategy: how to deal with problems like unemployment, job discrimination, bad housing, poor schools, which can be ameliorated but not solved by picket lines.

So long as there exist poverty, unemployment, slums, and inadequate schools in the United States, the Negroes will have a disproportionate share of them, and even a *proportionate* share of them is intolerable in a nation with such splendid economic potential. Civil rights groups, then, may begin to argue for a planned American economy. Such a reorganization of national wealth should be on the basis of justice rather than either luck or "ability"—which in our culture is too often defined as the ability to make money.

Among the more exciting possibilities in the development of SNCC these next few years is the creation of a new populism in the South, linking black and white people on the basis of common interests. At this point, it is little more than a dream. But what *has* taken place in the past year is that the original handful of white Southern students in SNCC—Jane Stembridge, Bob Zellner, Sam Shirah, Sandra Hayden—shows signs of a spectacular increase. Hundreds of white Southern-born students at Southern colleges have begun to take part in the civil rights movement, from attending meetings to walking on picket lines. At a SNCC Executive Committee meeting in Atlanta in early 1964, twenty-five Southern white students suddenly appeared, already organized, ready to go back to their colleges and universities throughout the South. They expect to build upon the growing belief among young white Southerners in racial equality, as well as to constitute themselves a radical spearhead on other social issues.

If this nucleus can do as SNCC did, first gather support in the colleges, and then move into the white communities, this will be the boldest move yet to attack the race problem in the South. Perhaps more important than anything else will be the *example* of white and Negro students working together, creating those situations of intimate contact which choke out prejudice.

Among other speculations about the future of SNCC is whether it will fulfill a promise it now contains in blurred form: to recognize that there are other supreme human values, along with that of racial equality, which deserve attention. For *any* society, whether totally white, or totally black, or perfectly mixed, can be controlled by an elite of power, can ignore the most wretched poverty, can destroy the right of protest, can engage in the mass murder of war.

Perhaps such a promise is not for SNCC alone to make good but for all of us, since the entire nation, shaken by the civil rights movement, has been granted a moment of grace in which to reflect on its past and its future. The history of our country—and indeed of all countries—seems to be a kind of stumbling through the darkness, continually banging into the furniture of the universe, and able to tell where we have been only by counting our bruises. In times of social disorder, however, there are moments of illumination when it becomes possible to see not only the problem at hand, but beyond it. Almost always, no one is ready; the flash comes, we blink and gasp, and then the darkness closes in again after we have been able to see our way for one step further, but no more.

Now, in the 1960's, in the United States, the terrain is lit up for a brief historic moment by the storm of the Negro revolt. We can, as in reform movements of the past, take one step forward, and then wait for the next flash of upheaval. Or we can take this opportunity to look hard, not only deep inside the race question, but beyond it, to other issues of justice and freedom.

12. An Independent Radicalism

In early June, 1964, twenty-five black Mississippians climbed into a bus and travelled a thousand miles to Washington, D.C. Their purpose was to warn the Federal government of impending danger; to ask for protection for themselves and the seven hundred Northern college students who were going to spend the summer in Mississippi.

The President was out of town, delivering a Commencement Address, and the Attorney General was unavailable. From the stage of the National Theatre, a short walk from the White House, the delegation from Mississippi addressed themselves to several hundred citizens sitting in the audience, to a "jury" of distinguished writers and educators, and to the television cameras. What they told that day, in dozens of variations, was a story of police brutality and intimidation, of complaints to the F.B.I. and the Justice Department, and of no help.

Mrs. Fannie Lou Hamer told of her beating in Winona and Mrs. Louis Allen of the shotgun murder of her husband outside her home. A fourteen-year-old boy told of being kicked and slapped by police, and of how he first "got started." "One day I was just standing on the street, watching a demonstration. The police came. They said, 'All you niggers move.' One hit me in the stomach with a club. I said 'OOMP!' And I joined the movement."

Jimmy Travis of SNCC told how he was shot, almost fatally, just outside of Greenwood. Asked for suggestions on what might be done to help, he replied: "We need federal marshals to be sent down this summer."

A parade of constitutional lawyers came to the stand and testified about the powers of the Federal government to protect citizens against attack on their constitutional rights. Professor Robert J. Harris of the University of Michigan Law School quoted at length from an 1880 decision, *Ex parte Siebold,* in which the Supreme Court affirmed that the national government could execute its laws "on every foot of American soil." How many marshals should be sent to Mississippi for the summer, he was asked? "I don't think you could have too many."

William Higgs, Mississippi's lawyer-in-exile, tall, blond, soft-speaking, hard-hitting, came to the microphone. He pointed to the different treatment by federal authorities of a bank robber and a brutal policeman, though both were violating federal law, and noted the F.B.I.'s power, by statute, to make arrests. He was asked if he was not contradicting the Attorney General of the United States, who had said the F.B.I. was just an investigative agency. Higgs replied: "I am."

The transcript of the day's testimony was sent to President Johnson and to Attorney General Kennedy. There was no response.

On June 21, 1964, exactly thirteen days after that plea to the President in Washington, James Chaney, an eighteen-year-old Negro from Meridian, Michael Schwerner, a twenty-five-year-old white CORE organizer in Meridian, and Andrew Goodman, twenty, a summer volunteer just arrived from the Oxford, Ohio, orientation session, disappeared in Neshoba County, Mississippi, after their arrest on a traffic charge by local police. The F.B.I. and the Justice Department responded with their usual slowness to civil rights workers' requests for help. This time, the delay turned out to be fatal. The F.B.I., notified at 10 P.M. that night about the disappearance of the three, did not show up in Philadelphia until almost twenty-four hours later.

With the Mississippi Summer Project about to begin, and the three still missing, COFO asked that the Federal government send marshals to protect Negroes and whites engaged in civil rights activity. Attorney General Kennedy, Deputy Attorney General Nicholas Katzenbach, and Assistant Attorney General Burke Marshall all pleaded a lack of constitutional authority under the American federal system. This prompted a group of distinguished law professors, headed by Professor Mark Howe of the Harvard Law School, to issue a statement reprimanding the Attorney General, and pointing to the government's powers in Sections 332 and 333, Title 10 of the U.S. Code. But no protection came.

In mid-August the bodies of the three young men were found, bullet holes in their chests, buried in a hastily-dug grave near Philadelphia, Mississippi. The body of James Chaney was mutilated by a beating so terrible that the pathologist who examined him said he had only seen such damage in high-velocity accidents such as airplane crashes.

Meanwhile, the Mississippi Summer Project had begun, an operation like nothing in the nation's history. Through the spring of 1964, college students from all over the country were being interviewed by SNCC and CORE. Seven hundred of them showed up at Oxford, Ohio, for an orientation session organized by the National Council of Churches. There, young veterans of the Black Belt tried to give them realistic pictures of the dangers they faced. They were taught how to protect themselves from injury without responding violently. They talked passionately about their own fears, their indecision, their dreams. Then they climbed into buses and cars and headed south.

The volunteers were mostly white, northern, middle-class. The staff people—mainly SNCC, some CORE, a few

SCLC—were generally Negro, Southern, sent by lower-class parents to Negro colleges, from which they darted off into the movement. Together, in clusters, they fanned out across Mississippi: to "easy" Northern towns like Holly Springs; to "tough" little cities in the Delta, like Clarksdale, Greenwood, Vicksburg, Indianola; to places on the Gulf Coast like Biloxi and Natchez; and to dozens of other spots throughout the state.

They lived, by ones and twos, in a room or a corner of a room, with a Negro family which had made the offering, most likely, at a mass meeting in the church, on a night when the "collection" was not of dimes and quarters, but of beds. Some flopped on cots, or on the floor, in a dilapidated, rented "Freedom House." By day they went out canvassing, door-to-door, in the Negro neighborhood, tramping through the mud and dust of unpaved streets, talking to fearful, friendly, curious people about registering to vote, or about sending their children to something called "freedom school."

The nerve center for all the summer activity was a long, narrow, store-front office, COFO headquarters in Jackson, where somehow, through a confusion of telephones, typewriters, and people moving in and out, contact was maintained with the projects throughout the state. Shifts of volunteers, twenty-four hours a day, manned the "WATS line" (Wide Area Telephone Service, a costly system which allowed unlimited long distance phone calls all over the state). On July 8, not an untypical day, a digest of the WATS line report read as follows:

McComb: SNCC Freedom House bombed; two injured.

Hattiesburg: The Rev. Robert Beech of the National Council of Churches arrested on false pretense charge after allegedly overdrawing his bank account $70. Bail set at $2000.

Ruleville: Volunteer bodily ejected from county circuit

clerk's office for accompanying local woman to voter registration.

COLUMBUS: Three volunteers arrested on trespass charges after stopping at a gas station for a soft drink.

CLARKSDALE: Bomb threat.

HATTIESBURG: Bottle thrown at picnic by passing car.

HOLLY SPRINGS: Civil rights worker arrested. Reckless driving.

CLARKSDALE: Police chief in LaFayette tells Negro cafes not to serve volunteers.

VICKSBURG: Bomb threat.

Multiplying this day by seventy (the approximate number of days of the summer project) would give at least a capsule picture of some of the difficulties.

But there was more to the summer. There were the seven hundred student volunteers, being toughened and educated in a way that no book-learning could accomplish. Also, several hundred Northern professional people—doctors, nurses, lawyers, ministers, teachers—spent time in Mississippi, a break from the pattern of summer vacations on the seashore or in the mountains. The doctors and nurses were part of a new phenomenon which seemed to grow up overnight, called the Medical Committee for Human Rights. It brought to Mississippi what Dr. Jack Geiger of Harvard University called a "sympathetic medical presence." As for the ministers, they were everywhere: on picket lines, in Freedom Houses, at mass meetings.

The lawyers formed an efficient corps such as had never been seen before in the civil rights troubles of this decade: they moved like basketball players from one trouble spot to another, getting people out of jail almost as fast as police put them in (perhaps the shadow of the Philadelphia Three lent urgency to their pace). William Kunstler, one of the legal mainstays of the movement these past five years, wrote after the summer about the changes wrought in those who go South:

> The transformation does not come overnight. I can still recall with shame my earnest recommendation to a brother attorney during the Freedom Rider trials that he not address our clients at a mass meeting. "A lawyer must remain aloof," I told him. . . . Three years later, I realized that I was playing a fool's game and that my advice was worse than worthless. No member of a great social movement can remain untouched by the forces that drive it. . . . The law did not change in Mississippi last summer, but the lawyers who journeyed there did.

The Mississippi Summer had an effect impossible to calculate on young Negroes in the State. Thousands of them wore SNCC buttons through the summer (one fifteen-year-old girl in Clarksdale was expelled from school in the fall because her button was "too big," the school authorities said; with the aid of a Radcliffe girl who had befriended her in the summer she got a scholarship to go to high school in Massachusetts). Around SNCC's summer office in Greenwood, and at all the other headquarters in the state, Negro youngsters gathered, following staff members like Pied Pipers through the streets. Freedom Schools sprang up like wildflowers all over Mississippi, until 2000 were attending over thirty schools. SNCC's Charlie Cobb had pursued the idea with quiet persistence as plans were being made for the 1964 summer, and Staughton Lynd, a young Yale historian, became administrator for the schools. At the Oxford orientation, Lynd warned the youngsters who were slated to be Freedom School teachers:

> You'll arrive in Ruleville, in the Delta. It will be 100 degrees, and you'll be sweaty and dirty. You won't be able to bathe often or sleep well or eat good food. The first day of school, there may be four teachers and three students.

> And the local Negro minister will phone to say you can't use his church basement after all, because his life has been threatened. And the curriculum we've drawn up—Negro history and American government—may be something you know only a little about yourself. Well, you'll knock on doors all day in the hot sun to find students. You'll meet on someone's lawn under a tree. You'll tear up the curriculum and teach what you know.

And that is how it was. By orthodox educational standards, the teachers were unqualified, the students were backward, and it was hard to point to concrete results. But nine-year-old Negro children sounded out French words whose English equivalents they had not yet discovered, and one group of youngsters struggled to understand *Portrait of the Artist as a Young Man* by James Joyce. They learned about Frederick Douglass, wrote letters to the local editor about segregation, and discussed the meaning of civil disobedience. Some wrote short stories about their lives, and others wrote poems.

The object of the Freedom School was not to cram a prescribed amount of factual material into young minds, but to give them that first look into new worlds which would, some day if not immediately, lead them to books and people and ideas not found in the everyday lives of Mississippi Negroes. They didn't always succeed, but even their failures were warmed by the affection that sprang up everywhere between teachers and students—both aware that they talked with one another inside a common cradle of concern.

One afternoon in Jackson, a visiting folk singer brought the students of a Freedom School out into the sun-baked street back of the church, formed them into a huge circle, and taught them an Israeli dance chant imploring the heavens for rain to help the harvest. Older Negroes passed by, sat on porches, listened to their children utter strange words and dance this strange dance. The young ones seemed to understand; they were beginning, for the first time in their lives, to reach beyond their street, beyond their state, to join in some universal plea.

A University of Chicago graduate student taught in Vicksburg:

> It was hard. Youngsters hung around the school, slept there. Every morning, they were like corpses on the floor. To start class, you had to clean them out. The school was cramped, noisy. We used role-playing a lot. Kids would portray three generations of Negro families, and we learned history that way. We sat in a circle rather than the usual classroom format, to stress the equality of teacher and student. I read to them from Thomas Wolfe's *You Can't Go Home Again* and from Martin Luther King's *I Have a Dream,* then had them write speeches as if they were Senators urging passage of the civil rights bill. I tried to extend the idea of oppression beyond race. If you pick on a small kid with glasses—I asked—and beat him up, aren't you acting the same as these white supremacists?

One teacher spent a whole hour with his students discussing the meaning of the word "skeptical." He urged them not to accept everything he said. "Check up on me! Be *skeptical.*" He was talking to youngsters whose high school classroom was wired so that at the flick of a switch the principal could listen in on any class in the school.

A slim blonde girl from Skidmore taught French to teenagers. "I try to do the whole class in French, use pantomime a lot. . . . I soon realized these kids had never had contact with a white person before. Maybe that's the greatest thing about this whole experience. If nothing else is accomplished, it's been a *meeting,* for both student and teacher."

There was spasmodic harassment of the Freedom Schools. One day, the blonde Skidmore girl was picked up by police and held for several hours. Violence spluttered around the COFO office in Jackson one ugly Saturday night; a dance hall where teachers and students were spending the evening was sprayed with bullets by a passing car, and a Negro boy was wounded.

In the rural areas, the danger was greater. A church used as a Freedom School in the little town of Gluckstadt was burned to the ground (when the teachers arrived on the scene, fifteen youngsters were waiting under a tree for class to begin). Still, two white girls lived alone in a hilltop house out in the country, thirty miles from Canton, without a telephone, and held a Freedom School there. And in McComb, so dangerous that the Justice Department pleaded with the Mississippi Project not to send anyone there, a Freedom School was attended regularly by a hundred children.

The Freedom Schools challenged not only Mississippi but the nation. There was, to begin with, the provocative suggestion that an entire school system can be created in any community outside the official order, and critical of its suppositions. The Schools raised serious questions about the role of education in society: Can teachers bypass the artificial sieve of certification and examination, and meet students on the basis of a common attraction to an exciting social goal? Is it possible to declare that the aim of education is to find solutions for poverty, for injustice, for racial and national hatred, and to turn all educational efforts into a national striving for these solutions?

And while the youngsters were going to Freedom Schools, their parents were participating in another kind of experiment: the formation of a new political party outside the official party apparatus of Mississippi, a phenomenon which was soon to draw national attention, called the Freedom Democratic Party.

The start had been made in the fall of 1963, when Aaron Henry and Ed King ran for Governor and Lieutenant Governor on the "Freedom Ballot" and polled 80,000 votes outside the official polling booths. That had proved that Negroes *wanted* to vote. And so, the idea grew: if it was such painful work adding, one by one, to the 20,000 or so Negroes officially registered, why not bypass the whole Mississippi machinery and set up a new party, open to all, with no rigamarole? And why not send Freedom Democratic Party delegates from Mississippi to the Democratic National Convention in Atlantic City in August, 1964, to claim those seats traditionally held by white Mississippians who kept Negroes out of the Party machinery?

All through July and August summer volunteers joined regular SNCC, CORE, and SCLC staff people to canvass the Negro communities of Mississippi for "Freedom Registrations," in churches, on porches, along country roads. To register, a person only had to fill out a form with nine simple questions about age, residence, and citizenship. As the deadline of August 24 approached, the registrations pouring into the COFO office in Jackson reached 60,000. In August, conventions were held, first on the county level, and then in congressional districts, to elect delegates to the FDP state convention in Jackson.

On the eve of the state convention, Joseph L. Rauh, labor attorney, counsel for the Americans for Democratic Action, and member of the Credentials Committee of the Democratic Party, arrived in Jackson. He had agreed to argue the case before the Credentials Committee at the Democratic Party Convention in Atlantic City, to seat representatives from the Freedom Democratic Party rather than the regular Mississippi delegation.

Sitting in a crowded little cubicle at the COFO office in Jackson, Rauh and Bob Moses went over final plans for the challenge. For Rauh to convince the Credentials Committee, it was important that the Freedom Democratic Party follow all regular procedures and show up as a strong and well-organized group, and he asked Moses anxiously: "How will the Convention be tomorrow?" Moses, with his characteristic tendency to understatement, just nodded his head slightly.

Next day, the State Convention of the Mississippi Freedom Democratic Party gave Rauh his answer. It was a beautifully-organized, crowded, singing assembly of laborers, farmers, housewives, from the farthest corners of Mississippi, and made the political process seem healthy for the first time in the state's history. It was probably as close to a grass roots political convention as this country has ever seen. Most delegates were Negroes, but there were a few whites: one was Edwin King, Mississippi-born white minister at Tougaloo College; another was a husky former fisherman from the Mississippi Gulf Coast. Ella Baker gave the keynote address, a passionate promise that, whether recognized at Atlantic City or not, the Freedom Democratic Party would grow to be a powerful political arm of the movement in Mississippi. With Dr. Aaron Henry of Clarksdale presiding, a slate of delegates was chosen to the National Democratic Convention, and a state chairman of the Party was elected: Lawrence Guyot, a veteran field secretary of SNCC. (Guyot never made it to Atlantic City, because the city of Hattiesburg decided to put him in jail, exactly at this time, on an old disorderly conduct charge arising from a demonstration.)

In Atlantic City, the presence of the Freedom Democratic Party contributed just that streak of honesty and moral concern which is customarily absent at national political conventions in the United States. Here was an issue so clear in its implications for American democracy that it shoved aside for a few days, in newspapers and on television screens all over the nation, the usual shenanigans surrounding the selection of candidates and adoption of a platform. The Democratic Party now could decide to recognize as delegates from Mississippi the all-white regular group, elected by machinery which had excluded Negroes all along the line. Or it could recognize the mostly black delegation, painstakingly chosen in meetings up and down the Mississippi countryside, and backed now by the physical presence of a thousand black Mississippians just arrived in Atlantic City.

Joseph Rauh argued the case before the Credentials Committee (of which he was a member) cogently, eloquently; he had worked very, very hard on this and it was clear that he was personally involved. He summoned Mississippi Negroes to testify before the Committee: Mrs. Hamer and others delivered moving accounts of their experiences trying to register, and of the iron-clad exclusion of Negroes from the regular Democratic Party of Mississippi. Martin Luther King and James Farmer also testified.

Rauh and the Freedom Democratic Party did not expect to get a majority vote of the Credentials Committee to seat the FDP delegates, but the hope was to get the eleven votes needed for a minority report, because then it would be possible to present that report for approval on the floor of the Convention.

The behind-the-scenes politics of the next few days was frantic. Lyndon Johnson, eyeing the coming presidential election, did not want to alienate Southern votes by favoring the Freedom Democratic Party. Through Hubert Humphrey, who wanted to be Vice President, Johnson began making compromise offers to the FDP in the hope that acceptance would avoid a fight on the convention floor. The FDP was willing to compromise on the terms laid down by Congresswoman Edith Green of Oregon, who along with Rauh formed the hard core of its support on the Credentials Committee. She had proposed that all members of the two rival delegations who would swear loyalty to the national ticket in the presidential elections be seated, with the votes divided among them. However, just when the FDP had succeeded in lining up enough members of the Credentials Committee behind this proposal to assure that it would go out onto the floor, the Administration offered a much weaker compromise: two seats at large (not as representatives of Mississippi) for Aaron Henry and Ed King, and a willingness to seat every member of the white Mississippi delegation who was willing to support the national ticket in the election. This offer fragmented the solidity of the Credentials Committee minority, which was lining up behind the Green proposal.

Joseph Rauh and Edith Green now met with the Freedom Democratic Party delegation to urge them to accept the Administration offer. Green and Rauh were clearly shaken and uneasy. They were being pressured by Humphrey, Walter Reuther of the United Auto Workers, and the hierarchy of the Democratic Party. On the other side, they faced, not only the anger of the SNCC youngsters who had helped organize the FDP, but that of the FDP delegates, for whom this token offer of recognition was too much like the usual bone thrown to Negroes who showed signs of revolt. And perhaps a third pressure was simply their own traditional view that politics is "the art of the possible."

But SNCC and the FDP were born in struggles for "the impossible." The politics of the FDP was not traditional politics, and its members were not politicians. Fannie Lou Hamer spoke out angrily against accepting the compromise, and her fellow delegates went along. On a hand vote, they agreed unanimously to reject the administration offer. With support gone now in the Credentials Committee for a floor fight (only Edith Green seemed willing now to stick it out to the end) Bob Moses urged a sit-in on the convention floor.

That night, television screens all over the nation showed unprecedented scenes of Mississippi Negroes (who had managed to get passes to the floor from friendly delegates) occupying seats in the Mississippi section in defiance of the whole officialdom of the convention. One was physically ejected by the Sergeant-at-Arms, but the rest linked arms, and supporters surging around managed to get in the way of the police, until orders came to the police to stop the evictions. When the convention session ended, the successful sit-in was celebrated in a giant rally outside, and a snake-dance along the boardwalk.

At another meeting the next day, Aaron Henry asked his fellow members of the FDP delegation to reconsider their refusal to accept the compromise. Leading figures of the civil rights movement arrived to argue for acceptance: Martin Luther King, James Farmer, Bayard Rustin. But here the difference between SNCC and the other civil rights groups was made clear: SNCC's was a politics of protest, not of working within the orthodox frame. Its attitude towards compromise was in the spirit of the old abolitionists, of Wendell Phillips. Phillips understood that the eventual outcome of any social struggle was a compromise, but he also understood that in order for that compromise to take place at the highest possible level, the social reformer must maintain his position to the end. "If we would get half a loaf," he said, "we must demand the whole of it."

SNCC was carrying the distinction between the agitator and the politician into politics itself, and the "old-timers" in civil rights and national politics could not understand this agitational politics. The SNCC mood was dominant in the Freedom Democratic Party, not only because SNCC workers were by far the most numerous among all civil rights groups working in Mississippi, but also because SNCC, more than any other organization, remained close to its soil, to the poverty-stricken, rural, black countryside, reflecting the temper of the people living there. When the FDP delegation voted on reconsidering the compromise, the vote was 60-4 against.

Many liberals all over the country, following the externals of the conflict over television, could not understand why the compromise was rejected. The FDP and SNCC leadership did not succeed in making their position clear. Perhaps the conditions in Atlantic City were too hectic; perhaps they themselves were not sure. After the excitement, they could reflect on the difference between the FDP and the ordinary political party. For one thing, in American politics there is the tendency to judge victory and defeat by keeping score of seats, votes, memberships. A radical protest movement is more concerned with the degree to which the movement has expressed its emotions honestly, regardless of immediate consequences in winning votes and offices. To a great extent, this is because a mass movement recognizes that its "victory" ultimately depends on the way it represents fully and unashamedly the temper of its constituents, and not whether it offends its far-off supporters. The SNCC staff gathered in Washington understood, and the FDP delegates themselves sensed, that their power depended on how true they remained to the grief of the Delta, and not to the politicking in smoke-filled rooms.

At Atlantic City, the FDP learned most about itself. It had never acknowledged clearly how strong was its disaffection from the regular politics not only of Mississippi but of the nation. During the summer, it had become enthralled with the idea of ousting the regular delegation to the convention by demonstrating *its* superior loyalty to Lyndon Johnson as against the Mississippi Democrats' obvious sympathy for Barry Goldwater. This was an inaccurate rendering of the FDP mood, which was not really "loyal" in the traditional political sense to *any* candidate of the Establishment, whether Democratic or Republican. The FDP became dazzled for a while by its own pre-convention hoopla about "loyalty" to Johnson. Its signs read "All the way with LBJ" when it still felt anger at Johnson's failure to give protection in Mississippi. The FDP never made sufficiently clear to itself or to the nation that its chief reason for demanding seats at the Convention was not its greater loyalty to the national Democratic Party, but its position as true representative of that 45 per cent of Mississippi's population which was Negro.

This confusion was reflected at a COFO staff meeting in

Jackson in August, where SNCC people themselves were divided between a majority willing to wage civil disobedience at the convention if the Freedom delegation was not seated, and a minority which suggested "playing the game of politics" so as not to lose too many political friends. It was also reflected in the fact that even Edith Green's acceptable compromise at the convention was based on the administering of "loyalty" oaths. Confusion was resolved when the administration compromise was offered and the FDP and SNCC people realized suddenly how far they had come along the road to being absorbed in that political mainstream which they had always believed was polluted; at this point they reacted instinctively with an overwhelming "No!"

In the end, despite what some liberals considered a failure to grasp emblems of success—two seats on the floor—the Freedom Democratic Party came out of its Atlantic City experience both wiser and stronger, split off in an unfortunate way from some liberal supporters like Joe Rauh, but firmer than ever in its ties with the people back home, and ready to organize those people into an even greater fighting force.

When the election of 1964 was over, and Lyndon Johnson had registered his smashing victory over Goldwater (by a margin so great that his desperation at the Atlantic City convention over the FDP challenges seemed, in retrospect, irrationally intense) the FDP turned to its next step. This was to challenge the seating of the five segregationist Mississippi Congressmen at the opening of Congress in January, 1965.

The United States Constitution, in Article I, Section 5, provides that the House of Representatives "shall be the Judge of the Elections, Returns and Qualifications of its own Members." In Title 2 of the U.S. Code a legal procedure is outlined by which American citizens may contest an election and present evidence to the House. In accordance with this, Mrs. Fannie Lou Hamer, shortly after the November election, sent to Jamie L. Whitten, who had been "elected" to Congress from the Second Congressional District, a notice of intention to contest his election.

Mrs. Hamer's argument was simple and her documentation powerful. Jamie Whitten did not deserve to represent the Second District of Mississippi because Negroes constituted 52.4% of the adult population of that district, yet only 2.97% had been permitted to register to vote, because of a pattern of intimidation, murder, and official restraint. Her challenge contained the statistics in detail for each county, a history of disenfranchisement in Mississippi, and a long list of incidents of violence against Negroes.

At the same time, challenges were filed in two other Mississippi Congressional Districts by Mrs. Annie Devine, a CORE worker and leader in the Canton Negro community, and Mrs. Victoria Gray, an SCLC voter registration director and a housewife in Hattiesburg. All three women had tried to run in the November elections and were kept off the ballot. They had run in "Freedom Elections" and polled large votes cast by Negroes in their districts.

When Congress opened on January 4, 1965, Congressman William Fitts Ryan of New York stood up as the oaths were about to be administered to the new membership, and objected to the seating of all five Congressmen from Mississippi. In an astonishing display of support, fifty Congressmen stood up with him. According to established House procedure, Speaker John McCormick, presiding, then administered the oath to everyone else so that the sworn-in members could decide what to do about those being challenged. Now Ryan rose again, hoping to introduce a motion that the Mississippi delegation not be seated until the House Committee on Administration (which deals with contested elections) could decide whether they were rightful representatives of their districts.

However, Representative Carl Albert of Oklahoma rose at this point, and Speaker McCormick recognized him. Now the view of the Johnson administration was clear, for Albert and McCormick were the Administration's spokesmen in the House. Johnson's weight, exerted on the overwhelmingly Democratic House, could have been used to get a majority for Ryan's motion to keep the white Mississippians out of their seats until a final decision were made. But Representative Albert's motion was quite different: to seat the regular Mississippi delegation until the dispute was finally resolved. Despite Johnson's easy victory at the polls, and despite the evidence in November that the South was no longer solid but split between "liberal" and "conservative" sections, Johnson was evidently still unwilling to ruffle Deep South politicians.

A test of how many Congressmen were behind William Fitts Ryan and Edith Green came when Mrs. Green asked for a roll-call vote on Albert's request to close debate on his motion. To open up debate would mean opportunity to air before the House and the nation the whole miserable history of Negro disenfranchisement in Mississippi and thus create an atmosphere which would then make it hard for Northern Congressmen to vote to seat the Mississippi delegation. Congressman James Roosevelt of California, according to a press release from his office, had prepared a speech in the event of such open debate, in which he would say:

> This House must speak upon its honor to the people of the United States. We are beyond politics in the ordinary sense; we are beyond the contentions of party and program that ordinarily concern us. We must speak upon politics in the very highest sense; we must speak upon the way a free people governs itself; we must speak upon the meaning of the words and the spirit of the Constitution, we must speak upon what to an American is the most terrible of political facts—that some Americans are not free men. . . . We dare not let men pretend to a seat in this honorable House who have been chosen by a closed vote in a closed society. If we do, we betray this House and the people of the United States and the Constitution they wrote for us.

As a result of the roll-call vote, debate was closed and the House went on to approve Albert's motion to seat the Mississippi regulars. But in that roll call 149 Congressmen stood with the FDP, not enough to win (the vote was 276 to 149), but far more than anyone had expected. More than their own inner conviction was responsible for such a display of support for the Negro challenge; often, such conviction must be brought out of hiding by demonstrative action. In the days before the opening of Congress, hundreds of FDP people had visited Congressmen to appeal for their support. On opening day, Negroes by the hundreds from Mississippi lined the tunnel leading into the House so that all Congressmen-elect had to file past them as they entered. Mrs. Hamer, Mrs. Devine, and Mrs. Grey tried to enter the House to take the seats they asserted were rightfully theirs. They were barred by the officer at the door. The effect, however, was to bring the issue visibly to Congress and to the nation.

Though the five Congressmen from Mississippi had been seated, the challenge continued in accordance with the provisions of Title 2. The three challengers had forty days to take testimony to support their challenge; then forty days were granted for argument by the other side, and then ten days for rebuttal, after which the House Committee on Administration was supposed to weigh the evidence and make a decision.

Thus, the next forty days were historic ones for the state of Mississippi. Armed with the statutory power to subpoena anyone in the state who could throw light on the elections, a hundred volunteer lawyers from all over the country took depositions for the FDP in hearings to bring out the evidence. Registrars and sheriffs were queried pointedly about those kept from voting in their counties. Negroes filled thousands of pages with their accounts of terror, intimidation, and subterfuge in connection with their attempts to register. When it came time for forty days of hearings held by the regular Congressmen, there were none; they had decided simply not to recognize the challenge.

Sometime in July, 1965 (after all the stages of the challenge had been exhausted in fulfillment of the law's requirements), the House Committee on Administration would decide what to do about the challenge, and report to the full House of Representatives. And three forces would face one another: the Mississippi regulars, the Freedom Democratic Party, and the Administration. SNCC and the FDP thus prepared once more to confront Congress, the Administration, and the American public with the moral question of whether racism in Mississippi would once again get the tacit support of avowed liberals at the head of the American government.

What *was* the Freedom Democratic Party by mid-1965? There were Lawrence Guyot, young philosophy major from Pass Christian, Mississippi, and Fannie Lou Hamer, of Ruleville—both veteran SNCC staff members, as Chairman and Vice-Chairman of the FDP. With them, running from time to time as candidates of the Party in "freedom elections," were Mississippians who had been active in other organizations: Aaron Henry of Clarksdale, NAACP state chairman; Mrs. Gray of Hattiesburg, with SCLC; and Mrs. Devine of Canton, who had worked for CORE. The research and publicity was being done by a hard-working crew of young people, black and white, some from Mississippi and some from elsewhere, mostly staff members of SNCC. Out in the field, registering people and organizing the party, were young Negroes from the area, and white volunteers, many of whom had come down in the summer and stayed on. And at the base of the party were tens of thousands of Mississippi Negroes (and a handful of whites) who had registered and voted in the "freedom elections."

This was a new kind of politics the FDP was engaging in, something that might be called *protest politics,* because it exerted its force both *against* and *within* the traditional politics.

Other reform movements in the American past had wrestled with the problem of dealing with an American party system which excluded the underprivileged. Many, trying to work within the frame, had been swallowed up by it: the Locofocos in the Jacksonian Democratic Party; the Populists in the Democratic Party of Bryan; the Progressives, in the parties of Woodrow Wilson and Theodore Roosevelt; the radicals of the thirties, in the cautious experimentalism of Franklin D. Roosevelt. Others, noting this absorption process, and trying to remain outside, stayed small, and then were assimilated anyway or petered out (as did the Liberty Party in the Republican Party of Lincoln and the Progressives of Henry Wallace). As a result, some radical groups, like the Industrial Workers of the World, had avoided politics altogether.

The FDP was trying a new synthesis of the old approaches: to register Negroes to vote, while making clear the limitations of the ballot box in eradicating the poverty which lay near the root of race hatred in Mississippi; to demand representation within the Democratic Party while fighting the tokenism of that party and the lack of democracy in the whole American party system: to elect leaders to office, while maintaining a suspicion of *all* leadership, in the knowledge that power corrupts the best of men and women. The FDP hoped that somehow it could maintain this tension between means and ends by never losing contact with the sources of its moral strength—the sharecroppers and housewives and barefoot children of the Black Belt.

SNCC itself came out of the summer with certain questions: where now, and what next? Its staff of 150 had grown to over 200; it had a national reputation as a band of young people in blue overalls who stood in the forefront of the civil rights struggle in the deep South. Through the summer, although its major attention was being concentrated on Mississippi, SNCC had skeleton crews working in Southwest Georgia, Alabama, and Arkansas. Everyone knew that the Summer

Project of COFO, while including hard-working people in CORE and SCLC, and supported by northern organizations like the National Council of Churches, was being manned largely by SNCC.

The NAACP had gone its own way pretty much during the summer, and its estrangement from COFO was open, although individual officers of the NAACP, like Aaron Henry, remained prominent in COFO affairs. In April, 1965, the national office of the NAACP announced that it was officially withdrawing from COFO, and Aaron Henry joined in the announcement. Many local NAACP people, nevertheless, would probably continue to work with COFO, as the most effective force in the state. Petty jealousies, rivalry, and conflict over tactics had always existed among the groups in COFO, and continued among SNCC, SCLC, and CORE. During times of crisis, however, they seemed to be able to work together, even in the midst of disagreements.

Six months after the Summer Project ended, in February and March of 1965, Selma, Alabama, gave evidence both of the organizational frictions and the basic fraternity-in-action between SNCC and Martin Luther King's Southern Christian Leadership Conference. SNCC had been working in Selma for two years, with local leaders like Mrs. Amelia Boynton and the Reverend James Bevel of SCLC. When Dr. King came to Selma in February, fresh from winning the Nobel Peace Prize, he not only aroused local people to their highest pitch, but brought national and world attention to Selma. Negroes in that town, marching peacefully to the county courthouse seeking to register to vote, were attacked again and again by Sheriff Jim Clark and his club-wielding volunteer posse, or by Colonel Al Lingo's state troopers. The following incidents took place:

FEB. 8: Ivanhoe Donaldson of SNCC and the Reverend James Bevel of SCLC were prodded with electric poles and beaten when they led a group of Negroes up the steps of the county courthouse bearing a petition asking for the right to register without encumbrance. Bevel was in bad condition and was sent to the hospital. (In the hospital, he was chained to the bed.) Fifty-seven of the Negroes in the demonstration were arrested.

FEB. 10: One hundred and seventy-five Negro high school and college students marching to the courthouse were turned around by Sheriff Clark and taken on a forced march out into the country. They were prodded and hit all the way by posse members with billy clubs and electric poles. Some were beaten when they fell to the ground exhausted.

FEB. 16: Sheriff Clark clubbed a Negro man and woman near the county courthouse.

FEB. 18: In the town of Marion, Alabama, thirty miles from Selma, Negroes marching out of church to protest the arrest of a civil rights worker were clubbed by state troopers. A U.P.I. dispatch described the scene:

> About 400 Negroes met in the Zion Methodist Church across the street from the courthouse and, after praying and singing, started out the door two by two for the courthouse. Local police and 50 state troopers were waiting for them in the darkness. About 100 Negroes had left the church when Police Chief T. O. Harris, using an electric loudspeaker, told them "You're going to be arrested if you don't disperse. Go back to the church." Instead of moving, the Negroes began praying. Harris warned them several more times. Then the troopers moved in. At first they pushed the Negroes back, shouting "Move! Move!" Suddenly there were screams and cries and clubs flashed in the darkness.

FEB. 26: Jimmy Lee Jackson, a twenty-six-year-old unemployed mason who had been beaten and shot in the stomach by a state trooper the night of the Marion demonstration died in a Selma hospital.

MAR. 7: A column of Negroes starting out on a march from Selma to Montgomery to protest discrimination in Alabama was stopped by state troopers and posse men on a bridge just outside of Selma, and when they knelt to pray they were clubbed and gassed. John Lewis of SNCC, leading the march, was hospitalized with a fractured skull.

MAR. 9: The Reverend James Reeb of Boston, who had come to Selma to protest police brutality, was clubbed on a street in Selma by white men. He died two days later.

Through this entire month of demonstrations and police brutality, the President and the Department of Justice, charged with enforcing the law, maintained the same attitude of verbal concern and general passivity that is described more fully in Chapter 9 of this book. It was the same reaction as to the triple murder of Schwerner, Chaney, and Goodman in Mississippi: the dispatch of more F.B.I. agents and Justice Department lawyers, who looked on and took notes while people were being beaten, the initiation of several prosecutions of policemen accused of brutality, and all of this accompanied by a plea that the federal government was powerless to take preventive, protective, action.

On March 7, when news of the clubbing and gassing on the bridge reached the White House, a full month after trouble had started in Selma, and civil rights groups were clamoring for President Johnson to act, the White House responded that Johnson "was keeping fully informed about the latest developments at Selma," that it had observers on the scene, and that there was no additional comment. Attorney General Katzenbach claimed that he could not know before the march that Alabama troopers would behave as they did; hence no preventive action had been taken. In view of the record of Sheriff Clark and Al Lingo over the past few years, and the order given by Governor Wallace to stop the march, it was an incredible statement.

Meanwhile, the Voice of America, responding to protests all over the world about what was happening in Alabama, broadcast in thirty-eight languages to more than one hundred countries a set of statements about federal constitutional powers which can best be described as misleading. The Voice broadcast the fact that the Alabama police who clubbed demonstrators on the bridge had acted on Governor Wallace's orders, and added: "Regardless of his motives, it is important to note that Governor Wallace had every right to make this decision" because "it is a fact that under the United States Constitution the police powers belong to the states, not to the Federal Government." A constitutional lawyer might have asked the Voice of America: Does a governor have a legal right to issue an order to police to violate a federal right like the right of peaceable assembly? Does not the federal government have some police powers—those it needs to enforce federal law? And do not these powers explain the existence of the F.B.I., the establishment of federal prisons, and the right of arrest given by law to F.B.I. men and federal marshals?

The Voice of America went on to state inaccurately the conditions under which the President had a right to call out troops, saying he could do this only when state or local authorities were "actively resisting federal court orders or defying federal laws". Actually, Section 333, Title 10, of the U.S. Code gives the President the right to send troops simply when a state is "unable" to protect people's constitutional rights.

The death of northern minister James Reeb, coming on top of the succession of police actions in Selma, brought spontaneous cries of outrage from all over the nation, demanding that the federal government act. Within twenty-four hours after the news of Reeb's death, thousands of people marched in New York and New Jersey to sites of federal buildings, asking that Johnson move. Two hundred students sat-in on the eleventh floor of the Federal Building in Boston, 2000 marched in Los Angeles, and meetings and rallies took place in many other cities. Reaction in Europe, Africa, and Asia was also strong.

Several days later, Johnson responded. He delivered a remarkably eloquent and vigorous speech to a joint session of Congress on behalf of Negro rights, and asked for a strong voting bill to eliminate the subterfuges and schemes used by states to deprive Negroes of the right to register and vote. In addition, following up a federal court order in Montgomery permitting the proposed civil rights march from Selma to Montgomery, Johnson ordered several thousand National Guardsmen and U.S. Army troops to protect the marchers.

When the 50-mile march took place, during the third week in March, with a hard core of three hundred marchers from the Selma area, and many thousands of whites and Negroes joining from other states as it neared Montgomery, it had superb federal protection. With soldiers in jeeps and on foot, helicopters and piper cubs overhead, it was certainly the best guarded civil rights activity in the nation's history.

Still, when the march was over, and the troops were gone, the basic demand of the civil rights movement remained unanswered: day-to-day protection by a special corps of federal agents, who would use a combination of persuasion and the power of arrest to protect constitutional rights and prevent violence. (Almost as a symbolic expression of this need, the day after the dispersal of the troops a white woman driving Negroes back to Selma was shot and killed.) What the events in Selma showed was the power of demonstrative protest in forcing the national government to take decisive action. What it also showed was the traditional reluctance of politicians to move *unless* pressured by a set of disastrous events and an accompanying wave of indignation.

In the midst of all this, SNCC in the spring of 1965 was trying to decide its own future. After the Mississippi Summer, it held a number of staff meetings to discuss what SNCC's role should be in future months and future years. One thing was clear: the SNCC organizational structure no longer fit the realities. It was based on SNCC's original position as a coordinator of student groups, so that both the "Coordinating Committee" and the smaller Executive Committee represented such groups. However, student groups had dwindled and SNCC now consisted of a large staff of professional organizers working in deep-South communities. It was now determined that this staff of over two hundred would become the basic decision-making body in SNCC, that it would meet about four times a year to lay down basic policy, and the Executive Committee would be drawn from these staff people working in the Black Belt.

A number of SNCC people, anxious to avoid the "iron law of oligarchy" that they had seen operating in other organizations, and determined to keep power near its base in the Black Belt, argued against an emphasis on the Executive Committee as a group of "leaders," and urged that the whole staff participate continually in decision-making. Their view was only partly followed, since the Executive Committee was given strong powers between staff meetings, and a three-person Secretariat of top officials was set up: James Forman was Executive Secretary, John Lewis as Chairman, Cleveland Sellers as Program Chairman.

But the spirit of the "anti-organization" view was shown in the kind of persons elected to the new Executive Committee in early 1965. Many of them were Negroes from Mississippi, including Mrs. Hamer of Ruleville, Jesse Harris of Jackson, Dorie Ladner of Hattiesburg, Silas McGhee of Greenwood, LaFayette Surney of Ruleville, Hollis Watkins of Summit. At a week-long staff meeting in Atlanta, again in keeping with the strong mood of "populism" in SNCC, it was decided that instead of issuing a call for thousands of northern volunteers for the summer of 1965, a series of "People's Conferences" would be held in Mississippi, Alabama, Arkansas, and Georgia. At these Conferences, local people would decide on programs and personnel for their areas.

All this reflected SNCC's stubborn insistence that it

would not go the way of so many other reform groups, that it would stick close to the soil of discontent from it sprang. And it declared openly SNCC's transition from a student group based in Negro colleges to a band of organizers in Southern communities.

SNCC still hoped to recruit students from Negro colleges in the South, and so used some staff people as "campus travellers" to organize students. Also, it maintained a cordial relationship with an energetic new organization of students at predominantly white Southern colleges that was determined to do for the white colleges and the white community what SNCC had accomplished in the Negro communities. This was SSOC, the Southern Students Organizing Committee.

SNCC's radicalism continued to be misunderstood and maligned by those who saw in it "sinister" and "subversive" and "Communist" elements. In fact, except for a few white and Negro students who had read a little Marx and espoused some vague form of "socialism," SNCC people simply could not be fitted into the customary ideological categories. SNCC people did want to revolutionize society as they knew it, but they did not conceive of doing this by an armed uprising; their tactics remained nonviolent, though militantly demonstrative. They did want a system drastically different from the one they saw operating in the United States, but they saw no model for such a system in any country in the world, and when pressed couldn't really describe what would be the features of the new society they hoped to establish. This fresh and independent radicalism baffled journalists, who kept trying to describe the SNCC mood in terms of the 1930's, not comprehending that this was truly a new phenomenon the nation was watching.

Columnists Rowland Evans and Robert Novak, syndicated in the *Herald Tribune* and other newspapers, found sinister implications in the fact that several SNCC leaders visited Africa at the invitation of Guinea's President Sekou

Toure, or that Bob Moses once accepted an invitation to speak at a dinner sponsored by the left-wing weekly *The National Guardian.* In SNCC outlook they saw "a startling and frightening parallel to the revolutionary movements in Africa."

It seems to me that there is one element of truth in the "parallel" between SNCC and revolutionary movements abroad which frightens Evans and Novak so much. That is, SNCC represents the closest thing we have in the United States to that militant mood of change which one finds in emerging nations abroad. For that, the nation should be grateful, because many of our mistakes in foreign policy might be corrected if we had a better understanding of the revolutionary spirit of Africa and Asia, and the SNCC people provide us, at home, with a sample of that spirit. In both cases, the basis is the same: a movement with hungry, harried people has a militancy hard to purchase. Also, such a movement is impatient with worries about ideology. It understands what it sees and feels—bread, land, a policeman's club, a friend's hand—and is impervious to sophisticated talk about doctrinal bogies.

The same parallel can be found in the attitude toward Communists and Communism. No country in the world has less cause to worry about communism, or more paranoic fear of it, than the United States. The talk about "Communist" influences in SNCC comes mostly from people who simply don't know the organization or the people in it. SNCC is fundamentally a group of Black Belt and Northern Negroes who are angry at American society and determined to change it, but who have had little or no contact with formal radical ideologies or movements. Here and there there may be one or two people at intermediate levels on the SNCC staff who've read a little Marx and are consciously sympathetic with one or another communist or socialist governments in the world.

Those journalists who see "conspiracies" or "infiltration" are working from second- or third-hand information.

Most middle-class white Americans simply have not had those experiences which make many Negroes hostile to a society which preaches equality and practices murder, which produces huge wealth, and leaves millions without the simple necessities of life. And so (forgetting that this country, long before Marx, had a tradition, however unpopular, of radical protest) these white Americans attribute this native-born hostility to "communism."

Perhaps, too, they suspect—and rightly—that even if the SNCC people could be shown a "Communist," they would not be upset. For one thing, SNCC workers are young, and they have grown up in a world where there is no longer any single meaning of "Communism" or "Communist," where varieties of communism develop in different parts of the world; the term, therefore, has lost both specific meaning, and the capacity to alarm.

The accusers (both liberals and conservatives), it turns out on closer inspection, cannot point to genuine "Communists" in SNCC, but to people who belong to organizations which are connected with other organizations which include people who might possibly be Communists! It is the McCarthy approach all over again, where five suspicions strung together become a certainty.

There was talk, for instance, about SNCC's "connection" with the Southern Conference Education Fund, a long-time militant civil rights organization in the South that had on occasion contributed a tiny amount of money to SNCC. And SCEF was to be looked on with suspicion because one of its leading figures was Carl Braden, who had refused to answer questions about Communist affiliations put to him by the House Un-American Activities Committee. It has been curious to see liberals on one day denounce that Committee and the next day accept its assumptions.

Another of these rickety "connections" was made in the newspapers between SNCC and the National Lawyers Guild. When the Atlantic City Convention was over, the Freedom Democratic Party planned its next move not with liberal attorney Joseph Rauh, but with liberal-radical attorneys William Kunstler and Arthur Kinoy. These were two brilliant and seasoned lawyers. However, Kinoy's membership in the National Lawyers Guild became an object of deep concern among some newspapermen. (The Guild's chief sin, it turned out, was to include lawyers who had defended Communists in trials.) But the legal aid from Kunstler and Kinoy no more meant an FDP tie with the Guild than the FDP's earlier use of Rauh meant an FDP tie with the Americans for Democratic Action. It has been hard for journalists, still quivery with the suspicions and the timidity engendered by the McCarthy era, to understand the honest, pragmatic approach of SNCC and the FDP to working with other people, an approach which asks no questions except: will you work your head off for our cause?

One story might illustrate SNCC's way.

In the spring of 1964, as plans for the Mississippi Summer were being made, a representative from the Legal Defense Fund of the NAACP came to a SNCC Executive Committee meeting with a warning: if COPO was going to use National Lawyers Guild attorneys in Mississippi, then the Legal Defense Fund, Inc., (known in the movement as the "Inc. Fund") would withdraw its offer of ample financial resources and large staff to help the Summer Project.

The SNCC Executive Committee, as the dominant group in COFO, discussed this. It had no special loyalty to the National Lawyers Guild as an organization; in fact, it knew little about the Guild. But Guild lawyers had helped in time of need; Bob Moses pointed to some imaginative work done by Attorney Ben Smith of New Orleans, a Guild member, when they were in a tight spot in Mississippi. Besides, there was an instinctive SNCC reaction against anything that sounded like bullying, or bribery. There would be enough legal work in Mississippi to require all the help that could be secured. SNCC decided overwhelmingly to reject the suggestion that Guild lawyers be turned away.

This decision posed two dangers which "sensible" and "practical" people would have worried about. One was that the movement would lose the services of the NAACP Legal Defense Staff when this was badly needed. The other was that the continued association, slim as it was, with the National Lawyers' Guild would hurt SNCC's reputation nationally.

What happened, of course, was that neither of the dangers eventuated. The Guild's lawyers worked in the Summer Project. The "Inc. Fund's" lawyers also worked in the Summer Project. Both groups were inestimably helpful. And SNCC came out of the Mississippi Project with an enhanced reputation for its accomplishments.

SNCC read lessons in this: that ultimately allies must come to your side on the basis of a joining of their needs and yours, and not because of some subsidiary issue, as magnified as it might be, verbally; that in the end, the strength of an organization comes from what it accomplishes, and not from its associations, real or imagined; that the best way to deal with name-calling is to drown it in a crescendo of constructive activity. For SNCC there was a special source of confidence: *its* power depended, finally, not on what the political higher-ups or the liberal Establishment or the press thought of it, but on its ability to organize ordinary people into a striking force for social change. If it could do that effectively, the "important" groups and individuals would give way.

SNCC's new radicalism comes from nowhere in the world but cotton fields, prison cells, and the minds of young people reflecting on what they see and feel. So it is expressed in no ancient books, but in odd bits of conversation, which reflect not a precise doctrine but an emotion. There is Charles Sherrod: "Our country is sitting on a powder keg. . . . It makes me mad, that some of us have to sweep and wait tables and work all night and go to school and they got thousands, yea, millions, yea, billions, of dollars. . . . We got to find ways, leverages, of moving the government. We may have to demonstrate for jobs. You know we may have to bring some bones up from the South and say: Johnson, feel my bones. You know —I'm hungry, Johnson, feel my bones!"

And Stokely Carmichael: "Yes, I would like to see the government take over U.S. Steel, General Motors, all the big corporations. I'd like to see more than one hundred people control over 60 per cent of the industry. I'd like to see all these plantations divided up until everybody who was on the plantation had his plot of land, because like Mrs. Hamer said: "Who the hell's land is it anyway?"

These snatches of talk pulled out of context and out of whole lives give only a hint of what it is about SNCC that worries traditional liberalism. They suggest a kind of socialism, but to put it this way freezes what is really a fluid attitude, directed at ending deprivation and equalizing wealth, but completely open about ways to do this.

What *really* makes SNCC a threat to American liberal society is that quality which makes it a threat to *all* Establishments, whether capitalist, socialist, communist, or whatever: its rejection of authority; its fearlessness in the face of overwhelming power; its indifference to respectability. It constantly aims to create and recreate, out of the bodies of poor and powerless people, a new force, nonviolent but aggressive, honest and therefore unmanageable. It wants to demonstrate to the nation not what kind of "system" people should believe in, but how people should live their lives. So its radicalism is not an ideology but a mood. Moods are harder to define. They are also harder to imprison.

This makes SNCC unpredictable for the future, for it sets

difficult goals for itself: to defy authority within as well as without, to resist temptations offered by friends as well as by enemies, to constantly refreshen its radicalism from springs of both anger and love. In any event, if it continues as before, it will crush accusations under the weight of its sacrifices.

Index

Abernathy, Ralph, 50, 53, 129, 134, 169
Adams, Patrolman John Quincy, 119
Aelony, Zev, 175, 183
African nations, emergence of, 18
Alabama
  registration laws in, 153
Albany, Georgia, 2, 11, 146
  and U.S. government, 123, 136
  voter registration in, 123, 136
  described, 124
  test of ICC ruling in, 126-128
  truce of Dec., 1961, 131, 133
  desegregation in, 135
  federal indictments of civil rights workers in, 211-212
Albany Movement
  formation of, 128
  boycott of buses, 133
  and Judge Elliott, 204
Albany State College for Negroes, 125-126, 129
Albert, Carl, 259
Alcorn, James L., 64
Allen, Louis, 74
Allen, Mrs. Louis, 242
Allen, Ralph, 138, 139, 140, 182-183
  on race, 184
Allgood, Clarence W., 204
American Civil Liberties Union, 197
American Friends Service Committee, 34
American Jewish Conference, 212
Americans For Democratic Action, 251, 272
Americus, Ga., 11, 182-183
Anderson, Candie
  on sit-ins, 16
  and Nashville sit-ins, 20, 21
  on bombing of Looby home, 22-23
Anderson, William G., 29, 128, 131
  found guilty of disorderly conduct, 134
  and federal indictments, 211-212
Anniston, Ala., 42-44
Ashley, Stephen, 76
Athens, Ga., 42
Atlanta, Ga., 2, 11, 42, 213, 238
  student movement, 17
  sit-ins, 25
  arrests in, 39
Atlanta Conference, 37
Atlanta *Constitution*, 25, 53
Atlanta University, 34
Attorney General. *See* Kennedy, Robert F.; U.S. Department of Justice
Augusta, Ga., 42

Baker, Ella
  background of, 32-33
  in Raleigh, 33
  in Atlanta, 34, 35
  at Highlander meeting, 59
  in Hattiesburg, 104, 106
  on role of Negroes in SNCC, 186
  at FDP state convention, 252
Baldwin, David, 152, 155, 159
  Selma speech, 165-166
Baldwin, James, 167
  in Selma, 152, 155, 159, 164
  Selma speech, 166
  on role of whites in civil rights movement, 186
Barbee, William, 49
Barnett, Ross, 196
  on Negro difference, 51
  Supreme Court ruling, 201
Barry, Marion, 38
  and Nashville sit-ins, 19
  elected Chairman, 34
  on sit-ins, 35
  appearance before Democratic Platform Committee, 1960, 36-37
  favors direct action, 59
  holds workshops on nonviolence in McComb, 68
Baton Rouge, La., 172-173
Beech, Robert, 245

Belafonte, Harry, 60, 66
Bennett, Myrtis, 76
Bergman, Walter, 43
Bevel, Diane Nash, 20, 38, 44, 45, 79, 80
  favors direct action, 59
  works full time for SNCC, 60
Bevel, James
  on direct action and violence, 14
  on Looby home bombing, 23
  works full time for SNCC, 60
  speaks in McComb, 68
  in Jackson, 79, 80
  speaks in Ruleville, 93
  injured in Selma, 263
Bickel, Alexander, 208
Bigelow, Albert, 42
Biloxi, Miss., 25, 245
Birmingham, Ala., 42, 43
  Freedom Riders arrested in, 45
  school board, 204
  bombing in, 213
Black, Charles, 209
Blackwell, Randolph, 89
Block, Sam, 5
  in Greenwood, 83, 84-86, 87-88, 91
Blues for Mister Charlie, 164
Bond, Julian, 18, 38, 142
  and Atlanta sit-in, 17
  poem by, 35
Boynton, Amelia, 12, 148, 161, 163, 263
Boynton, Bruce, 148-149
Boynton Case, 41
Braden, Anne, 169
Braden, Carl, 271
Branton, Wiley, 90
Brazier, James, 138
Britt, Travis, 69-70
Brooks, Paul, 47, 60, 79
Brown, Luvaghn, 80-81, 84
Browning, Joan, 129, 132
Bryant, C. C., 66
Burney, Robert, 143
Bus boycott, 1, 18

Cambridge, Md., 8, 11
Cameron, John, 121
Camilla, Ga., 11
Campbell, Cull, 135
Campbell, Janie, 76
Campbell Junior College, 76
Capell, Arthur, 153
Carey, Gordon, 41
Carmichael, Stokely, 40, 98, 274
  background of, 55-56
  on Parchman penitentiary, 57
Caston, Billy Jack
  attacks Moses, 68
  trial of, 69
  owned truck Hurst drove, 73
Chaney, James, 243, 265
  beating of, 244
Charlotte, N.C., 213, 238
Charlotte Observer, 52
Chase, Oscar, 108, 114, 115-117
Chatfield, Jack, 143, 144, 145
  shooting of, in Dawson, 141
  arrest in Albany, 141-142
Chatmon, Thomas, 136
Chattanooga, Tenn., 23
Chestnut, J. L., 159
Civil disobedience, 13, 28-29
Civil Rights Act of 1866, 194
Civil Rights Act of 1957, 206, 207
Civil Rights Act of 1960, 206, 207
Civil Rights Act of 1964, 206, 207-208, 230
Civil Rights Commission, 205-206
Clark, Jim, 12, 149, 226, 263-265
  described, 153-154
  on Freedom Day, 157-158, 161-162
  possibility of arrest of, 195-196
Clarksdale, Miss., 11, 245
Cleveland, Miss., 82
Cobb, Charles, 99, 247
Coffin, William, 53
Colleges
  and SNCC workers, 9
  need for reform in, 231-235
Colleges, Negro
  and sit-ins, 30
  and civil rights movement, 235-236
Collins, Norma, 129
Columbia, S.C., 25
Communism
  and SNCC, 226-228, 271
Compromise of 1877, 65, 198-199, 214

Congress of Racial Equality (CORE), 37, 77, 81, 91, 186, 215, 239, 244, 263
 and sit-ins, 23, 29
 and Freedom Rides, 41-42, 55
 and forming of COFO, 79
 in Hattiesburg, 104-105
 and Freedom Walk, 175
Connor, "Bull", 44, 45
Conway, Jack, 229
Conwell, Kathleen, 138
Cotton, MacArthur, 5, 70, 97, 104
Council of Federated Organizations (COFO), 79-80, 215, 244
Cox, Courtland, 56
Cox, William, 204
Crawford, James, 142-143
Crow, Carl E., 134

Dammond, Peggy, 138
 on gathering in Lee County, 144
 on courage in the South, 145
Daniels, Carolyn, 12, 139
 home shot into, 141
Danville, Va., 11, 12, 180-181
Dawson, Ga., 11
Day, Peggy, 13
Debs Case, 202-203
deLissovoy, Peter, 181-182
Democratic National Convention, 1964, 257
Dennis, David, 102, 105
 asks for federal protection, 90
 car shot at, 91
Devine, Annie, 258, 260-261
Diamond, Dion, 56, 76, 171
 bedroom fired into, 77
 arrest in Baton Rouge, 172, 174
Diggs, Ivory, 76
Direct action, 14, 59, 219-220
Dissent, 235-236
Dix, Dorothea, 225
Dollie, Mama, 145, 146
Donaldson, Ivanhoe
 transports food to Mississippi, 87
 in Henry-King campaign, 99, 100
 injured in Selma, 263
Douglass, Frederick, 3, 248
Dugger, Ronnie, 150
Dunbar, Leslie, 207, 213
Durden, Judge, 134
Durr, Clifford, 169
Durr, Virginia, 169

Eastland, James, 93, 204
Economic pressure
 on Negroes, 86
Economic reform, 228-231
Eisenhower, D. D., 199
Elliott, J. Robert, 204
Ellis, Frank, 204
Ellison, Ralph, 235
Enforcement Act of 1870, 194
Enterprise Journal (McComb), 73
Erikson, Erik
 on identity crisis, 5, 6, 7
 on young rebels, 14
Eubanks, Leotus, 76
Evans, Rowland, 269
Evers, Medgar, 93, 213
Ex parte Siebold, 243

The Faith of a Heretic, 2
Farmer, James, 1
 and Freedom Rides, 42, 51
 on Freedom Riders and jails, 57
 testifies before Credentials Committee, 253
 urges FDP to accept administration compromise, 255
Federal Bureau of Investigation, 210, 211, 242-243
 failure of agents to act, 193, 195, 206
 and civil rights crises, 196
Fellowship of Reconciliation, 41
Ferry, W. H., 230
Field Foundation, 58, 81
Fleming, Carl, 148, 179
Food Drive, Mississippi, 86-88
Forman, James, 11, 18-19, 81, 83, 142, 216, 231
 background of, 5, 60
 deliberate harshness of, 8
 chosen Executive Secretary, 60, 268
 asks President Kennedy for protection in Mississippi, 90
 in Greenwood, 91, 92
 in Ruleville, 93

in Hattiesburg, 111, 112-113, 117
in Albany, 127, 129
in Selma, 149, 151, 152, 155, 158, 160, 161-162, 165
Frankfort, Ky., 25
Free expression, 224-225
Freedom Ballot Campaign
directed by Moses, 99-101
Freedom Chorus, 4
Freedom Democratic Party
formation of, 251
state convention, 251
in Atlantic City, 253
votes to reconsider administration compromise, 255-257
philosophy behind, 256-257
and seating of Mississippi Congressmen, 257, 260-261
its protest politics, 261-262
Freedom Ride, 42
Freedom Singers, 132
Freedom schools, 247, 249
Freedom Walk, 175-180, 193

Gaines, Shirley, 135
Gaither, Tom, 23, 24, 39, 79
and Freedom Rides, 41
Garrison, William Lloyd, 3, 8, 9, 237
Gay, Ben, 126
Geiger, Jack, 246
Georgia
as area of activity, 11
Glover, Jesse James, 97
Gluckstadt, Miss., 250
Gober, Bertha, 132, 136
jailed and expelled, 128-129
arrest at railway terminal, 130
Golden Rule (ship), 42
Goldwater, Barry, 256
Goodman, Andrew, 243, 265
Gordon, Bruce, 156
Gore, Bob, 175, 177
Gray, Fred, 179
Gray, Victoria, 121, 258, 260-261
Green, Edith, 253-254, 257, 259
Greenberg, Jack, 202
Greene, George, 91
Greensboro, N.C., 2
first sit-in, 16
effect of sit-in, 17-18
Greenville, Miss., 2, 11, 82
Greenwood, Miss., 11, 12, 13, 82-83, 245. *See also* Leflore County
Gregory, Dick, 213
aids in food drive, 88
in Greenwood, 92
in Selma, 150-151
Gregory, Lillian, 150
Guyot, Lawrence, 5, 84, 95, 102, 104, 106
background of, 107
on whites in civil rights movement, 187
and Freedom Democratic Party, 252, 261

Haley, Richard, 175
Hall, Blanton, 128-129
Hall, Prathia, 12
in Selma, 154, 157
Hamer, Fannie Lou, 13, 188, 196, 253, 260-261, 268, 274
joins Movement, 93-94
arrest in Winona, 94
becomes field secretary, 95-96
in Hattiesburg, 103, 104, 113
runs for Congress, 121
in Washington, 242
in Atlantic City, 253
contests election of Jamie L. Whitten, 257
Hancock, Milton, 92, 115
Hansen, Bill, 135, 182, 193
on march to Jackson, 175
excerpts from diary, 177-178
arrest in Alabama, 180
marriage to Negro, 185-186
Hardy, John, 58, 66
and McComb school, 58
beaten by registrar of Walthall County, 70-71
shotgun fired into bedroom of, 77
Harrington, Michael, 228
Harris, Don, 182
Harris, Elijah, 134
Harris, Fred, 98
Harris, Jesse, 104, 268
at trial of Diane Bevel, 80-81
on march to Jackson, 175
Harris, Robert J., 243

Harris, Rutha, 132
Harris, Walter, 134
Hattiesburg, Miss., 2, 11, 101
Hayden, Casey, 177, 182
Hayden, Sandra, 10, 239
  background of, 12-13
  in Albany, 129, 133-134
Hayden, Tom, 77, 129, 133-134
Hayes, Curtis, 68, 76, 82, 102
Heilbroner, Robert, 230
Henry, Aaron, 105, 263
  protests shooting of Travis, 90
  damage to home and drugstore, 91, 92
  runs for Governor, 99, 250
  and Freedom Democratic Party, 252-255, 261
Higgs, William, 203, 243
Highlander Folk School, 58-59
Holloway, Frank, 50, 51-52
Hollowell, Donald, 134
Holly Springs, Miss., 81-82, 245
Holman, Carl, 29
Holsaert, Faith, 144
Holt, Len, 34, 180
Houston, Texas, 25
Howe, Mark, 244
Hugh, Matthew, 92
Humphrey, Hubert, 253-254
Hurst, E. H., 68, 72, 73, 74

Identity crisis, 5-7
Indianola, Miss., 245
Industrial Workers of the World, 262
Interstate Commerce Act of 1887, 206
Interstate Commerce Commission ruling on terminals tested, 126-128
Itta Bena, Miss., 96

Jackson, Eliza, 211
Jackson, Emanuel, 134
Jackson, Jimmy Lee, 264
Jackson, Miss., 11, 79, 213, 245
  violence in, 25
  and freedom rides, 40
  arrests in, 51
  jail conditions in, 52
  freedom school in, 248-249
Jacksonville, Fla., 25
Jail conditions, 96-97
  in Jackson, 52
  in Georgia, 132
Javits, Jacob, 209
Jenkins, Tim, 81
  and voter registration, 58, 59
Jet, 66
Johnson, Bernice, 132, 136
Johnson, Lyndon, 36, 215, 243, 253, 256, 259
  and Selma violence, 265
Johnson, Paul, 98, 103
Johnson, Warren, 211
Jones, Annette, 136
Jones, Charles
  at Rock Hill, 38
  in charge of voter registration work, 59
  works full time for SNCC, 60
  in Albany, 126, 127, 130, 133, 134
  in Terrell County, 139
Jones, Willie Mae, 130
Joyce, James, 248
Justice, 225-226

Katzenbach, Nicholas, 198, 244
  and Selma violence, 265
Kaufmann, Walter, 2
Kennedy, John F., 36, 191
  calls Gov. Patterson, 46
  statement on Alabama violence, 49-50
  protection requested from, 90, 175
  sends troops to Oxford, 199
  appointment of judges by, 203-204
  early delay on civil rights, 205-206
Kennedy, Robert F., 59, 191, 243-244
  assured Alabama would protect Freedom Riders, 46-47
  action on Freedom Ride violence, 49
  calls for "cooling-off period", 52
  protection requested from, 90, 104
  defense of judicial appointments, 205
  and authority to protect civil rights workers, 208
Kennedy Administration
  and civil rights, 190-191, 208

Keyserling, Leon, 228
King, C. B., 29, 135, 193, 211
  runs for Congress, 136
King, Ed, 34, 60
King, Edwin
  runs for Lieutenant-Governor, 99, 250
  and Freedom Democratic Party, 252, 254
King, Lonnie
  at Atlanta sit-in, 25
  asks for federal protection, 44
King, Martin Luther Jr., 1, 29, 33, 34, 53, 249
  organizes SCLC, 32
  speaks in Montgomery, 50
  in Albany, 130-131, 134
  on need for Executive action, 210
  criticism of economic system, 229-230
  and Freedom Democratic Party, 253, 255
  in Selma, 263-264
King, Slater, 29
  vice-president of Albany Movement, 128
  in Albany, 130, 134, 136
  charged by U.S. government, 211
King, Mrs. Slater, 135, 193, 211
Kinoy, Arthur, 272
Knoxville, Tenn., 23
Ku Klux Klan, 25, 49
Kunstler, William M., 212, 246, 272

Ladner, Dorie, 268
Lafayette, Bernard
  in Jackson, 79
  in Selma, 147, 149
Lafayette, Colia, 149
Larner, Jeremy, 31
Laurel, Miss., 81, 82
Laursen, Per, 129, 133-134
Lawson, James, 33, 34
  and Nashville sit-ins, 21-22
  on Freedom ride, 51
Lawyer's Committee on Civil Rights, 117
Lee, Bernard, 129
Lee, Herbert, 72-73, 74, 75, 170, 192
LeFlore, Greenwood, 90
Leflore County, Miss.
  described, 83-84
  stops distributing surplus food, 86
  voter registration drive in, 90
LePrad, Paul, 21
Levinson, Stanley, 32
Lewis, Ike, 76
Lewis, John, 5, 11
  harshness of, 8
  and Nashville sit-ins, 19
  and Freedom ride, 42, 45, 48
  in Hattiesburg, 104, 105, 110
  in Selma, 149, 150, 265
  Washington speech, 190, 208, 211, 212, 215, 217
  and violence, 222
  elected chairman of SNCC, 268
Liberty, Miss., 11, 67
Liberty Party, 262
Lingo, Al, 160, 178, 179, 263-265
Little Rock, Ark., 18, 199
Lockett, Winston, 175, 178, 179
Locofocos, 262
Long, Worth, 149
Looby, Z. Alexander, 22-23
Lowell, James Russell, 8
Lowenstein, Al, 99
Lucy, Autherine, 169
Lunney, Robert, 117, 118, 119
Lynd, Staughton, 229, 247
  describes Negro colleges, 235-236
Lynd, Theron, 105, 111-112
Lyon, Danny, 162

McCollum, Salynn, 127
McComb, Miss., 58, 75, 170
  Freedom school in, 250
McCormick, John, 258-259
McDew, Charles, 13, 19, 76
  reaction to Greensboro sit-in, 18
  in McComb, 74, 75, 170, 171
  in Magnolia, 76
  arrest in Baton Rouge, 172-174
  marriage to white girl, 185
McGhee, Silas, 268
McGill, Ralph
  on sit-ins, 27-28
McKinnie, Lester, 79, 81
MacNamara, Norris, 107
Madison, James, 219

Mahoney, Bill, 55, 56
describes Parchman penitentiary, 56-57
Malcolm X, 213, 222
Manchester Guardian
on SNCC and Communists, 227
Marion, Ala., 264
Marshall, Burke, 58, 197, 199, 244
Mass communication
and civil rights movement, 7-8
Matthews, Zeke, 131
attitude to Negroes, 138
on voter registration, 139
May, Samuel, 8
Medical Committee for Human Rights, 246
Meharry Medical School, 23
Memphis, Tenn., 23, 213, 238
Miller, Dotty, 177
Mississippi
as area of activity, 11
conditions of Negroes in, 64
registration law in, 66
Mississippi Food Drive. *See* Food Drive, Mississippi
Mississippi Free Press, 79
Mississippi Summer Project, 1964, 242, 244
Mitchell, Danny, 225
Monley, Father, 81-82
Montgomery, Ala., 26
bus boycott in, 1, 18
Freedom rides, 47-49
Montgomery Advertiser
statement by Auburn University students in, 53
its reporter attacked in Selma, 163
Moore, Amzie, 64, 66, 79
Moore, William L., 174-175
Moses, Donna Richards
in Hattiesburg, 103, 104, 107
Moses, Gregory, 63
Moses, Robert Parris, 11, 18, 66, 102, 142, 186, 251, 272
background of, 5, 62-63
harshness of, 8
effect of Greensboro sit-in on, 17
describes SNCC office, 35
sets up voter registration schools at McComb, 58, 59-60
describes voter registration in Liberty, 67
in McComb, 67-68, 170, 171
files charges against Caston, 69
on Britt and Hardy incidents, 71-72
on murder of Herbert Lee, 72, 73
and march in McComb, 75
in Magnolia, 76
on voter registration campaigns, 77, 78
in Jackson, Miss., 79, 81
on Sam Block, 84
and Mississippi food drive, 87, 88-89
in Greenville, 89
in Greenwood, 91-92
in Itta Bena, 97, 98
directs Henry-King campaign, 99
in Hattiesburg, 103, 104, 111, 112, 117-121
asks Robert Kennedy for protection in Hattiesburg, 104
on whites in Movement, 188-189
directs Mississippi summer program, 215
on SNCC and political associations, 226-227
urges Convention sit-in, 254
speaks at *National Guardian* dinner, 270
Moses v. *Kennedy,* 203
Mount Olive Church, 139

Nash, Diane. *See* Bevel, Diane Nash
Nashville, Tenn., 2, 213, 238
sit-ins, 16, 19-21
Nashville Banner, 22
Natchez, Miss., 245
The Nation, 210
National Association for the Advancement of Colored People (NAACP), 32, 37, 81, 215
effects of sit-ins on, 29
and forming of COFO, 79
and Albany Movement, 127, 128
estrangement from COFO, 263
Legal Defense Fund, 272
National Council of Churches, 96, 104, 263

and Mississippi summer project, 244
National Democratic Convention, 1960
Barry appears before Platform Committee, 36
National Guardian, 270
National Lawyers Guild, 272-273
National States Rights Party, 49
National Student Association, 34, 37
Neblett, Carver
in Terrell County, 140-141
in Selma, 163
on march to Jackson, 175
New Leader, 31
New South, 51-52
New York Times, 52
Nonviolence
and lack of federal protection, 212-213
SNCC's view of, 220-224
Nonviolent Action Group, 56
Norris, Mildred W., 118
Notre Dame Conference
conclusions on voting rights, 209-210
Novak, Robert, 269

Oak Ridge, Tenn., 23
O'Boyle, Archbishop
objects to Lewis' speech, 190
O'Neal, John, 103
Orangeburg, S.C.
CORE classes in, 23-24
sit-in, 24
Ouillet, Father Maurice, 150, 165
Oxford, Miss., 199
Oxford, Ohio, 244

Parchman State Penitentiary
Freedom Riders in, 40
conditions in, 54-55
Patch, Penny, 138
in Terrell County, 139
on Southwest Georgia, 144-145
Patterson, Eugene, 53
Patterson, John, 46-47, 49, 53
Pauling, Linus, 230
Peacock, Willie, 5, 176
in Greenwood, 83, 85, 86, 91
Peck, James, 41, 42, 43
Pegues, O. C., 82
Pemberton, John, 197, 199
Perdew, John, 183
Perkins, Mother, 98
Person, Charles, 43
Phillips, Rubel, 98
Phillips, Wendell, 3, 8, 9, 237, 255
Piel, Gerard, 230
Pike County, Miss.
"Nonviolent High" opened, 76
Pine Bluff, Ark., 11
Polier, Shad, 212
Ponder, Annelle, 94, 95, 105
Populists, 262
Potter, Paul, 77
Poverty
and the civil rights movement, 228-231, 239
Pratt, John, 105, 117, 118
Prescod, Martha, 87
Pritchett, Laurie, 128-130, 131, 136, 141
Private property, 230
Progressives, 262

Quarterman, Ola Mae, 133

Rabinowitz, Joni, 212
Race Relations and American Law, 202
Raines, James Griggs, 138
Raleigh Conference, 33, 220
Randolph, A. Philip, 1
Rauh, Joseph L., 251-253, 272
Reagan, Cordell, 14
in Albany, 123, 127, 132, 134
described, 124
in Terrell County, 139
Reconstruction in Mississippi, 64
Redding, Saunders, 236
Reeb, James
murder of, 265
reactions to death of, 266-267
Reunion and Reaction, 65n, 198
Reuther, Walter, 254
Richards, Donna. *See* Moses, Donna Richards
Richardson, Gloria, 8
Richmond, David, 16

Richmond, Va., 27, 213
Richmond News Leader, 22, 26
Ritter, Norman, 47
Robinson, Harold, 76
Robinson, Reggie, 58, 66
Rock Hill, S.C., 2, 38, 42
Rogers, Willie, 96-97
Rollins, Avon, 180
Roosevelt, James, 259
Rousseau, Jean Jacques, 219
Ruleville, Miss., 13, 82
Rustin, Bayard
  organizes SCLC, 32
  Freedom Rider in 1947, 41
  Moses talks with, 63
  on poverty, 229
  and Freedom Democratic Party, 255
Ryan, William Fitts, 258-259

Samstein, Mendy, 5, 107, 108
Sasser, Ga., 11
Schwerner, Michael, 243, 265
Screws case, 194
Searles, A. C., 130
Sellars, Cleveland
  elected Program Chairman of SNCC, 268
Selma, Ala., 2, 11, 12
  description of, 147-148
  events of Feb.-March, 1965, 263-266
Selma-Montgomery march, 266-267
Shaw University, 33
Sherrod, Charles, 144, 184
  background of, 5
  in Georgia, 11
  at Rock Hill, 38, 39
  works full time for SNCC, 60
  described, 123
  in Albany, 123, 126-127, 133
  describes conditions in Albany, 125-126
  on Terrell County jail, 131
  on effects of Albany demonstrations, 133
  on social change in Albany, 136
  and registration in Terrell County, 139
  speech in Terrell, 139-140
  on Southwest Georgia, 145-146
  wanted whites in Movement, 181
  on Communists in SNCC, 227
  on poverty, 274
Shirah, Sam, 10, 182, 239
  on march to Jackson, 175
  wires Gov. Wallace, 179
  advice to whites in Movement, 185
Shuttlesworth, Charles, 43, 53
Siegenthaler, John, 46, 48
Singer, Felix, 56
Singing
  and civil rights movement, 4
Sit-ins
  effects of, 26-28. *See also* names of cities.
Sitton, Claude, 179, 180, 207
Smelley, Joe, 160, 163
Smith, Ben, 272
Smith, Frank, 228
  in Holly Springs, 81-82
  in Greenwood, 91
Smith, Rev. R. L., 79
Smith, Ruby Doris, 90
  reaction to Greensboro sit-in, 17-18
  at Rock Hill, 38
  on violence in Anniston and Birmingham, 44
  on Freedom Ride, 45-46
  on arrival in Montgomery, 47, 48
  on jail conditions, 54, 55
The South and the Southerner, 27-28
Southern Christian Leadership Conference (SCLC), 37, 81, 91, 104, 105, 186, 215, 245, 263
  and sit-ins, 29
  and Ella Baker, 32
  provides money to SNCC, 33
  turns down cooling-off period, 53
  and forming of COFO, 79-80
Southern Conference Educational Fund, 37, 271
The Southern Patriot, 169
Southern Regional Council
  report on Freedom Rides, 43-44
  administers Foundation money, 81
  and judicial appointments, 203-204
Southern Students Organizing Committee, 269

Southerners, White
and the law, 210-211
in SNCC, 239-240
Stembridge, Jane, 38, 239
on human relationships, 7
first office secretary, 10, 35
describes Raleigh meeting, 33
on "coordinating", 36
on Atlanta sit-in, 39
returns to school, 60
works with Moses, 63
Steptoe, E. W., 68
Stewart, Lamar, 133
Student Nonviolent Coordinating Committee (SNCC)
budget, 10
organization of, 11, 34-35
purposes, 34
credo on nonviolence, 220-221
work-study programs, 234
reorganization of, 1965, 267-268
SNCC staff
numbers, 3
background of, 9-10
salaries of, 10-11, 13
living conditions of, 12
threat of violence to, 12
The Student Voice, 35
Students for a Democratic Society, 129
Sullivan, L. B., 48
Sullivan, Terry, 56
Supreme Court. *See* U.S. Supreme Court.
Surney, Lafayette, 5, 113, 268

Taconic Foundation, 58, 81
Taitt, Lenore, 129
Talbert, Robert, 76
Tappan, Lewis, 9
Taylor, Ben, 87
Taylor, Lana, 39
Terrell County, Ga.
conditions in, 138
Thomas, Henry, 45
Thomas, Norman, 230
Touré, Sekou, 269-270
Travis, Brenda, 69, 72, 74-75, 170
Travis, James
shot near Greenwood, 89-90
in Washington, 243
The Triple Revolution, 230-231
Truman, Harry, 37
Trumpauer, Joan, 56
Truth, Sojourner, 3
Turner, Bessie, 80
Turnbow, Hartman, 92
Tyson, Sheriff, 57

United States
identity crisis, 6
political structure, 218-220
U.S. Code
Section 241, Title 18, 195
Section 242, Title 18, 194-195, 199
Section 332, Title 10, 244
Section 333, Title 10, 199-200, 244, 266
Section 3052, Title 18, 195
U.S. Congress, 218-219
House Rules Committee, 219
House Un-American Activities Committee, 56, 227
U.S. Constitution
First Amendment, 192, 224
Fourteenth Amendment, 65, 192, 198, 205
U.S. Department of Justice, 59, 71, 92, 162, 205, 206, 242
and voter registration in Hattiesburg, 105
fails to enforce law in Albany, 127
failure to help in Selma, 158, 160-161, 162, 164, 265
refuses protection to civil rights workers, 193, 197-198, 208
prosecution of civil rights workers in Albany, 211, 212
and Chaney-Schwerner-Goodman murder, 243
U.S. government
in Mississippi, 90
failure to help in Albany, 123, 127, 129, 136
SNCC interpretation of its powers, 192
special agents for South proposed, 196-197, 200
response to civil rights crises, 199
warned of trouble in Mississippi, 242

U.S. Supreme Court, 1
  decision of 1954, 18
  Boynton case, 41
  ruling in Gov. Barnett case, 201
  ruling in Debs case, 202-203
  Ex parte Siebold, 243
Urban League, 81

Vanderbilt University
  expels Lawson, 22
Vick, Lee Chester, 76
Vicksburg, Miss., 82, 245
Vivian, Rev. C. T., 52
Voice of America, 266
Voter registration
  Mississippi law, 66
  Alabama law, 153
  drives. *See* names of cities.

Walker, Wyatt, 53
Wallace, George C., 175, 179, 196, 265-266
Wallace, Henry, 262
Ware, Charlie, 193, 211
Warner, Clinton, 29
Washington, D.C., March on, 190
Watkins, Hollis, 76, 268
  in McComb, 68
  in Hattiesburg, 82, 102
Weaver, Claude, 100
Weinberger, Eric, 175, 177, 180
Weld, Theodore, 3, 9
Wells, James, 76
West, E. Gordon, 204
Wharton, Vernon, 64
White, Byron, 49
White, Theodore, 226
White students
  reactions of Negroes to, 137-138
Whitten, Jamie L., 257-258
Wide Area Telephone Service, 245
Wilkins, Roy, 1
Williams, Avery, 108, 163
Williams, James, 183, 193
Wingfield, Charles, 136-137
Winona, Miss., 94-95, 207
Winston Salem, N.C., 28
Wofford, Harris, 58
Wolfe, Thomas, 249
Wood, Mrs. of Hattiesburg, 12, 103, 106-107, 117
Woodward, C. Vann, 65n, 198
Wright, Irene, 125, 127
  on Albany Movement, 128
  on effects of Albany demonstrations, 133
Wright, Marian, 92
Wright, Stephen, 21
Wyckoff, Elizabeth, 55

Yancey, Bobby 235-236
Young, Whitney, 29
Young Man Luther, 5-6
Young Women's Christian Association, 34, 37

Zachary, Francis, 119-121
Zellner, Bob, 10, 182, 239
  in McComb, 74, 75, 170-171
  in Albany, 129, 133-134
  background of, 168-169
  arrest in Baton Rouge, 172-174
  on walk to Jackson, 175
  praises Claude Sitton and Carl Fleming, 179
  arrest in Alabama, 179-180
  in Danville, 180-181
Zellner, Dotty, 182
Zwerg, James, 47-49